THE TRIBE OF

Ashbery and Contemporary Poetry

THE TRIBE OF JOHN

Ashbery and Contemporary Poetry

Edited by Susan M. Schultz

The University of Alabama Press

Tuscaloosa and London

The University of Alabama Press
Tuscaloosa, Alabama 35487-0380
All rights reserved
Manufactured in the United States of America

∞   .

The paper on which this book is printed meets the minimum
requirements of American National Standard for Information
Science-Permanence of Paper for Printed Library Materials,
ANSI Z39.48-1984.

Library of Congress Cataloging-in-Publication Data

The tribe of John : Ashbery and contemporary poetry / edited by
    Susan M. Schultz.
        p.   cm.
    Includes bibliographical references and index.
    ISBN 0-8173-0767-2 (alk. paper)
    1. Ashbery, John—Criticism and interpretation.   2. American
poetry—20th century—History and criticism.   3. Ashbery, John—
Influence.   I. Schultz, Susan M., 1958–   .
PS3501.S475Z87   1995   ,
811'.54—dc20   94-28820

British Library Cataloguing-in-Publication Data available

Contents

Foreword

A Short Article or Poem in Response to the Work

George Bradley

You kept waiting for it to happen all the time. It never did,
　　　　but it would; it was like the sun, endlessly put out.
So many messengers arrived, there was no time to cut off all their
　　　　heads. They would have to do it for themselves.
Everybody was gaga about what you were up to: bubbles rose among
　　　　the distorted noses pressed against the glass.
You thought and thought about it until finally nothing needed
　　　　to be done. Then you threw out all the plants.
The orange juice on his Metallica tee-shirt served as a kind
　　　　of foil, setting off an enormous penis. Something
　　　　he did before leaving had made a mess on the floor.
　　　　The stain was indelible and spreading, and suddenly you
　　　　realized you loved the little snot to distraction.
Armed with advice from Betty Crocker, she was completely normal
　　　　in a 50's way and an odd choice. She told you everything
　　　　she knew anyhow, and it was what you knew, too.
The primrose path at this end of the garden got narrower and
　　　　narrower. Night fell, and it disappeared altogether.
　　　　Then it was set on fire, to be placed among the stars.
They were always worming their way in under the windows and
　　　　around the door, sweet lamentations shaped like
　　　　violin scrolls or the corbels of an overly ornate facade.
The melisma of cembalos seemed as intricate as ever, until somebody
　　　　in the audience went absolutely ape and you found
　　　　you had lost the knack of listening to the end.
We have reserved a brand new Chevy Blazer, worth $15,000,
　　　　in your name or a toaster-oven, but you must claim
　　　　your prize in person at Heritage Village.
It was pleasant to recall the days of childhood awkwardness,
　　　　before you had been gifted with this fucate fruit
　　　　and forced off toward the horizon.

As if you had set out years ago under a mild sky, only to come
        calling now at this frigid extreme of tundra and
        tar-paper shacks . . . a lot could be said about
        your entrance into it, a tentative anchorage.
And so once again you were marooned among the mannequins, left
        with Volume One of a two-volume encyclopaedia and
        provisioned with your version of the daylight, which
        could not help itself and cannot thank you enough.

Acknowledgments

MY DEEPEST THANKS go to the contributors for their dedication to this project, and in many cases for their friendship. Henry Hart invited me to guest edit an Ashbery issue of *Verse*, from which this collection grew and ramified. Eyal Amiran provided wise counsel early on. Charles Bernstein, Rob Wilson, Marjorie Perloff, Janet Bowdan, Alfred Corn, and Peter Nicholson offered advice and encouragement to me at various stages of the project. Nicole Mitchell, of The University of Alabama Press, was enthusiastic and supportive from the first, as were Hank Lazer and Alan Golding, whose detailed comments made this a much better book. I want to thank my friends and students at the University of Hawaii for their help, tangible and otherwise, as well as my parents, Martha J. Schultz and the late Frederick W. Schultz, for their tolerance and support.

Permissions

Permission to quote from the following works has been granted by their copyright holders:

Charles Altieri. "Ashbery as Love Poet," from a special issue of *Verse*, © copyright 1991. Reprinted by permission of the publisher.

John Ash. Excerpt from "Nympheas," from *The Branching Stairs*. Permission granted by Carcanet Press Limited.

John Ashbery. Excerpts from "Night" from *The Tennis Court Oath*, copyright © 1962. Permission granted by University Press of New England. Excerpt from "They Dream Only of America," from *The Tennis Court Oath*. Permission granted by University Press of New England.

"On Autumn Lake," "Fear of Death," from *Self-Portrait in a Convex Mirror* by John Ashbery. Copyright © 1972, 1973, 1974, 1975 by John Ashbery. Used by permission of Viking Penguin, a division of Penguin Books USA, Inc.

"Self-Portrait in a Convex Mirror," copyright © 1974 by John Ashbery,

Excerpts of "Holy Ghost" and "Of Poetry" from *Death Is the Place,* copyright © 1989 by William Bronk. Reprinted by permission of the poet.

Excerpts from *Vectors and Smoothable Curves: Collected Essays,* copyright © 1983 by William Bronk. Reprinted by permission of the author.

Excerpts from five letters to John Ernest by William Bronk. Reprinted by permission of the author.

Excerpts from William Bronk's response to "Poetry Society of America Survey," copyright © 1991 by William Bronk. Reprinted by permission of the author.

Excerpts from a letter written by William Bronk to Cid Corman, 18 January 1967, copyright © 1967 by William Bronk. Reprinted by permission of the author.

Excerpts from *Living Instead* by William Bronk. Copyright © 1991 by William Bronk. Reprinted by permission of North Point Press, a division of Farrar, Straus & Giroux, Inc.

Clark Coolidge. Excerpt from "Echo & Mildew," from *Space,* copyright © 1971. Reprinted by permission of HarperCollins Publishers, Inc.

Thomas Fink. "Minimalist," from *Surprise Visit,* copyright © 1993, The Domestic Press. Reprinted by permission of the publisher.

John Gery. "Ashbery's Menagerie and the Anxiety of Affluence," from an earlier version published in a special issue of *Verse,* © copyright 1991. Reprinted by permission of the publisher.

Jorie Graham. Excerpts from "The End of Beauty," copyright © 1987 by Jorie Graham. First printed by The Ecco Press in 1987. Reprinted with permission.

Ann Lauterbach. Excerpts from *Before Recollection,* copyright © 1987 by Princeton University Press. Reprinted by permission of Princeton University Press. "Mountain Roads," "Broken Skylight," "A Documentary," "Prom in Toledo Night," "The Elaborate Absence," from *Clamor.* Copyright © 1991 by Ann Lauterbach. Used by permission of Viking Penguin, a division of Penguin Books USA, Inc.

David Lehman. Excerpt from "One Size Fits All: A Critical Essay," from *Operation Memory,* copyright © 1990. Permission granted by Princeton University Press.

Stephen Paul Miller. "Periodizing Ashbery and His Influence," forthcoming in 1996 from Duke University Press in a volume tentatively entitled *Culture and Surveillance: The Seventies Now.* Permission granted by Duke University Press.

Cherríe Moraga. "And Then There's Us," from *Loving in the War Years, lo que nunca pasó por suslabios,* copyright © 1983 by South End Press. Used by permission of the publisher.

Donald Revell. "Purists Will Object: Some Meditations on Influence," from a special issue of *Verse,* © copyright 1991. Reprinted by permission of the publisher.

David Shapiro. Excerpts from *House (Blown Apart),* copyright © 1988. Permission granted by The Overlook Press.

Marjorie Welish. Excerpts from "The Lure" and other poems from *Handwritten* (copyright © 1979). Reprinted by permission of the poet. Excerpts from "Respected, Feared, and Somehow Loved"; "Carpet Within the Figure"; "The Diaries Began"; and "Skin," from *The Windows Flew Open,* copyright © 1991. Permission granted by the poet.

John Yau. Excerpts from "After Moving," "Genghis Chan: Private Eye" from *Radiant Silhouette: New and Selected Work, 1974–1988,* copyright © 1989. Reprinted with the permission of Black Sparrow Press.

Abbreviations

IN CITATIONS throughout the text, John Ashbery's books of poetry are abbreviated as follows:

AG	*April Galleons*
AWK	*As We Know*
DDS	*The Double Dream of Spring*
FC	*Flow Chart*
HD	*Houseboat Days*
HL	*Hotel Lautréamont*
RM	*Rivers and Mountains*
RS	*Reported Sightings*
ShTr	*Shadow Train*
SoTr	*Some Trees*
SPs	*Selected Poems*
SPCM	*Self-Portrait in a Convex Mirror*
TCO	*The Tennis Court Oath*
TP	*Three Poems*
VN	*The Vermont Notebook*
W	*A Wave*

THE TRIBE OF JOHN
Ashbery and Contemporary Poetry

Introduction

Susan M. Schultz

AMONG CONTEMPORARY POETS, John Ashbery is at once the most consistent and the most various. It is a mark of Ashbery's pervasive presence that so many of the poets he included in *The Best American Poetry, 1988*, which reprinted the hundred poems of the year that Ashbery most liked, sound like him, or—that is—like one of him. There is a meditative Ashbery, a formalist Ashbery, a comic Ashbery, a late-Romantic Ashbery, a Language poet Ashbery, and so on—even, as Charles Altieri shows us here, a love poet. No poet since Whitman has tapped into so many distinctly American voices and, at the same time, so preserved his utterance against the jangle of influences. Of course, as in an intricate Venn diagram, these Ashberys overlap; form inspires comedy and meditation (as in "Farm Implements and Rutabagas in a Landscape").

Curious then, especially in the light of Ashbery's many honors and awards, including the Pulitzer and MacArthur awards, that there has been so little critical attention to his work; John Shoptaw's *On the Outside Looking Out: John Ashbery's Poetry* (Harvard University Press, 1994) is the first full-length study since David Shapiro's quirky introduction, published in 1979 (before *April Galleons, Flow Chart, Hotel Lautréamont,* and *And the Stars Were Shining*). Ashbery criticism has also failed to catch up with its subject, generating itself out of a value-ridden set of terms that does readers of contemporary poetry a disservice. Too many discussions of Ashbery's work are based on a simple dichotomy of good or bad, the writer's point of view determined by his or her part in the contemporary comedy of poetic manners. Ashbery suffers from his refusal to join the current generation of poet-critics, almost certainly the best since the New Critics of the 1930s through the 1950s. His only published criticism, aside from the as-yet-unpublished Norton Lectures, has been about modern and contemporary art or appears in the form of short jacket blurbs for his friends. For better or worse, he operates outside the self-consciously political field negotiated by poets from the right (New Formalists), the left (Language writers), or what now amounts to the old guard (practitioners of free verse). That he publishes in the organs of all factions' journals (from the conservative *Poetry* to the radical *Sulfur*) may only confuse matters. "Fence-sitting" is not every poet's "aesthetic ideal," as Ashbery claims it is in "Soonest

Mended," from *The Double Dream of Spring*. He has become an awkward presence both for the proponents of the "real" and for those who believe that language is even more slippery and deceptive than Ashbery perceives it to be. As Linda Reinfeld reports, "He recently remarked that he is not a Language poet because he believes that language finally depends on references to meanings generated outside language."[1]

Harold Bloom, for many years Ashbery's chief promoter in the world of literary criticism, writes (typically), of "Ashbery's finest achievement to date";[2] conversely, the New Formalist advocate Mark Jarman calls readers like Bloom "dishonest," the poetry "a kind of musical noise, something like the easy listening jazz of the Windham Hill productions."[3] Even as perceptive and canny a critic as Charles Altieri, who sets Ashbery within the context of the 1970s in *Self and Sensibility in Contemporary American Poetry* (1984), falls back on the label "the major poet of our minor age."[4] And Charles Molesworth, who goes some distance toward investigating the politics of Ashbery's reputation, believes that his reputation depends upon "a weariness with moral and political fervor in poetry now that the 1960s are past."[5] "What stands behind Ashbery's rather sudden success d'estime [*sic*] is the triumph of a poetic mode," Molesworth argues. "A mode demands less aesthetic energy than a truly individual style but usually offers more gratification than the average school or 'movement.' "[6] So, Molesworth begins the important work of situating Ashbery within cultural and professional parameters but finally spends more energy in bemoaning Ashbery's mode than in explaining it.

Both Bloom and Helen Vendler vaunt Ashbery not so much for himself but as the revisionist of a larger tradition; he is the latest link in a chain that includes Whitman and Stevens. (I do not intend to dismiss their crucial work to fit Ashbery into a genealogy of American poetry; instead, I wish to push that genealogy forward, to recontextualize Ashbery's work in a contemporary framework.) Bloom, especially, uses Ashbery's work toward his own ends, as the proof-texts for his own poetics of influence, first elaborated in his 1973 book *The Anxiety of Influence: A Theory of Poetry;* his criticism since that book's publication is often overtly personal. For example: "Ashbery's *persona*, at least since his great book *The Double Dream of Spring*, is what I remember describing once as a failed Orphic, perhaps even deliberately failed."[7] The critic's standard of judgment, then, is the critic's standard of judgment; Ashbery is great because Bloom claims that he is. Doubtless Bloom's criticism benefited Ashbery in the short term, giving him a name to put up against "Stevens" or "Crane" or "Whitman" or "Dickinson," but in the long term, this self-enclosed method denies Ashbery a "visionary company" among his peers and followers. He is pulled out of contemporary literary history, rather than being submerged in it.

Vendler, too, creates genealogies for Ashbery, noting in a 1981 *New Yorker* review of *As We Know* that, "in short, he comes from Wordsworth, Keats, Tennyson, Stevens, Eliot; his poems are about love, or time, or age."[8] She then asserts, however, that "it is no service to Ashbery, on the whole, to group him with Stevens and Eliot; when he echoes them most compliantly, he is least himself." Like Ashbery, or like a good lawyer, Vendler here makes a statement and then pulls it partway back; the suggestion of a genealogy remains, even as it is complicated by the notion that Ashbery is best when he is himself, whoever that is. Vendler's review bears the promising title "Understanding Ashbery" and undertakes the task of teaching a mode of reading that is not, like Bloom's, dependent on a knowledge of Ashbery's precursors. The virtue of Vendler's method (or lack of one) is that it is accessible to readers who are not also critics or academics. More than any other critic, Vendler has introduced and fought for Ashbery as a public poet, one who should be widely read as a barometer of contemporary language and "the moral life." But the problem with her strategy is that it is every bit as idiosyncratic as she conceives Ashbery to be. As she writes in her review of *Flow Chart*: "In my own case, by entering into some bizarrely tuned pitch inside myself, I can find myself on Ashbery's wavelength, where everything at the symbolic level makes sense." In other words, reading Ashbery is tantamount to being Ashbery (or being Vendler, who echoes Keats's definition of negative capability): "The irritating (and seductive) thing about this tuning in is that it can't be willed; I can't make it happen when I am tired or impatient. But when the frequencies meet, the effect on me is Ashbery's alone, and it is a form of trance."[9] Having made her effort, she comes to acknowledge that "it is discouraging to be Ashbery, because the very culture of which he is the linguistic recorder cannot read him, so densely woven is the web of his text."[10] Vendler's reviews are marvelous descriptions of Ashbery's poems and the process of reading them, but like Bloom's essays, they do not situate him in our time.

One might expect poet-critics to do better, as they tend to be more engaged with their own time than with anyone else's. For the most part, they do acknowledge—happily or not—Ashbery's importance. Much of their work is, however, more value-ridden than informative or analytical. Consider Mary Kinzie, who writes in *The Cure of Poetry in an Age of Prose: Moral Essays on the Poet's Calling* (1993): "Ashbery is the passive bard of a period in which the insipid has turned into the heavily toxic."[11] Mark Jarman, among other New Formalist critics, laments Ashbery's influence wherever he sees it; in a recent review-essay in the *Hudson Review,* "The Curse of Discursiveness," he bases his harsh invective against Ann Lauterbach, Robert Creeley, and James Tate on their resemblances to Ashbery, in particular the Ashbery of *Flow Chart* (1991). Where these poets go right, according to Jarman, they ignore Ashbery's mode entirely. The invective is so strong, one surmises, because Ashbery's presence is so large—Jarman even calls him "Emperor Ashbery" at one point, alluding to his nakedness, but also to his power. Jarman, like Irvin Ehrenpreis in 1975, allows that "there is room in our literature for John Ashbery"; he just wants to avoid that room and fears contamination of the rooms that he and his colleagues inhabit. That Ashbery is adept at using forms such as the sestina makes him even more dangerous to New Formalist critics; this may be the reason why John Gery here finds Ashbery's influence evident even in the fact that so many contemporary poets attempt to ignore him altogether.

David Lehman's important collection of essays on Ashbery's poetry, *Beyond Amazement* (1980), which includes work by poets and critics such as Douglas Crase, Marjorie Perloff, John Koethe, Lehman, and others, set out to refute the countercritics and argued against the notion of Ashbery's inaccessibility (and unteachability) by presenting cogent practical criticism of the poems. The ten contributors to the volume performed able close-readings that served as courtroom (or classroom) defenses of their client; Lehman calls the opposition the plaintiffs, which says a good deal about the polemical purpose of the collection.[12] Lehman, who often traffics in such metaphors, sets out as the leader of the first expedition into unknown—but guessed at—territory: "If, however, the longitude and latitude of Ashbery's poetry are now thought to be known, the territory itself remains a dark continent."[13] Ashbery, Lehman contends, is misunderstood and even hated, but he finds some solace in the fact that at least Ashbery has *hostile* readers: "No other poet of our time has managed so consistently to polarize his public, to arouse opposite reactions—as though there could be no middle road, as though it were impossible to respond to an Ashbery poem with a complacent nod or shake of the head."[14] Lehman et al. rest their case on the positive side of the divide.

Lehman, recognizing that Ashbery's work largely defies our means of analyzing it, sent his contributors a series of questions intended to elicit a new kind of criticism, one that would do justice to Ashbery, rather than hang him by his poetic thumbs. Lehman's questions included the following, the strength of which lies in their simplicity: "Is there a method by which to extract the sense and flavor of an Ashbery poem?" "Does Ashbery's poetry yield meanings, or does it militate against the very possibility of articulating them?" "What mileage does he get out of his habit of rapidly shifting gears in a poem?" "With a poet as reluctant to repeat himself as Ashbery, what unifying principles, tactics, figures, or concerns are there in his poetic output?"[15] The essays Lehman collected prove these questions to be valuable, and yet I'm struck by the way in which these "new" questions echo old ones posed by New Criticism, stressing as they do the "extraction" of meaning, the "unifying principles" that might exist behind Ashbery's seeming randomness, the coherent set of "concerns" that he might have, and so on. Aside from one question about the New York school of poets—"Of what use is the label 'the New York School of poetry' for understanding the very different writers . . . frequently grouped under that heading?"[16]—Ashbery remains a solitary figure. This question, in its very wording, suggests that the proper response of the critic is to find Ashbery poetically unattached, and that the label is an empty and useless one for poets so "very different" from one another.

We must, according to Lehman's subtext, take or leave Ashbery on his own terms; the collection is meant to defend him against detractors but not to put him in the New York school or any other context. While most of the essays are not New Critical in their method, they treat the poet himself as a well-wrought urn, reading him, like the good New Critical poem, only on "his own" terms. Even Keith Cohen, in his article "Ashbery's Dismantling of Bourgeois Discourse," ultimately resorts to a value- and personality-based criticism. In writing about Ashbery's *Three Poems,* which dismantles notions of the "poetic" by being in prose, Cohen asserts, "What is amazing in 'The System' . . . is that, taken phrase by phrase, no other contemporary poem would seem so humdrum, so vapid. Each sentence seems another fatuous building block of a tiresome, transparent metaphysical argument."[17] Not only is this contention arguable in the extreme (I, for one, find the poems anything but humdrum or vapid, even taken sentence by sentence), Cohen has no ground on which to base his discussion of "bourgeois discourse" or poetic value. His criticism, therefore, becomes as idiosyncratic as Ashbery's poetry is thought to be, based on subjective criteria that are not self-conscious enough to frame the argument in the context of Ashbery's time, and ours. This strategy focuses Lehman's book nicely but also leaves the ground open for further investigations into Ashbery's relationship to his own time, and to the poets who follow him.

Harold Bloom's 1985 Chelsea House collection of essays on Ashbery doesn't so much build on Lehman's foundation as it adds more bricks to it; Bloom's stated purpose is to "address Ashbery's difficulty" and "to achieve a new balance and justice in the evaluation of Ashbery."[18] Bloom's agenda is, as ever, to ensure Ashbery entrance into the Romantic, Bloomian canon. The contributors to the book are friendly to Bloom's thesis; they include Douglas Crase, Charles Berger, Helen Vendler, John Hollander, and Bloom himself (who contributes two essays along with his "Editor's Note" and "Introduction"). According to Bloom, "Ashbery has been misunderstood because of his association with the 'New York School' of Kenneth, Koch, Frank O'Hara and other comedians of the spirit"—in other words, with his peers.[19] His real place is with his precursor, Stevens: "Like his master, Stevens, Ashbery is essentially a ruminative poet, turning a few subjects over and over, knowing always that what counts is the mythology of self, blotched out beyond unblotching."[20] In other words, Ashbery is alone in his time, and his work mythologizes that loneliness; there is "a clear descent from the major American tradition that began in Emerson," that other solitary singer.[21] The strength of Bloom's approach is that he provides us with a narrative of influence—but that narrative works backward rather than forward onto the post-Ashbery landscape where we now are, to a certain extent. As Andrew Ross writes here, "Bloom, more than anyone, has successfully written Ashbery into that kind of heroic story which explains all of the contradictions and discontinuities of a writer's work in terms of *idiosyncrasy.*" But the idiosyncrasies in Ashbery's work—namely, *The Tennis Court Oath,* which Bloom calls peculiar,[22] become embarrassing lapses from the tradition, rather than provocative additions to it. In this new volume, that peculiar work becomes key to a different understanding of Ashbery, an understanding that depends upon the use of his influence by members of the Language school of poets, in particular, Charles Bernstein. For them, ironically, everything not in *The Tennis Court Oath* is considered dubious—they like the discontinuity of discontinuity, whereas Bloom favors the continuity of discontinuity.

The aftermath of Bloom's collection was an important, if not frequently alluded to, turn in Ashbery criticism, namely, S. P. Mohanty and Jonathan Monroe's 1987 review in *diacritics* of it and Ashbery's book *A Wave.* Rather than regard Ashbery as a solitary quest-hero, in the Bloom and Vendler mode, they claim that "the business of explaining Ashbery becomes a significant kind of cultural self-definition."[23] Even more than that, and this is to raise the stakes considerably, "What is at stake in the criticism of Ashbery . . . is the meaning and status of what it is to be 'American,' a charged index, if ever there was any."[24] Mohanty and Monroe seek nothing less than a recasting of Ashbery as a poet more interested in the social than in the private realm: "The central concern of Ashbery's poetic career can only be defined as the self-world relationship, with an investment in exploring the features of a social voice and identity as they can be genuinely available today."[25] Or: "It may thus be suggested that all life is for Ashbery social life, the stuff of history."[26] In stating their case this way, Mohanty and Monroe reaffirm another divide, that between "social" and "private" realms; perhaps for effect, they neglect the way in which the social *is* the private in Ashbery, the private profoundly social (hence the many competing voices in *Three Poems*). As they must, Mohanty and Monroe acknowledge and then argue against Bloom. While theirs is an important effort to call Bloom's assumptions about Ashbery into question and to open Ashbery to other modes of criticism, Mohanty and Monroe still find their "proof-texts" entirely *in* Ashbery's work and not in the world that informs that work. They focus, for example, on Ashbery's use of clichés, which are social constructions (the macros of the masses), but they do not discuss the function of particular clichés in American culture. Nor do they explain what these clichés do for Ashbery in his exploration of the social world. They are quite right and renovative in their claim that "to limit the question of memory in poetry to one of agonistic conflicts passed on *within* poetry from one generation to the next needlessly risks a further deepening of poetry's continuing isolation from other modes of discourse and from the public at large."[27] But their countercriticism is insufficient to make the case work; the review-essay format obviates from the start the possibility of development, though it opens the field for others.

The Tribe of John: Ashbery and Contemporary Poetry will take the criticism I've discussed thus far as a prolegomenon; the focus of these essays, however, is on Ashbery's work as context more than on his work as text. Not only does this collection open up the field of "Ashbery criticism" to other poets who have been influenced by him, but it also aims to break the safe of methods that have been employed in that criticism. Thus, for example, Stephen Paul Miller and Andrew Ross place Ashbery in his (and our) historical and cultural periods. Fred Moramarco traces Ashbery's own history and proposes his own "flow chart" of the poet's career. Each writer illuminates the poetry in a practical way, but the contributors also, at times quite contentiously, take on the goals and methods of the nascent Ashbery industry. Those critics who discuss influence do so with deft indirectness; they refuse to accept the models (especially the Bloomian one) by which we usually measure it. Their evasions (or swerves, to use Bloom's term) are telling and grow stronger as the volume goes on, culminating with Charles Bernstein's aside, found some distance into his long poem:

> For the purpose
> Of your request I'm including this
> Sentence about the influence of John
> Ashbery.

John Gery tropes Bloom, revising the "anxiety of influence" into "the anxiety of affluence." "Ashbery," Gery claims, "deconstruct[s] the very tradition Bloom describes, thereby opening up the field of language for those poets who follow."

John Koethe, who bemoans Ashbery's lack of a good influence, writes below of Douglas Crase, whose work he thinks important: "What Crase does in a way is receive Ashbery into the body of American poetry that is the common property of all poets, rather than let his work remain the private preserve of those who feel a temperamental affinity with it, or have some special relation to it." Koethe's essay appeared in a special issue of *Verse* (Spring 1991), out of which this collection grew and ramified; many of the writers here (including Jonathan Morse and John Gery) have chosen to answer his article in these pages, rendering a portion of the book into a sometimes contentious dialogue between contributors. My hope is that such contention will serve to focus future discussions of Ashbery's influence, or lack thereof, even as it creates a book that is more dialogue than univocal statement.

Several contributors question the importance of influence in their thinking about Ashbery and contemporary poetry. James McCorkle writes of the relationship between Ashbery and Ann Lauterbach: "Rather than casting this relationship between Ashbery and Lauterbach within the dynamics of Harold Bloom's formulations of influence, Ashbery and Lauterbach share in a concern for the condition of the lyric moment. . . . Thus, Ashbery is part of our horizon of understanding, and any poetry now being written will implicitly respond to the poetics his poetry represents." This is to agree with Lauterbach herself, who remarked in an interview, "My affinities to Ashbery are certainly there, although I think of myself as more psychological in tone and perhaps more intent and intense; I do not have his laconic, insouciant, inclusive temperament. As I think Ashbery is our great poet, it would be odd not to have learned from him, but as with all great presences, the question is: what part to learn?"[28] Perhaps the strongest attack on influence is John Ernest's; his essay is curious and provocative in the way it treats two poets—Ashbery and William Bronk—who begin from the same place but diverge radically on their way to very different destinations. Ernest undertakes an anatomy of influence theories, only to declare "that narratives of influence colonize individual poets and poems, assuming critical authority over them in the name of conceptual manifest destiny." Our reading, according to Ernest, is necessarily historical, and influence is allegory not history; "by emphasizing the privacy of their separate enterprises," Ernest argues paradoxically, "they reemphasize the social nature of the poetic experience."

These essays do more than argue influence and methodology, however; they do the valuable, if old-fashioned, task of helping us to read poems, beginning with essays by Jonathan Morse and Charles Altieri on Ashbery's use of clichés and on his little-noticed love poetry. Their means of doing so, however, are not old-fashioned; most of the criticism in this book could have been written only after deconstruction, which swept the profession in the late 1970s and early 1980s; the advent of intertextual criticism (which becomes a kind of influence study of texts on other texts); and of Language poetry, which attained its maturity in the 1980s and which—paradoxically—takes deconstruction as intention, seeking to unravel and deconstruct the syntax that confines us in a worldview characterized by consumerism and right-wing politics. Nowhere in these essays do we find a heroic Ashbery questing after the dark tower of canonicity; whatever heroism there is, is textual. As Andrew Ross writes, in an essay that puts Ashbery firmly in a cultural and art-historical context: "They [techniques of collage and montage] do not constitute a medium through which authors can transfigure their traditional role of alienated commentator . . . authors lose the power to elevate themselves as source and origin of all the transformative impulses that inhabit the text." Ashbery's voice, in other words, triumphs not because it is a "voice" in the traditional sense of the term but because it is writing that is generated from other writing, "an incident of disturbance," as Donald Revell describes it here.

Even more radically, Ross and Shoptaw argue that Ashbery—the Tennis Court Ashbery, that is—"presents . . . an alternative to the politics of content which would limit that kind of poetic commentary to a mere ethics of *opinion*." Ashbery shows us, in other words, how *mediated* and material language is. Ross, for one, turns on its head the argument for Ashbery's idiosyncrasy; he argues that Ashbery's importance may be based less on his idiosyncrasies than on his conventionality. In Ross's work, as elsewhere, Ashbery enters his own age not so much as a prophet but as an apostle, or what Donald Revell once described to me in a letter as an "apostle of indeterminacy." As John Gery puts it, "It is essential to regard the 'acquiescence in indeterminacy' in Ashbery's work not only as characteristic of his poetic method but as inherent in his vision of experience, a vision that allows for a multiplicity of readings." Gery's readers and writers include Clark Coolidge, John Yau, Jorie Graham, and Marjorie Welish. Finally, as Jonathan Morse writes, he is "the lyricist of what in us is most typical of all."

Ashbery, more than any contemporary poet, has self-consciously examined the categories by which we define writing, whether poetry or prose, fiction or nonfiction, lyric or epic. James McCorkle, for one, suggests that we can still talk about the lyric, rather than arguing, like Charles Bernstein in *A Poetics* (1992), that there is no difference between poetry and prose. Yet his lyric is inclusive rather than exclusive, contains multitudes rather than moments of time; McCorkle writes: "Poetic language, for both Derrida and Ashbery, would arguably be able to saturate space. . . . To drench or saturate inscribes excess or the possibility of overflowing and invokes a libidinal energy no longer centered upon the self. This saturation and porousness begin a reconsideration of the lyric." That McCorkle's definition might apply more to prose than to lyric poetry is only appropriate in a discussion of a poet whose *Three Poems* were in prose and whose *Flow Chart* contains lines that dwarf Whitman's. Poetry, this anthology claims, can itself be criticism; the Foreword, by George Bradley, and the Afterword, by Charles Bernstein, are both essay-poems. The poet-critic, like Ashbery's wandering "I's" and "you's," can be the same person, and at the same time.

We are also thrown back on the notion of influence. As I reread the opening of this Introduction, I wonder if it isn't truer to claim that "influence," as a critical term, ought to be deflected from Ashbery's person or even his poetry onto the particular field of contemporary language that informs his work more completely than it does any other poet of his generation. Ashbery's real importance may lie in the fact that we cannot separate his work from the language we use each time we think about the world—about its shopping malls, its movies, its art, its dreams of transcending itself, and even about our criticism of Ashbery (much of *Flow Chart* is devoted to a critique of the critics). This discovery may make it harder, though not I trust impossible, to write literary history, but it may also force us to think of such history as part of a larger concern, where poetry and history cannot be separated, as they so often are. I hope that this book will provide some of the trailheads.

Notes

1. Linda Reinfeld, *Language Poetry: Writing as Rescue* (Baton Rouge: Louisiana State University Press, 1992), 24.

2. Harold Bloom, introduction to *Modern Critical Views: John Ashbery* (New York: Chelsea House, 1985), 6.

3. Mark Jarman, "The Curse of Discursiveness," *Hudson Review* 45, no. 1 (Spring 1992): 158.

4. Charles Altieri, *Self and Sensibility in Contemporary American Poetry* (Cambridge: Cambridge University Press, 1984), 19.

5. Charles Molesworth, *The Fierce Embrace: A Study of Contemporary American Poetry* (Columbia: University of Missouri Press, 1979), 182.

6. Ibid., 181.

7. Harold Bloom, "Measuring the Canon: 'Wet Casements' and 'Tapestry,' " in *Modern Critical Views: John Ashbery* (New York: Chelsea House, 1985), 221–22.

8. Helen Vendler, "Understanding Ashbery," *New Yorker*, March 16, 1981, p. 120.

9. Helen Vendler, "A Steely Glitter Chasing Shadows," *New Yorker*, August 3, 1992, p. 73.

10. Ibid., 76.

11. Mary Kinzie, *The Cure of Poetry in an Age of Prose: Moral Essays on the Poet's Calling* (Chicago: University of Chicago Press, 1993), 17.

12. David Lehman, introduction to *Beyond Amazement: New Essays on John Ashbery*, ed. David Lehman (Ithaca: Cornell University Press, 1980), 17.

13. Ibid., 15.

14. Ibid., 16.

15. Ibid., 18.

16. Ibid.

17. Keith Cohen, "Ashbery's Dismantling of Bourgeois Discourse," in *Beyond Amazement: New Essays on John Ashbery*, ed. David Lehman (Ithaca: Cornell University Press, 1980), 143.

18. Bloom, *Modern Critical Views*, "Editor's Note" (no page number).

19. Ibid., 6.

20. Ibid., 7.

21. Ibid.

22. Ibid., 6.

23. S. P. Mohanty and Jonathan Monroe, "John Ashbery and the Articulation of the Social," *diacritics* 17, no. 2 (1987): 37.

24. Ibid.

25. Ibid.

26. Ibid., 42.

27. Ibid., 55.

28. Molly Bendall, "Ann Lauterbach: An Interview," *American Poetry Review* 21, no. 3 (May/June 1992): 23.

PART I

New Readings of Ashbery

1 | Typical Ashbery

Jonathan Morse

> There's always a problem of running time in historical movies, and you need the clumsy apparatus of player identification, "Lenin, meet Trotsky," and characters telling each other things that we know they already know. The Word can take you back with much less effort. . . . It's simpler to consider these names as just the names of characters. They're all recognizable as types.
>
> —Michael Herr, *Walter Winchell*

JOHN ASHBERY, too, is just the name of a character. The Ashbery who is the occasion of a special issue of *Verse* called "John Ashbery's Influence on Contemporary Poetry" is simultaneously (among other things) a poet and a writer of popular journalism, a solipsist who nevertheless writes love poems to an Other, an influence on some poets, and a poet influenced by others. If he could somehow stand out from any of these categories, we would call him a Renaissance man: a kind of character whose role is to transcend character. But Ashbery is not at all at home with transcendence. On the contrary, the convex mirror of Ashbery's multiplex referentiality places the poet on equal terms with every other item in the universe he has created out of souvenirs. Reading Ashbery by reflection, watching the poet continually darken and brighten as he moves through the shadows of the verbal decor, we learn that the thing we call "Ashbery" as we read is only one more item in the room. Amid his collections of words, Ashbery is at home in the typical. What is really original about Ashbery, perhaps, is only his awareness of typicality. Who else in English has thought so tenderly, so optimistically, of the meaning latent in the clichés his readers live by?

I

> There's a probability excess. Plus which we don't have our victims laid out where we'd want them if this was an actual simulation. . . . You have to make allowances for the fact that everything we see tonight is real.
>
> —Don DeLillo, *White Noise*

There it is on the page in the cliché: the meaning, ready to be made readable by subsumption into typicality.

I teach in a high school
And see the nurses in some of the hospitals,
And if all teachers are like that
Maybe I can give you a buzz some day,
Maybe we can get together for lunch or coffee or something.

To read this opening passage from "The Wrong Kind of Insurance" (HD 49–50) is to begin trading in a verbal Confederate money: a currency whose basis in fiat has become transparent to history. Who is speaking, under what authority of meaning? Because the poem has allowed us to see through its language, we no longer trust it to tell us. "I," the entity whose signature is affixed to the bill, is mired in some terrible predicament, but he has only words written on paper to tell us what that predicament is trying to be. Lurching from subject to subject in midsentence but never escaping from cliché, he seems to speak a radically inauthentic language: the language of a poetry performing "in an arena where the simulacrum (the prime time TV melodrama, for example) exerts increasing control over the way business is actually done in the 'real' world."[1]

The floor plan of that arena comes to us from Marjorie Perloff, with the help of Jean Baudrillard. But of course we began knowing our way around as soon as we opened the page to Ashbery. Ashbery's prefabricated blocks of language are, after all, remnants of a culture whose distinctive characteristic is that it makes us think we once knew it. Like Don DeLillo's simulated disaster, it is a type—a *read* type—of the modern. Ashbery's clichés aren't representative communications from any imaginable history because they aren't capable of representing anything, but as read texts they possess simulacra of meaning, and those simulacra have given them a function: to typify. Specifically, they typify themselves. In the act of being read, they are the words of a pure poetry—that is, a poetry cut off from everything but the verbal. Bound to the customs of a particular tribe living in a particular place at a particular time, they keep us from communicating with any tribal entity except ourselves, reading.

Perloff has perceived that historiographic irony. But to do so she has had to stand outside the arena of the simulacrum. To recognize irony, to recognize cliché as cliché, is after all to avail oneself of an understood standard of authentic meaning. Somewhere in the ideal reading of "The Wrong Kind of Insurance" is a word named *right,* without quotation marks. But that word remains in deep background. Coming vaguely into view when the book is opened to its poem, *right* is never more than a silent complicity between the poet and his reader, alluded to but never explicitly mentioned. Not for Ashbery the straightforward decisiveness of a Saddam Hussein, whose quadruple colossal statue of his hand grasping a sword is specifically a casting because casting allows for the realization of the desire to achieve a perfect fit between intention, built form and the inner experience of the outside world. . . . The knowledge that in every little bump and squiggle which can be seen, felt and maybe even stroked, these were, are, and will always remain His arms is mesmerizing. The effect must not rest on a lie any more than the divine image on the Turin Shroud can afford to be shown by carbon-dating tests to be a fourteenth-century fake.[2]

No; the shroud and the monument can pass current for reality in a command economy, but Ashbery has trouble issuing commands. Least monumental of poets, Ashbery concedes at the outset that he is writing fiction; that "The Wrong Kind of Insurance" is an assemblage of words whose only guarantee of meaning is the ephemeral consensus of a particular social class at a particular moment in its history.

The poem's point is that this chatter is the world. It cannot be transcended, not even in the painful revision of Wordsworth's Immortality Ode, which forms the core of "The Wrong Kind of Insurance." In a world which exists, like Ashbery's, only to acknowledge its verbality, the ground of existence can never be more than yet one more word. What Wordsworth felt in periphrasis as

> joy! that in our embers
> Is something that doth live,
> That nature yet remembers
> What was so fugitive!

could be given a succinct name by Stevens's Man on the Dump: "the the"; but naming is something Ashbery can't do. A name is a reference to something unique; it implies that there can *be* something unique. But the function of Ashbery's words is only to typify. His poem's "Yes, friends" is an utterance in generic context: a voice from a television set in its darkened room, saying that we are all lost in type together, spectators whose function is only to guess that we *are* spectators, passive before the world's play.

> Yes, friends, these clouds pulled along on invisible ropes
> Are, as you have guessed, merely stage machinery,
> And the funny thing is it knows we know
> About it and still wants us to go on believing
> In what it so unskillfully imitates, and wants
> To be loved not for that but for itself [.]
>   (HD 50)

And yes, we are friendly all the way to the end of the program. Warm words go with the genre. But investments in typicality always leave us in debt, with a net loss of the "the," the definite article. When the set goes dark, we are left only with what Ashbery calls "that emptiness that was the only way you could express a thing" ("The New Spirit," TP 12).

II

That, at any rate, is the cliché. Just as there are novelists whose created worlds notoriously mean only the *à clef*—D. H. Lawrence, John Dos Passos, Thomas Wolfe—Ashbery is ordinarily known as an artist who lives in a wholly contingent universe consisting solely of culture. To think of Ashbery and of the novelists in that way is to generate a complementary pair of modes of biography. Novelists rewrite their extraverbal life into a descriptive grammar of themselves; Ashbery sublimates all that is nonverbal of his life onto the page, becoming (as Milton said a poet must) himself a true poem. Within the poem, as Ashbery says in "The Wrong Kind of Insurance," "all of our lives is a rebus." To read a rebus, we must leave the page and refer elsewhere, reaching back in memory as we rethink the association between things and the sounds we represent them with. It is a gesture of tribal solidarity. But to think of Ashbery as the creator of the rebus, faithfully drawing the picture words forth from himself, is to see him as one of those "poets so private they speak for us all,"[3] a citizen of Byzantium.

Sharing our language, a writer shares our perceptions; some such formulation is the ordinary assumption that makes reading possible. But the typicality of Ashbery's language is a more general matter than that. For Ashbery is a poet of the ancient Platonic lineage, one whose object—whether or not he has consciously articulated it—is to escape language and its clichés, abandoning to the forever baffled efforts of mere reading the vain effort to represent reality in words. While the reader is left holding a squirming body of interpretation, the poet makes his escape to Byzantium with his booty of the ineffable. That much of a conclusion, at least, is available to reading.

"The Tomb of Stuart Merrill," for instance (SPCM 37–39), is constructed of a nested series of allusions to French politics and *Our Boarding House,* a comic strip from the 1930s about a blowhard of the W. C. Fields type who is given to quoting Kipling. In the crypt, however, Stuart Merrill himself, an American-born French symbolist poet, remains expatriated from representation. To be a subject of one of Ashbery's *tombeaux* is to be translated into the alien.

Worse: the specific text of this French poet's epitaph is a letter in English prose. Read in quotation marks as if it has existed prior to being translated onto the page, this text comes to warn us that we will never be able to read through words all the way to significance. " 'After I read one of your poems,' " say the words, " 'I'm always tempted to read and reread it. It seems that my inexperience holds me back from understanding your meanings.' " The addressee is presumably the character named John Ashbery, an extrapoetic personage hovering somewhere off the page. But of course it is impossible for us readers outside Byzantium to be sure. "You" is a potent word for Ashbery; it is the central term of his great love poems. Other important words are "understanding," "meaning," and "hold back." Whatever its origins off the page, therefore, the letter as read has become a part of the ritual that lies at the heart of Ashbery's poiesis: a perpetual tribute of nostalgia offered to "you," the lover absent in time. The poet's memory and the reader's letter yearn equally, establish themselves in a common emotion, merge "I" and "you" in a single hypostasis. That, if anything, is the poem's *clef*: an extrinsic datum of the poem's origin in the poet. But of course the letter waiting to descend on the page is forever too soon to be read. All of us are held back by inexperience.

In that respect we share a culture which extends outward from poetry to pervade the American sensibility, whose clichés Ashbery has taken for his own typicality. When something descends on the supermarket in *White Noise* and rearranges the shelves, a new and terrible inexperience holds back the shopping carts.

> There is a sense of wandering now, an aimless and haunted mood, sweet-tempered people taken to the edge. They scrutinize the small print on the packages, wary of a second level of betrayal. The men scan for stamped dates, the women for ingredients. Many have trouble making out the words. Smeared print, ghost images. In the altered shelves, the ambient roar, in the plain and heartless fact of their decline, they try to work their way through confusion. But in the end it doesn't matter what they see or think they see. The terminals are equipped with holographic scanners, which decode the binary secret of every item, infallibly. This is the language of waves and radiation, or how the dead speak to the living.[4]

At the tomb of Stuart Merrill, however, a poet writing in a foreign language, the codes are less infallible. There we are given to read only the fragments of a grammar, an unfinished question followed by the answer to a question which remains, terribly, unasked.

> The canons are falling
> One by one
> Including *"le célèbre"* of Pachelbel
> The final movement of Franck's sonata for piano and violin.
> How about a new kind of hermetic conservatism
> And suffering withdrawal symptoms of same?
>
> Let's get on with it
> But what about the past
>
> Because it only builds up out of fragments.
>   (SPCM 38)

In the terror of the unasked, unaskable question there lies the cultural symptomatology we share with this poet of our time. Ashbery speaks out of his characteristic wistfulness, DeLillo out of an emotion a little simpler. There are differences. But we probably read both texts through eyes blurred in the same way by the emotion of recognition. At last, we think: somebody knows that "Let's get on with it" is a command waiting for Godot; at last somebody understands. We even have our own clichés to help us typify what we are reading—words like "alienation" and "paranoia" and "the condition of postmodernism"—and these clichés are capable of taking the place of actual read experience. In fact, the impression I get when I talk with readers of Ashbery is that many of his poems achieve their typicality not as experience but as retrospect. Having fully entered memory, they exist there solely as the experience of having been read, like *Look Homeward, Angel* at the age of seventeen. They are synecdochic; they have come to stand for the entire range of experiences that we call nostalgia.

III

Understanding this typicality in historical terms, John Koethe has been able to fit Ashbery to a chronological table of differentiae as follows:

> The exemplary poem of thirty years ago was characterized by a strong speaking voice. . . . [I]ts style was marked by literalness, a clipped diction, an avoidance of indeterminacy, an insistence on the concrete and the particular, and the calculated refusal of rhetorical effect. It rarely acknowledged its status as writing, and its attitude toward the impulses of romanticism was one of irony and condescension.
> The generic poem of today seems quite different.[5]

Koethe goes on to apply such words as "nostalgic," "passive," "tenderness," and "[dissociation] . . . from everyday ideas of rationality and control" to the present era of poetic history—the era par excellence of John Ashbery, a poet whose influence on other poets (this is Koethe's thesis) has therefore yet to define itself. The poet Ashbery has been present in our language, leaving us tokens of himself; now the poet Koethe must account for the way he nevertheless keeps vanishing before our advances on him, like an image in a convex mirror. Considered that way, as a recuperative historical construct, Koethe's strangely effaced Ashbery is a realization in critical form of what Emily Dickinson said about the way we take in the world:

> Perception of an object costs
> Precise the Object's loss—

> Perception in itself a Gain
> Replying to it's Price—[6]

But Ashbery has revised that text.

In "Houseboat Days," for instance (HD 38–40), Dickinson's generalization is qualified by love for the phenomenal, reluctance to complete the exchange of perception for thing. Holding back from consummation, the life that works out its autobiographical terms in this poem begs memory not to abandon it. The poem's economy requires nostalgia, the sense of remembering Byron through the sound of Berlioz, the sense too that perception is only provisional, since time and memory have always already had their way with whatever could have existed before perception entered their world, bearing love.

> A little simple arithmetic tells you that to be with you
> In this passage, this movement, is what the instance costs:
> A sail out of some afternoon, like the clear dark blue
> Eyes of Harold in Italy, beyond amazement, astonished.
> Apparently not tampered with.
>   (HD 40)

If a poem can be a performative utterance of its own mode of reception, then these lines from "Houseboat Days" want to be what Stanley Burnshaw calls "a poem of self-discovery within the purview of the culture."[7] The cultural role they perform is the monetization of desire: words creating a currency in the air between two persons, striking beauty out of evocation and allusion. Through the words' agency, we see the sail in the full panoply of its meanings, an array of associations embracing the entire universe, re-creating the wholeness of response that has not been ours since the days of Eden. In this poem, the sail is a moment's earnest of Stevens's Platonic source of value, the "the."

The moment is so powerful that while it holds us, we are willing to believe it is true, believe it is apparently not tampered with. But of course it has been tampered with, always; and *always*, adds the pedantic voice of critical theory, *already*. After all, Eden, a place of high standards where only unmediated perceptions are accepted, is not John Ashbery's dwelling. Ashbery is too much of a lover of associations for that. "I really can't explain why I enjoy using preexistent titles like 'Civilization and Its Discontents,' " he confessed to David Lehman, "except that I must have a sort of cuckoo instinct that makes me enjoy making my home in somebody else's nest."[8] So the sense of the sail must be tampered with by anticipation, association, and memory: the presence of other afternoons, other epic poems and program symphonies, some of them untouched by love. Ashbery's characteristic poignancy is only a generalization from that, a realization that poetry can never be pure enough to carry conviction beyond the sphere of the mutable. Finally, in fact, to read Ashbery is to acknowledge him as a poet of the fallen world, our representative from the land of Nod, the lyricist of what in us is most typical of all.

IV

Inter tot populi, tot scriptis, milia nostri,
　quem mea Calliope laeserit, unus ego.
(Amid all the myriads of our people, many as are my writings, I am the only one whom my own Calliope has injured.)
　　—Ovid, *Tristia,* trans. Arthur Leslie Wheeler

Ordered by the Emperor Augustus into exile on the shores of the Black Sea, Ovid, the sophisticated urban poet of *The Art of Love,* spent the rest of his career bewailing the catastrophe, in verse, and, also in verse, supplicating for pardon. But though Ovid's epistles from the empire's frontier are full of pathetic details, they remain discreetly vague about legal explanation. For diplomatic reasons, the pain they sing is a general pain: the song of a man self-condemned and far from home. We call them classics because they speak to a typical condition. But it is the nature of the classic never to solve the problems it elevates to typicality. Mozart and Sophocles offer us not help but only definitive reiteration.

The Bright Young Things of Evelyn Waugh's *Vile Bodies,* for instance, have Shakespeare at their disposal. They remember Shakespeare's words at a moment when the king of England also bears the title of Emperor of India, and they have been granted the privilege of seeing from a triumphant new perspective the land from which English soldiers and sailors, speaking Shakespeare's language, set out to rewrite the history of the world. But the words themselves remain only words.

Ginger looked out of the aeroplane: "I say, Nina," he shouted, "when you were young did you ever have to learn a thing out of a poetry book about: *'This scepter'd isle, this earth of majesty, this something or other Eden'?* D'you know what I mean? *'this happy breed of men, this little world, this precious stone set in the silver sea. . . .*

　" *'This blessed plot, this earth, this realm, this England,*
　This nurse, this teeming womb of royal kings
　Feared by their breed and famous by their birth. . . . '

"I forgot how it goes on. Something about a stubborn Jew. But you know the thing I mean?"
"It comes in a play."
"No, a blue poetry book."
"I acted in it."

"Well, they may have put it into a play since. It was in a blue poetry book when I learned it. Anyway, you know what I mean?"

"Yes, why?"

"Well, I mean to say, don't you feel somehow, up in the air like this and looking down and seeing everything underneath. I mean, don't you have a sort of feeling rather like that, if you see what I mean?"

Nina looked down and saw inclined at an odd angle a horizon of straggling red suburb; arterial roads dotted with little cars; factories, some of them working, others empty and decaying; a disused canal; some distant hills sown with bungalows; wireless masts and overhead power cables; men and women were indiscernible except as tiny spots; they were marrying and shopping and making money and having children. The scene lurched and tilted again as the aeroplane struck a current of air.

"I think I'm going to be sick," said Nina.

"Poor little girl," said Ginger. "That's what the paper bags are for."[9]

Clearly those paper bags have more value within the ambit of Waugh's satire than a volume of Shakespeare. The bags can at least serve human needs innocently, uncorrupted by will. Ideally unambiguous performatives, they are only what they do. Unlike words, they can offer the human no possibility of misreading truth, if and when truth ever comes. Evelyn Waugh, Catholic satirist, writes out of a rueful awareness that grace is too lucid to entrust itself to language.

But of course the Church's agenda isn't the only proposal for dealing with the paperwork of fallen words. Between Waugh's generalizing *parti pris* and Ovid's gentle *unus ego,* for instance, there comes John Ashbery, diffidently bearing clichés. "Where were you when it was all happening?" asks a voice in "Alone in the Lumber Business" (AG 23–24). And it adds, in an ominous weather report directed toward whoever it is that has been hanging around the Tree of Knowledge,

> Night is full of kindred spirits now,
> Voices, photos of loved ones, faces
> Out of the newspaper, eager smiles blown like leaves
>
> Before they become fungus. No time. . . .
> (24)

"Kindred spirits" is a cliché, but it is *our* cliché. After all, we need to think of ourselves as spirits, speaking and understanding spirits' language. We want individuation; we want to believe we matter; we want what T. S. Eliot, dipping himself icily into cliché for an ulterior motive, called "the evening under lamplight / (The evening with the photograph album)" ("East Coker," V). But the language of the typical cannot be repressed. On behalf of the fallen and the imperfect, it humbles itself to absorb the spirit. So, conducting a moral discourse with itself, the poem continues:

> No time to give credit
> Where it is due, though actions, as before,
> Speak louder than words. To dot the i's,
> Cross the t's and tie everything up
>
> In a loose bundle stamped "not wanted on the voyage."

The cliché is always there to absorb meaning, explaining in words that there can be something which speaks louder than words, the human agency that moves us to act and love and remember. Once there was an Eden, and we named the animals there, but now—no matter:

> There were flowers in a garden once,
> Monkey business, shenanigans. But it all
> Gets towered over. There would be no point
>
> In replying to the finer queries, since we live
> In our large, square, open landscape.
>   (AG 24)

No, there would be no point in replying. Here in the typical, we are free to become silent, humbly uncomprehending as the animals were just before the advent of their naming. Henceforth we will be as they.

> The bridge
> Of fools once crossed, there are adjustments to be made.
> But you have to settle in to looking at these things.

And the poem ends there. If it is a satire on cliché and the people who think in cliché, I suppose it is at least as effective as, say, Sinclair Lewis's. But it may not be a satire.

To satirize, after all, is to categorize, extending the individuality of character into type. Thomas Gradgrind becomes a way of thinking about the industrial revolution and the history of English philosophy, and Lemuel Gulliver's greatness is precisely that he is a representative man. But the individual comes first. At this point in our lives we may need F. R. Leavis to prescribe *Hard Times* for its high moral fiber, but when we were children, we could read *Gulliver's Travels* for its story alone. But where is the individuality in "Alone in the Lumber Business"?

It is there, but not referentially, transferred as a second approximation to something like plot or character. No. All that is real in Ashbery's work exists in the language itself. Forgoing the chance to say "Lenin, meet Trotsky," Ashbery's language operates abstractly, at the Platonic level of the typical. There, it appears, Michael Herr's generalization doesn't hold. The Word does require the effort of recalling one's collective immortality in the undifferentiated language from which our culture shapes its history. There, alone in the lumber business, we find ourselves wandering, lonely as an Ashbery protagonist, through a warehouse full of raw material. But it's *our* raw material—our clichés, our abstracted sentence rhythms, the epitomized history of our language. And that, perhaps, is the value of Ashbery's recycled speech. When we speak it, we are immersed in the typicality of ourselves.

Notes

1. Marjorie Perloff, "Making Poetic Sense in Media Society," *Verse* 8, no. 1 (Spring 1991): 60.

2. Samir al-Khalil, *The Monument: Art, Vulgarity, and Responsibility in Iraq* (Berkeley: University of California Press, 1991), 6.

3. Douglas Crase, "The Prophetic Ashbery," in *Beyond Amazement: New Essays on John Ashbery,* ed. David Lehman (Ithaca: Cornell University Press, 1980), 30.

4. Don DeLillo, *White Noise* (New York: Viking, 1985), 326.

5. John Koethe, "The Absence of a Noble Presence," *Verse* 8, no. 1 (Spring 1991): 24. It is easy enough to argue with this analysis on objective historical grounds. Thirty years ago was, to take only two examples out of many, the time of Sylvia Plath and John Berryman, who were anything but chary of rhetorical effect and nothing if not dissociated from rationality and control. But I take it that Koethe is primarily interested here in writing a different kind of history, one of his own growth into the language of the Ashbery era.

6. Emily Dickinson, *The Poems,* ed. Thomas H. Johnson (Cambridge, Ma.: Harvard University Press, 1955), no. 1071.

7. Stanley Burnshaw, "A Future for Poetry: Planetary Maturity," in *A Stanley Burnshaw Reader* (Athens: University of Georgia Press, 1990), 35.

8. David Lehman, "The Shield of a Greeting: The Function of Irony in John Ashbery's Poetry," in *Beyond Amazement: New Essays on John Ashbery,* ed. David Lehman (Ithaca: Cornell University Press, 1980), 111.

9. Evelyn Waugh, *Vile Bodies* (1930; reprint, New York: Delta-Dell, 1966), 169–70 (ellipses in original).

2 | Ashbery as Love Poet

Charles Altieri

In teaching John Ashbery, I stumbled upon a perspective that I think helps a good deal in showing how contemporary poets can make distinctive and important claims on our lives. I concentrated on treating his shy, indirect, often vague, and always understated work as offering fresh approaches to recurrent problems within the genre of love poetry.[1] By identifying what seemed fundamental to the genre, we could see clearly how contemporaries seemed to characterize what was distinctively contemporary about our imaginings of what love entails and about the emotional economies within which these imaginings had to function.

There are of course many ways to use generic considerations. I have chosen the love lyric because this genre is so directly connected to how the imagination engages textual energies for existential concerns—that is, to how we imagine affects how we pursue certain aspects of emotional lives. Such an orientation proves a dynamic way of teaching lyrics because it allows us to treat formal choices as testing exemplary existential possibilities, at least in terms of how we represent what is for most of us our deepest and most intense narcissistic experience. Simultaneously, we can use the generic background to position those choices historically. Once we tease out what seem the fundamental problems within the project of giving love a voice, we can use those as provisional constants that individual poets and historical epochs will treat in a variety of ways. Just as the structure of political relations imposes constant requirements on political thinking—for example, developing some way of negotiating the claims of individuals and the claims of collectivities—genres like love poetry must negotiate a recurrent set of issues fundamental to expressing, celebrating, and enduring the pains of love. Only then we will have means of talking about that variety which isolates significant differences and puts pressure on us to understand how the differences relate to cultural change—both as an expression of forces impinging on us and as a specification of ways we can respond to those changes with the fullest possible mix of psychic intensity and self-reflexive lucidity. Were we to read in terms of allegories generated by contemporary theoretical issues, we would condemn ourselves to collapsing all history into our own obsessions, and we would risk surrendering the possible authority of the art for the authority of theory. And were we to rely on close analyses of individual poets, we would have considerably fewer grounds for appreciating the pressures that the poets face and the responses that they develop.

There are two basic levels to this framework (so long as the framework is derived from Anglo-American poetic traditions). First I will isolate three tasks that I think virtually any convincing verbal expression of love must accomplish, and then I must elaborate the two basic sets of pressures that require innovations in that rendering. The first task of the love poet is the most daunting. For our culture the imagination of love is the imagination of human powers and needs at their most vital. Love is our imaginative angel, if not our god, so the poet must be able to project idealizations of the lover's states worthy of such investments. But love also involves constraining such narcissistic states so that we remain responsive to what for most of us is our richest experience of the claims of another person upon us, and of the intimacy that comes from adapting to those claims. Thus the second task consists in preserving an intimacy and a vulnerability in which we must risk our narcissistic defenses, at the very point where that narcissism finds its deepest gratifications. Love poetry must define the psyche at its greediest, while also directing that intensity toward someone on whom we confer the power to empty us of all our narcissistic resources. In poetry the lover's voice must define the rewards of desire while negotiating fears of all that the projected bonding can cause.

The third task then emerges from these contradictory impulses. For there is a phenomenon we might call "lover's time" implied in Wittgenstein's observation that one cannot feel deep grief or be in love for only a moment (although there are often only moments when one feels love). One cannot love another whom one treats as only a casual encounter. Instead one must confer a distinctive singularity. And that involves placing the other in relation to fears and needs shaped by past loves; it involves imagining the future as the ripening of what the lovers can plant within the lyric moments opened by responding to that singularity, and above all, it involves the risk that this future will exact the loss of both the self and the world that love composes. One might even say that much of what we can attribute positively to how love is constructed at any particular moment takes on its full power only under the lens of love's possible disasters, for it is by what we know and fear about loss that we measure what we have.

To see how these background conditions frame individual choices, we might glance quickly at some of the paradigmatic texts of the lyric tradition. The easiest way to project terms for the lover's intensity is to represent the beloved so as to make immediately visible the grounds for the lover's narcissistic satisfactions and, simultaneously, to establish the pull beyond the self that submits the satisfactions to a chain of dependencies. One thinks of the very different exalting agency of Spenser's lady, of Yeats's Maude Gonne with no second Troy to burn, and of the more direct sexual powers celebrated by poets like Maxine Kumin and Sharon Olds. Or poets can invoke those ideals as conventional contexts against which they develop a singular relationship, then use that relationship as a version of the sublime to celebrate a love taking the lover beyond everything limited by such conventions. The most obvious form of this device is Shakespeare's "My Mistress' eyes are nothing like the sun," but similar effects can be achieved in more sinister or more transcendental ways: for example in the threatening sexuality of Shakespeare's dark lady and in the elegant resisting intelligence that silently stabs the flea on whom Donne lavished his own desiring wit.

Once the erotic force is established, the love poet must make clear his or her means of relationship to it. Dramatically that usually involves elaborating a ritual center through which the love is exemplified and by which the example takes hold upon the lover's imagination. Consider how Sharon Olds uses sexual activity as an emblem of everything that binds voice to the deepest recesses of natural energy, while anchoring those energies within the temporality of married life. For other contemporaries the ritual center carries more general social force, ranging from Gary Snyder's casting his wife in relation to the intricate play of desire within an ordered, nurturing nature to Adrienne Rich's sense of the beloved as a heroic partner sharing the terrors of urban life and the demands of political struggle. Drama in turn must be tested by the voice that the poet manages to bring as a result of what occupies the imagination. How one speaks to and of the love is the basic test for who one becomes by opening oneself to such centers.

Who one becomes cannot be measured simply by the rendering of a dramatic moment. For the promise of enduring love requires also the possibility of enduring changes in character. So the ultimate demand on the love lyric, like the ultimate demand on love, is to provide convincing ways of marking how the agent takes on transformations opening new possible selves without losing the public life that the old self had managed to achieve. One way to do this is to concentrate on how the loving breaks free from certain modes of repetitive behavior, so that the beloved is no longer simply a substitute within an interminable romance plot; another is to project the transformations forward onto a modified future. Thus we find at one pole Sharon Olds celebrating the gulf between her husband and the patterns her father established for male behavior, and at the other we find Adrienne Rich seeking through her lover a relation to deep, enduring time that will provide the sustenance necessary for building new futures.

In this area, as in all areas of the love lyric, the speaker is likely to be haunted by constant possibility that our celebrating love opens us to a very different future within which love fails and life becomes a terrifying emptiness, with all time collapsed into one's present agonies. Thus in Shakespeare's sonnets love's demand for immortality is constantly juxtaposed with a terrifying sense of how the old patterns keep repeating themselves. And in most love poetry the failure to endure through time becomes the poet's richest instrument for learning what love could have been. For this cautionary note there is no richer contemporary instance than the concluding section of Robert Hass's *Human Wishes,* where the sense of becoming a stranger to one's life and the pervasive pressure of self-disgust mark by contrast the pervasive, intimate transformations of ordinariness that love brings.

A second level of analysis must go beyond the various ideas we have about loving to the qualities of voice by which we make those ideas means of exchange with the beloved. On the most elemental level the poet's act of speaking love must maintain a difficult balance between what makes the love singular and what establishes a place for it in the symbolic order. Unless the speaker can convince us that the beloved makes unique demands on language, the poem threatens to reduce the love to posture, and the relation to the other to a staging for certain roles that agents can fantasize for themselves. Yet as soon as one begins to speak one's love, one also begins to speak about it (in both senses of "about"), so there can be no singularity within language. The most the poet can do is at once speak within and against the language. So the condition of "sincerity" in love poetry demands an ability to hear the conventions one relies on and to alter them in some way (if only by a syntactic directness or by a metrical innovation). This is no easy matter because the cultural order has no stronger hold than in those areas where we most intensely seek imaginative identities. Eloquence is a trap, but there can be eloquent refusals of eloquence which make resistance to the dominant tropes a model for strengths and dispositions open to the full particularity of this love relationship.

Here, though, the author begins to encounter a pressure that makes it impossible to rely entirely on particularizing gestures. Love poetry will probably not make much of an impact on its audience if it is content to engage the beloved in his or her particularity. Because the lyric must engage the lives of other people, poets will be tempted to envision their loving as carrying some kind of metaphoric or exemplary force, if only as a measure of the difference that the love makes. Demonstrating one's seriousness as a poet becomes inseparable from demonstrating a seriousness as a lover responsive to the ways in which the beloved leads the imagination beyond particulars. Ironically the demands on the poet then turn out to echo some of the basic demands of love at its most intense. For in such moments the lover's responsiveness to the beloved is likely to extend beyond the particular, as if in calling us to the things of this world, love also calls us to metaphors for those things and invites us to imagine realms in which the excess that is metaphor becomes access to underlying erotic energies the poet can share with his or her audience. Thus for Spenser love is inseparable from experiencing a desire that yearns for absolute conditions only partially represented by the one loved; for Shakespeare's last sonnets that absolute becomes the state of a self able to reconcile the eye, the "I," and the "aye" of the lover's intensity (especially in sonnet 148); in Donne love merges with a more general sacramentalism that takes new secular forms in contemporary poetry; in Yeats the love rewards the dynamics of setting masks against the limited desires of the empirical self; and in poets as diverse as Whitman and Rich love sustains the possibility of a transformed political order.

Unfortunately this very sense of transcendental possibilities also proves love's most naturalizing trap. Given the intensity and focus of erotic desire, it is not surprising that for secular culture the subject position of the lover becomes one of the most exalted models of individual life at its fullest. But that appeal to idealization also threatens to subject the author to cultural fantasms confining the beloved to a set of functions within the symbolic order. So love poetry faces the challenge of having to handle both poles of this expansiveness — the sense of metaphoric extensions of self that erotic desire brings and an ironic grasp of the temptation then to love oneself in love so much that one loses sight of the beloved except in the symbolic functions which the poetry establishes. Behind every moment of love, there is likely to be a constant sense of vulnerability and fragility, since so much depends on so little.

I

Fully developing and assessing these categories would require comparative study of several poets. For now, though, I can concentrate only on Ashbery. Yet that should prove a substantial test of contemporary imaginative resources. Ashbery offers an exemplary sensitivity to the ways in which traditions become traps, yet in so doing, he also manages to resist the dangers of lyrically displacing the other as his vehicle for expressing love's exalting powers, for locating ritual centers that enable the poet to develop a voice at once intimate and self-celebrating, and above all for making temporal dimensions of love his metaphoric vehicle to exemplify a fully vital reflective intensity. First I will trace how he makes working against the romance imagination his means for celebrating the differences that love creates in one's sense of the world; then I will turn to a poem which defines the same complex of values from the other side, from the sense of all that the end of a love relationship reveals about possibilities and limits.

My initial example, the poem "As We Know" (AWK 74), seems at first an odd choice of an exemplary love lyric. Where does the lover manifest his or her power? Where is the intensity of the lover's voice, and how does it free itself from Ashbery's characteristic solipsism long enough to respond fully to what manages to make itself present as a distinctive "you"? Moreover, there is no clear ritual center of the poem establishing and reinforcing the bonds between the lovers. A complex sense of time we certainly have, but it seems as if all singularity is lost in the text's intricate web. Yet if we are willing to impose a dramatic continuity that Ashbery goes to some pains to suspend, we will find the poem defining a remarkably expansive minimalist sense of how love transforms a person's world.

The poem's opening is maddening, as maddening as wondering what happens to oneself when one is in love:

> All that we see is penetrated by it—
> The distant treetops with their steeple (so
> Innocent), the stair, the windows' fixed flashing—
> Pierced full of holes by the evil that is not evil,
> The romance that is not mysterious, the life that is not life,
> A present that is elsewhere.[2]

The indeterminate "it" introduces Ashbery's version of the basic site of romance: whatever makes love possible also makes it problematic by offering a domain that in fact the lovers cannot inhabit except in a fantasy of an alternative present distinguished by a full transparency. So the poet's vagueness takes on a disturbing concreteness, capturing at the edge of sense what seems to afford it an alternative life—evil in its distance from the quotidian present but by no means evil in what it promises or in the energies that it organizes.

Possibility itself then becomes Ashbery's ritual center for experiencing the intensity that love offers and for encountering its most disturbing challenges:

> And further in the small capitulations
> of the dance, you rub elbows with it,
> Finger it. That day you did it
> Was the day you had to stop, because the doing
> Involved the whole fabric, there was no other way to appear.
> You slid down on your knees
> For those precious jewels of spring water
> Planted on the moss, before they got soaked up
> And you teetered on the edge of this
> Calm street with its sidewalks, its traffic,
>
> As though they are coming to get you.
> But there was no one in the noon glare,
> only birds like secrets to find out about
> And a home to get to, one of these days.

One might speak here of the seductions of the wandering "it" as it modulates from the "we" to an equally ambiguous "you," and as it calls up the most intimate memories. Whatever "you" did, that doing marks a point of surrendering the self to some state of desire so intense that hunger leaves one alienated from everything quotidian. It is no wonder, then, that this section of the poem ends in a turning from desire to fear of punishment, and through that to an almost total isolation. But one factor remains located deeply within the "you" that makes possible a return to the "us," now capable of projecting a romance state fully within the flow of time. Ashbery's figure for that is the birds, which even in this light hold out the possibility of secrets, and a home sanctified by those secrets. But what are the birds a figure for within the psychological forces set in motion by the poem? I think they serve as external images of a doubleness within the "you" that will not be subsumed under the threat of the "they" and that calls the lovers beyond their fantasies to some enabling sense of their grounds. Thus Ashbery finds his means of connection to the beloved precisely where traditional love poetry finds its greatest difficulty—in distinguishing between the narcissistic ego and an other constructed in its language and its image. Here that problem takes center stage: the speaker must recognize the ways in which the "you" both gestures toward the other and projects the lover's desires. But at the same time this doubleness means that in a sense each must internalize the other, so that even one's most solipsistic moments become haunted by addresses to a beloved, addresses that keep alive the hope there is something that the isolated consciousness can share, something that Ashbery calls elsewhere the "permanent tug of a home."

Once such recognitions enter, there can be an alternative to the noon glare and the power that "they" wield in relation to it. The birds hovering on the edges of the scene evoke a competing light reduced to shadow by that glare, but at the same time made important precisely because those shadows provide access to a satisfying casualness usually figured within the romance imagination.

> The light that was shadowed then
> Was seen to be our lives,
> Everything about us that love might wish to examine,
> Then put away for a certain length of time, until
> The whole is to be reviewed, and we turned
> Toward each other, to each other.
> The way we had come was all we could see
> And it crept up on us, embarrassed
> That there is so much to tell now, really now.

Here the romance imagination initially captured within the landscape finds its alternative home as space yields to time, and as the "it" gets securely anchored in the history that the lovers share. This sense of time then becomes the poem's own ritual center, distinctive in its abstraction and in its capacity to be constituted in relation to any scene. Particulars matter a good deal less than the attitude one learns to take to those particulars.

This stanza begins with two passive expressions, as if the consciousness oppressed by the noon glare, by the sharp oppositions between romance site and grim reality, found itself contained by what the lovers' lives have built together. On that basis, they can turn to each other, locating through that turn the deep alternative to romance absolutes. Rather than immerse themselves in present moments that are elsewhere, the lovers can make their past a recurrent source of romantic connection powerful enough to carry even into the future. There need be no drama of absolute surrender, like the one in the second stanza, but there is a rich, subtle eroticism projected in the strange sense of embarrassment that the poem evokes, as if embarrassment were an effect of erotic plenitude. And grammatically it is just that. "Embarrassed" hovers between modifying the "way"—which now provides a clear referent for the "it"—and modifying "us" as we begin to feel the plenitude within that way. Awakened to that "us," the lovers can so engage one another that the isolated yearning can yield to a stunning contemporary recuperation of Whitman's "telling," now simply a function of the lovers' understanding the resources they carry with them.

The ultimate resource for this poem is its capacity to replace the present that is elsewhere with a sense of the "really now" that is at once act and description, form and content for an intensity that bonds the lovers. On the dramatic level within the poem, the "really now" emerges from the realization of how much the return to their own history yields as a vital present. On more abstract figurative levels, the expression suggests that as the lovers attune to their specific history, they reach a site where everything matters simply because of where they are. The talking itself creates and sustains the "now," leaving no residue and inviting no alienation. Then the relation between the "now" and its intensifier, "really now," creates a superb self-referential moment in which the reflecting consciousness manages to will what it is producing. Not only is there no supplemental romance site elsewhere, there is within the "now" a mode of eros that fully engages the will, in the process opening the "now" into a promise of future connection because the telling itself becomes a recurrent activity. The "now" shifts from referring to one moment to exemplifying a relation to all moments that can be absorbed within the history that the lovers create, and it does so while avoiding any single image or idea that would reintroduce the cycle of demand and alienation.

One crucial piece of that history now transformed is the poem's title. On one level "as we know" calls up all the banalities which constitute love's quotidian reality. "The way we had come" offers nothing remarkable, nothing not contained within standard lives as we know them. But what the title denies itself on the level of romantic content, it claims for itself in relation to the state of reflective activity achieved within the poem's "really now." This "now" has substance only as the lovers form a "we" in the process of telling itself, and the feeling of that telling locates love's center. A moment becomes "really now" only as two sensibilities contour themselves to it—temporally by yielding their attention and modally by recognizing that the very substance of the moment is two independent ways of knowing joined through the "as" of the telling. There a "we" is composed. And there the "as" offers up a last resource by referring indexically to precisely the poem's processes of intensification, as we read. "Really now" is the affirmation within the act of speaking—first between the projected lovers, then in the reader's own coming to appreciate what their speech involves.

II

What, then, do we know through Ashbery's transformations of the love lyric? One might say that he manages to redefine the entire process of lyric love by shifting attention from the dramatic scenes in which love is born or sworn to the kind of site where its enduring qualities can be celebrated. This is not a matter of proposing new ideas or images. It involves simply focusing on the form, the process, by which that love renews itself. Thus he manages to free lyric eros from the ironies that haunt its efforts to imagine idealized poses dramatically securing all the intensity that love brings, but also mocking the long-term bonds such states may produce. Where theatrical intensity had been, Ashbery seeks the much more quiet and subtle intensities that characterize mutual recognition of how the bonds of love hold and that allow one to participate fully in one's words. This sense is sufficiently rare and strange to warrant all the idealizations that the lyric tradition affords erotic love, but it remains so tied to processes that it need not displace the lover's intimacy for more idealized single states of intensity. Indeed Ashbery's lush abstraction is the counterpart to his shy asceticism. Uncomfortable with fantasized contents for his desires, he tries to locate lovers' discourse at its elemental levels, where the "really now" becomes the essential lyric cry of joy, a cry inseparable from the most casual exchanges.

The basis for this unique stance is Ashbery's subsuming the first and second tasks of love poetry under the third. Emphasis on the "really now" allows the lovers' temporality to account for the intensity love can bring and to define a mode of speech correlating that intensity with intimacy. At the same time it forestalls the temptation to idealize romance states because the ideal is nothing but a state within time—it cannot be abstracted from the telling of the way we had come. Any additional details attempting to flesh out this formal vision would only weaken the intensity by tying it to specific moments, thereby banishing others. Similarly, such details create problems for the speaking voice because they locate it within fantasy, and hence within a structure of demands that probably does not contour itself entirely to the other person. Such fantasies can create sublime states, and they can compose a ritual center around which lovers learn to adjust. Ashbery's is not the only important mode of celebrating love. But only his abstraction makes lovers' time a condition of lovers' discourse and thus frees that discourse to speak of and within an entire life.

One might generalize from this example to suggest that in this love poem the ritual center of the reflection calling love into this world manages to become its own mode of sacramentalism by the relationship it establishes to time. "As We Know" moves from a disruptive gulf between action and a desired sense of presence first back into the history shadowed by romance, then forward into a present tense that can be fully engaged. And then this present itself takes on a strange doubleness. If we can move from a "now" to a "really now," we can also imagine an instant that is inseparable from a future. Saying "really now" affirms the present and so attaches the will to what emerges within it, as we come to know. "Really now" then becomes not only a reference to one specific moment but an abstract form for how love allows the experience of all references to the present. The lovers affirm not only the moments that their story makes possible but also the condition of connectedness that their relationship projects for the flow of time. Love finds its sanction and its reward not in any moral or psychological or physical qualities specific to the lovers but in how they learn to bring all such qualities within the orbit of mutually affirmed desires. Modesty becomes its own access to a sublime moment in which the very form of lover's time becomes really present, if only as a shadow cast by the imperatives of the lover's demands.

III

I grow so idealistic in praising Ashbery's alternative to traditional idealizing that I need to right the balance by turning to his handling of the opposite side of the story, the process by which the telling becomes mere story and the "really now" modulates into a bare "this is all there is." Here then is "Frontispiece":

Expecting rain, the profile of a day
Wears its soul like a hat, prow up
Against the deeply incised clouds and regions
Of abrupt skidding from cold to cold, riddles

Of climate it cannot understand.
Sometimes toward the end
A look of longing broke, taut, from those eyes
Meeting yours in final understanding, late,

And often, too, the beginnings went unnoticed
As though the story could advance its pawns
More discreetly thus, overstepping
The confines of ordinary health and reason

To introduce in another way
Its fact into the picture. It registered,
It must be there. And so we turn the page over
To think of starting. This is all there is.
      (ShTr 46)

In so turning we begin to flesh out the background of needs and fears and self-divisions which by contrast makes the "really now" so satisfying a state. The dissatisfactions begin with this poem's maddening ambiguities: do we read the promise of starting at the end as a hopeful resolution based on recognizing that certain necessities of desire are all there is, or do we emphasize the reference to endings so that the frontispiece becomes little more than a blank page where one thinks of starting again while looking at a life that has nothing before it but the bare "this" of what once had elicited the vital desire of "As We Know"? Since there is no clear answer, I suspect we must try to understand how both stances have holds upon us, perhaps precisely because of the difficulties of facing the end of romances.

Here the speaker recognizes that there is nothing left to a romance, yet he also seems to want to treat that recognition as an imperative to attempt starting over. But it is hard to see how after such knowledge there can be another beginning for this relationship. Instead the tenuousness of that vague hope may become part of the problem. For hope becomes an aspect of the drive leading the lovers to attempt to recuperate themselves within stories of themselves. However the gap between the story and a sense of telling that creates a "really now" gets marked by the poem's play of subjunctives and by its relentless move toward increasingly simple, reductive syntax. Tense too tells its own tale about the difficulty of beginning again. The poem moves from a grimly determined resolution in the present, through the lovers' own sense of themselves in the past tense, to the desperate blend of present and future in the many meanings of "it must be there" (some of which barely restrain hysteria), to the absolutely bare, timeless, lifeless present of "this is all there is." This final "this" can be the most affirmative of indexicals, since it gathers into an otherwise inexpressible whole whatever the rendered experience offers.[3] But here that whole can consist only of the "there is," the marker of distance and inevitability.

Once we develop a feeling for what is at stake in the ending, we can go back to see how deeply the sense of distance and blank beginnings defines this lyric space. Ashbery often imagines love as a kind of weather or atmosphere which affects all the facts of an environment without materially changing any of them. Weather becomes a figure for pervasive interconnection between the psyche's life and that of its surroundings. But here the movement goes the other way. The psyche so pervades the weather that even weather becomes a riddle to itself. From the start the day is divided against itself—victim at once of forces it cannot understand and of its own efforts to compose a resistance to those forces. But resistance proves little more than a self-defeating nostalgia that puts pressure on the lovers to create a story for their love. This story, however, proves inescapably distant from what it would narrate, so we witness a victory of discretion over creative difference and an imposition of narrative time on the play of beginnings. It should be no wonder, then, that all the hope carried in these final lines is canceled by the underlying sense of an impersonal imperative, the one force that is incompatible with love. Once the "must" enters, starting becomes thinking of starting, and the blank page invites only the empty fact of all that cannot start again.

Yet even if in this poem all there is, is that oppressive "this," there does remain the thought of starting again. Here it is not much consolation. Nevertheless there is at least an echo of the irreducible hope at the core of any lyric experience; even as we find nothing in a concrete situation that allows an alternative to despair, we find in the pain both a memorial to the love we can live and a negative projection of why it matters so much never to lose hope in starting again. "Even now" is a state not absolutely distant from "really now." The darkest love poetry can become a ground that, in C. K. Williams's words, "is to be worked across not like a wistful map, but land."[4]

Notes

1. I want to acknowledge the genesis of this project in my reading the introductory chapter to Maeera Shreiber's dissertation on love poetry for Brandeis University. She too uses certain features of the idea of speaking one's love in poetry as a constant backdrop for setting off cultural changes, but we have very different constructions of the idea of love, and of the idea of poetry.

2. I offer a similar reading of this poem in my "Contemporary Poetry as Philosophy: Subjective Agency in John Ashbery and C. K. Williams," *Contemporary Literature* 33 (1992): 214–42.

3. I take this sense of the indexical "this" from Michael Levenson, *Modernism and the Fate of Individuality* (New York: Cambridge University Press, 1991), 74. I should add that grammatically "this" can serve as an exclamation that affirms individual intentionality. One finds that "this" best developed in Wittgenstein's understanding of how one suddenly sees how materials fit together. Here, of course, Ashbery plays against that exclamatory possibility, while in his "Soonest Mended" and "A Wave" he does use the exclamatory "this" to develop a positive sense of beginning.

4. C. K. Williams, *Flesh and Blood* (New York: Farrar, Straus & Giroux, 1987), 18.

3 | Coming Full Circle
John Ashbery's Later Poetry

Fred Moramarco

> The words have, as they
> always do, come full circle, dragging the meaning that was on the reverse side
> all along, and one even
> expects this, something to chew on. I'm rubber
> and you're glue, whatever you say bounces off me and sticks to you; in which gluey
> embrace I surrender. We are both part of a living thing now.
>
> *Flow Chart*, 25–26

WITH THE PUBLICATIONS of *Flow Chart* in 1991 and *Hotel Lautréamont* in 1992, John Ashbery's work appears to have come full circle. The books revert to the kind of disjunctive language characteristic of his earlier work, a language in which words are unhinged from their traditional referents and seem to float on the swells and ebbs of their meanings. But these books, of course, add the density of the thirty years' experience of living and writing that have intervened since the publication of *The Tennis Court Oath* (1962). *Hotel Lautréamont* is a collection of formally diverse and usually cryptic lyrics, influenced especially by French and Provençal poetic conventions as well as by the surrealistic predilections of their namesake, Isidore Ducase, who wrote under the name of Comte de Lautréamont, updated by Ashbery's unique and often astonishing sense of contemporaneity. Like *The Tennis Court Oath*, *Flow Chart* is a book of radical linguistic disjunctions, highly experimental, strikingly innovative, defying categories and creating a similar but much denser sort of metapoetry. At both the beginning and the later stages of his career, Ashbery has worked toward finding the language to express an awareness that exists on the axis between our "inner" and "outer" lives, between our personal lives as individuals and our collective life as a contemporary civilization. In this sense Ashbery's work is really not about language at all but about consciousness, which, for a poet, can be reached and conveyed only *through* language. He is interested in creating a body of work that is "a living thing" both for him and for his readers, and his most recent work is involved in ruminations about just what that living thing is, and what sort of legacy he will leave for posterity.

In his later work, Ashbery has attempted to measure the dimensions of that consciousness. From *Houseboat Days* (1977) through *As We Know* (1977) and *Shadow Train* (1981) to *A Wave* (1984), *April Galleons* (1987), *Flow Chart* (1991), and the extremely difficult *Hotel Lautréamont* (1992), this quest seems central, as does his desire to invigorate traditional poetic forms or discover new ones that can embody that consciousness. "Litany" from *As We Know* is a long poem printed as two columns to be read simultaneously; *Shadow Train* is an entire volume of sixteen-line poems consisting of four quatrains each; *A Wave* includes thirty-seven haiku, a description of a masque, and an innovative form of prose poem he calls "Haibun." These forms and the innovations that Ashbery brought to them have been "containers" for the shifting phantasmagoria that is contemporary experience. Ashbery often distills that experience into a kind of quintessential metaphor, as in this memorable passage from *Houseboat Days*:

> To praise this, blame that,
> Leads one subtly away from the beginning, where
> We must stay, in motion. To flash light
> Into the house within, its many chambers,
> Its memories and associations, upon its inscribed
> And pictured walls, argues enough that life is various.
> Life is beautiful. He who reads that
> As in the window of some distant, speeding train
> Knows what he wants, and what will befall.
> (HD 39)

"[L]ife is various. / Life is beautiful." These sweeping banalities do not seem simplistic in Ashbery because these observations (and others like them throughout the poetry) are embedded in imagery of intermittent light and motion that enriches and illuminates them.

Ashbery's longer works—*Three Poems*, "Self-Portrait in a Convex Mirror," "Litany," "A Wave," and now the exhausting and exhaustive *Flow Chart* as well as the mysterious and elusive totality of poems that make up *Hotel Lautréamont*—are variations and elaborations on just *what* life is, or at least what kind of metaphors he can come up with for it. In fact, the word "life" or one of its variants, and speculations about what it is or might be, punctuates these works with substantial regularity. The examples of these "life metaphors" in Ashbery's poetry are so numerous that even a highly judicious selection of them goes on for pages, but I have included a number in an appendix at the end of this chapter to emphasize the fact that despite his reputation as a "difficult" poet who is preoccupied with word games, his poetry remains closely tied to poetry's central mission: finding metaphors for life.

Flow Chart particularly seems to be the culmination of this dual focus of Ashbery's writing life: to express contemporary consciousness and to find metaphors that truly invoke a sense of what life is. Every fourth or fifth page of my copy of this 216-page poem is tagged to mark such a metaphor. A flow chart itself is, among other things, a metaphor for life, one thing leading to and affecting the next, all of the major life events linked in an inexorable and interconnected pattern.

In many of Ashbery's major works, the central metaphor embodies a specific conception of art and/or life, usually connoting something about the relationship of art and artists to the world around them. These metaphors have been drawn from nature ("A Wave"), sports ("The Skaters"), art itself ("Self-Portrait in a Convex Mirror"), religion ("Litany"), music ("Blue Sonata"), and, in *Flow Chart*, appropriately for the post-Reagan years, the corporate and institutional world. The metaphor of a flow chart resonates in a number of additional directions. On one level the poem appears to be about the relationship of both the writer and the reader to what the writer has written. In the case of a writer like Ashbery, that relationship is often a lifelong association. Many of the readers likely to read his books at this stage in his life have charted his development as a writer with something of the systematic organization of a flow chart. So the book is a metaphor as well for his life's work (his "published city" as he refers to it in the first line of the poem) and its ongoing relatedness to both himself and his readers. He speaks directly to those readers throughout the poem and about halfway through it, refers to them as "fellow members in the secret society" and feels comforted by the fact that "I've not outstayed my welcome, that on the contrary quite a few people are waiting / in the anteroom to shake my hand" (FC 102).

The metaphor encompasses as well the way a writer's work (or any work of art) is disseminated in the world—the way it finds its way from one reader to another through conversation, classrooms, media, other writing, and so on. How does an artist's work get from the inside of his or her head to becoming a part of a culture's awareness? And when and if it does become a cultural icon, where does it then fit in the larger scheme of things? What would a flow chart for the *Mona Lisa* look like, or for *King Lear?* These are huge questions, and they can evoke a heavy sense of dread in a writer—a feeling of the futility of one's art, especially in the contemporary world and especially for poets whose art form has been completely marginalized in a commodity-oriented society.

Ashbery persists in trying to find the poetry of this virtually untenable situation rather than to submit to a "new form of despair." The style and tone of *Flow Chart* bring the reader directly into contact with the consciousness that is embroidered throughout it and indeed throughout all of his work. He wants to capture the elusive consciousness that exists between the reader and the writer, what in a happier time would be the collective spirit of the age. He speculates about what the end of individual life might be like, but the existence of this consciousness, which does not exist within an individual, suggests the possibility of a "larger activity" beyond the "busyness" of life. Listen to the speculations (which are all words can be, as he observed in "Self-Portrait") about the nature of contemporary life that carry the reader into the poem:

> Still in the published city but not yet
> overtaken by a new form of despair, I ask
> the diagram: is it the foretaste of pain
> it might easily be? Or an emptiness
> so sudden it leaves the girders
> whanging in the absence of wind,
> the sky milk-blue and astringent? We know life is so busy,
> but a larger activity shrouds it, and this is something
> we can never feel, except occasionally, in small signs
> put up to warn us and as soon expunged, in part
> or wholly.
> (FC 3)

The "published city," the world of a writer's work, remains under construction as long as he or she lives. So the poem asks us to consider Ashbery's complete works (one of the poems in *Hotel Lautréamont* is called "*Oeuvres Complètes*") as a kind of a flow chart. It may be useful to actually visualize that flow chart as a kind of circle emanating from both the formalism of *Some Trees*, his first published book, and the innovative experimentation of *The Tennis Court Oath*, which secured his reputation as an avant-garde poet. Nearly all of the qualities we associate with Ashbery's mature voice are already present in those two books: the fascination with fixed French forms, the adaptation of surrealism to contemporary life and language, the playful and generative use of language, the unapologetic use of clichés and puns, the self-referentiality, the elusive narrative voice, its elusiveness heightened by shifting pronouns, the mixed diction and esoteric allusiveness. So a flow chart for Ashbery's "published city" might look something like figure 1.

In this flow chart the formalism of *Some Trees* and the surrealistic innovation of *The Tennis Court Oath* combine to produce the richly metaphoric *Rivers and Mountains* (with its central and seminal poem "The Skaters"), which leads to the quieter lyricism of *The Double Dream of Spring* (Ashbery's most personal volume), which in turn leads to a new kind of "reader interactive" prose poem in *Three Poems*, which produces the earned playful respite of *The Vermont Notebook*, which is then countered by the richly philosophical masterpiece *Self-Portrait in a Convex Mirror*. This is the most accessible phase of Ashbery's career, and it produced as well the eloquence of *Houseboat Days*, which gave way to the startling density of *As We Know*, the exhaustive innovation there reverting to the rigid formalism of *Shadow Train*, which trans-

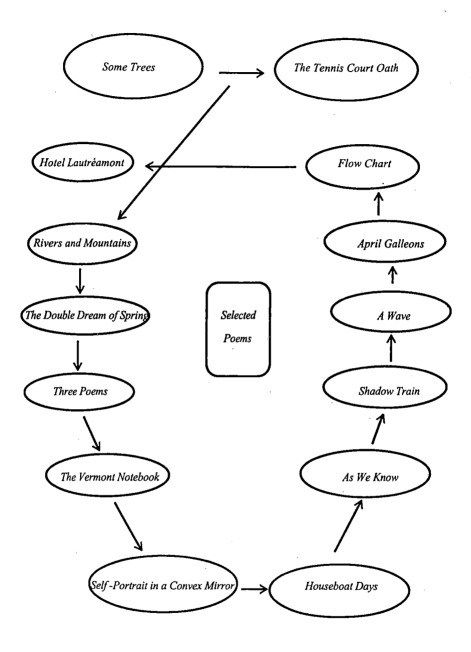

Figure 1. Flowchart for Ashbery's "published city"

forms into the meditative/philosophical mode of *A Wave,* which leads to the miscellany of *April Galleons* and then to the radical comprehensiveness of *Flow Chart* and the surrealistic reassertion of *Hotel Lautréamont.*

Flow Chart is surely Ashbery's least accessible book since *The Tennis Court Oath,* although it is also one of his most important. Few readers, other than those familiar with the successiveness of his work, will persevere through all of its 216 pages. Those who do, however, and who are familiar with Ashbery's earlier work will recognize familiar motifs and strategies. Thematically, the poem elaborates on several of his major lifelong concerns. I have already mentioned some of them: the idea of a collective consciousness, the self as the repository of that consciousness and the source of all human creativity, the relationship of artist and audience, writer and reader, the nature of "life" and its metaphors. In addition, Ashbery has been preoccupied by a sense of how the present differs from the past and of how elusive "the present" always is—a "now" that disappears even as we speak it. And he has always been focused on renewing language, literalizing and enlivening clichés, juxtaposing the banal and the profound, the eloquent and the ordinary. *Flow Chart* moves rapidly from one to another of these concerns, much as an airport landscape whizzes by during takeoff. Here, for example, are a few lines about, among other things, feeling at home in the strange world we live in:

> One wants, not to like, but to live in, the structure of things, and this is
> the first great mistake, from which all the others, down to the tiniest
> speck, bead of snot on a child's nose, proceed in brisk military fashion, encouraging
> to some on a chilly afternoon in March.
> (FC 54)

Many readers, encountering a passage like this, will share both the irritation and the exhilaration of Helen Vendler, who wrote in a *New Yorker* piece about *Flow Chart:* "By entering into some bizarrely tuned pitch inside myself I can find myself on Ashbery's wave length, where everything at the symbolic level makes sense. The irritating (and seductive) thing about this tuning is that it can't be willed."[1]

Paradoxically, to read *Flow Chart* attentively is to allow oneself to fall under that trance and submit to its nearly impossible demands, for it is an impossible poem to explicate or to paraphrase. To get into the spirit of reading it, a reader needs to develop a curiosity about the larger activity that shrouds life and to participate in the power of language to embody consciousness, which is otherwise only embodied in flesh and blood. It is a highly serious book, the summation of a life's work as a poet; at the same time, it is a contagiously playful book, because Ashbery never takes his own work as seriously as his critics do. In *Flow Chart* he satirizes weighty and pretentious criticism of his work, especially that which suggests that his art never "really comes to fruition," by contrasting it with the reality of the daily writing life. (One of the most characteristic things said about his work is that it approaches and recedes from "meaning.")

> And so I often take the afternoon off, read, write or gaze intently out of the window for long periods of time. And then you take tea in the afternoon, that is you make it and then drink it. Oh I'm so sorry, golly, how nothing ever really comes to fruition. But by the same token I am relieved of manifold responsibilities.
> (FC 39)

The nature of the relationship between a writer and his or her readers is puzzling and not very well defined, but it is distinctive, unlike any other human relationship. Very little has been written about it, but *Flow Chart* takes a brave stab at getting at it exactly:

> What we are to each other is both less urgent and more
> perturbing, having no discernible root, no raison d'être, or else flowing
> backward into an origin like the primordial soup it's so easy to pin
> anything on, like a carnation to one's lapel. So it seems we must
> stay in an uneasy relationship, not quite fitting
> together, not precisely friends or lovers though certainly not enemies, if
> the buoyancy of the spongy terrain on which we exist is to be experienced
> as an ichor, not a commentary on all that is missing from the reflection
> in the mirror. *Did I say that? Can this be me?*
> (FC 10)

Those italicized queries separate the voice of the poet from the language of the poem, the interior consciousness of the person from the exterior consciousness encased in art. In many ways, Ashbery has redefined for us, in the late twentieth century, the relationship between the individual talent and tradition that T. S. Eliot wrote so memorably about. The relationship between a poet and a poet's readers, though firmly rooted in two individual psyches, leaves the realm of the individual and becomes mediated and expressed through the medium of language in the historical space that evolves between them. It is, as Ashbery notes here, "an uneasy relationship" nearly, but not quite, indescribable, for it is described precisely and memorably in the language above.

Flow Chart is a cacophony of sentences rising and falling, building and deconstructing, swelling and imploding. What's this poem really about? we want to ask again and again as we read it. And we read it with the sense of hearing a whole range of contemporary discourses simultaneously, catching snatches of lucidity intermittently, but never quite grasping the whole of a particular sequence. Its nearest analogue may be Eliot's *Waste Land,* which was originally to be titled "He Do the Police in Different Voices." In *Flow Chart,*

Ashbery does a lot more than the police in different voices—he does art, history, poetry, business, academese, pop culture, music, slang, and folksiness of all sorts. The poem is a display of the polyglot discourses of our time. One of the reasons we need to go into a trance to read it is explained in the poem:

> For the discourse (and by discourse I mean
> *lively* discourse)
> to take place on a meaningful level, that is, outside someone's brain, a state
>   of artificial
> sleep would have to be induced, first of all.
>   (FC 198)

Artificial sleep (Isn't that what a trance is?) can give us the kind of "language dreams" that exist in *Flow Chart*. Though it is organized in sections and looks like a narrative, the poem remains open-ended, both allusive, pointing to Ashbery's past work and the literary traditions he emulates and extends, and elusive, impossible to pin down and categorize. Like life itself, it has lucid moments and long passages of inexplicable, disconnected activity; like life too, it is alternately exciting and boring, mysterious and obvious, fascinating and tedious.

The narrator of "Self-Portrait" had underscored the paradoxical nature of almost any art: how the fixed and finished quality of an art object works against its intention to capture life authentically. In that poem Ashbery demonstrated how the artist desires to convey his or her "self"—an individual consciousness—in forms that are inherently without consciousness: some paint on canvas, a block of wood, so many words upon a page. This paradox culminates in the poem's breathtaking description of Parmigianino's gesture as "pure / Affirmation that doesn't affirm anything." That description applies as well to the sum of Ashbery's achievement as a poet: at their deepest level his poems are metaphors for the fragile, mysterious, and transitory nature of life. As he puts it in *Flow Chart*, "life is after all very much what they are all about" (91). They awaken us to an eternal present where we can never arrive, and paradoxically can never leave. This is Ashbery's great functional theme: propelling us perpetually into the present that slips away as quickly as we get to it. But whether we're interested in continued travel in that direction or in finding a way out of the dilemma, the poem's final words offer a pointer: "It's open: the bridge, that way" (216).

His 1992 collection *Hotel Lautréamont* seems to pick up on this directive. Its first poem, "Light Turnouts," concludes with this life metaphor:

> One of us stays behind.
> One of us advances on the bridge

as on a carpet. Life—it's marvelous—
follows and falls behind.
    (3)

The poem underscores the way language expresses our collectivity and our connectedness with past, present, and future. The narrator begins addressing a ghost (both his readers to come and those writers of the past that he reads) and seeks his individuality, described in the poem as "shelter / in the noonday crowd," through his daily activities of reading and writing:

Dear ghost, what shelter
in the noonday crowd? I'm going to write
an hour, then read
what someone else has written.
    (3)

This is commonplace activity for a writer, and it's also a kind of withdrawal from an active, adventurous life, or a life of connectedness with others. That sort of life lies beyond the realm of reading and writing, but the writer's use of language and the reader's apprehension of it bind the two together in a perpetual cycle of human continuity and create a kind of alternate adventure that "matters," although how it matters remains as mysterious as "a shot in the dark." In fact, clichéd phrases like "a shot in the dark" are irrefutable evidence of how psychologically connected we are as human beings:

You've no mansion for this to happen in.
But your adventures are like safe houses,
your knowing where to stop an adventure
of another order, like seizing the weather.

We too are embroiled in this scene of happening,
and when we speak the same phrase together:
"We used to have one of those,"
it matters like a shot in the dark.
    (3)

The interaction between readers and writers continues beyond death; with the passing of each writer, a body of work remains that "follows and falls behind" the life and becomes its posterity. Ashbery's latest work seems very much focused on that which will follow and fall behind him.

This same sense of a collective consciousness that inhabits past, present, and future in nearly all of Ashbery's poetry is present as well in the work of Comte de Lautréamont, whose masterpiece, *Les Chants de Maldoror*, embodies the poles of the human spirit, its capacities for both good and evil subsumed in the extremities of the narrative. Like Ashbery, Lautréamont is "not con-

cerned to tell us what he thinks, but to create a text, an object designed to
show us how we all think."² Just as *The Tennis Court Oath* evoked the surrealistic spirit of Raymond Roussel, whose *Impressions of Africa* and *How I
Wrote Certain of My Books* provided an inspiration for the self-generative language of that work, so the spirit of Lautréamont hovers behind these late poems, demolishing our comfortable sense of individual reality and substituting
for it a bizarre conglomerate reality that is both mysterious and inexplicable,
unable to be domesticated and contained by the culturally acceptable art of
any given age. Alex de Jonge puts it this way: "Lautréamont forces his readers
to stop taking their world for granted. He shatters the complacent acceptance
of the reality proposed by their cultural traditions, and makes them see that
reality for what it is: an unreal nightmare all the more hair-raising because the
sleeper believes he is awake. . . . The desire to bring his readers to full consciousness, make them see who and what they are, underlies every word that
Lautréamont wrote."³

For Ashbery, reality is less a nightmare than simply a strange dream whose
meaning continually eludes us, no matter how much we analyze it. But apart
from that distinction, de Jonge's remarks apply to his poetry as fully as they do
to Lautréamont's. Certainly Ashbery's radically disjunctive language intends to
disturb our "complacent acceptance" of the world as we experience it; and
certainly he asks of his readers full consciousness and attentiveness, both to
the words as they appear on the page and to the history of associations both
they and the forms they are encased in carry with them. "It is an enormous
mistake," de Jonge continues, "to assume that language is something we ma-
nipulate; usually it is language that manipulates us. Since it is a collective phenomenon, the product of a tacit consensus on the part of the group, each individual is at the mercy of his language."⁴

Ashbery expresses the same idea more succinctly and with a good deal
more humor in the opening lines of the title poem, "Hotel Lautréamont":

> Research has shown that ballads were produced by all of society
> working as a team. They didn't just happen. There was no guesswork.
>   (HL 14)

"Hotel Lautréamont" is a central and emblematic poem and itself a life metaphor that envisions existence as a large surrealistic inn, characterized by repetition and diversity, by juxtapositions of the familiar and the strange. There is
a lot of tourist and hotel imagery throughout the collection—as if we are visitors to this exotic place called life, which Ashbery calls the Hotel Lautréamont,
a hotel with many different kinds of rooms and, more important, all sorts of
people and other creatures who wander around its corridors and lobbies in all
their exotic splendor and amazing strangeness. As one looks into the various

suites in the hotel, one can hear the innkeeper, the ghost of Isidore Ducase beckoning, as the narrator does in the poem "Elephant Visitors":

Here, try the gloom in *this* room.
I think you'll find it more comfortable
now that the assassins have gone away.
(96)

Formally, the title poem is a quadruple pantoum, each section consisting of four quatrains with repetitive and interlocking lines. A simpler version of this form occurs in the poem "Seasonal," a pantoum (four quatrains in which lines 2 and 4 of the first stanza recur as lines 1 and 3 of the succeeding stanza, and lines 2 and 4 of that stanza recur as lines 1 and 3 of the next stanza, and so on until lines 2 and 4 of the last stanza are the same [having come "full circle"] as lines 1 and 3 of the first stanza) where emphasis on four as well as the title underscores a seasonal motif that runs through the entire book. Of course, the seasons themselves are emblems of sameness and diversity. Here are a few examples:

a box in which four seasons will again fit
just as they did once before fire took the sky
("A Driftwood Altar" 82)

                        The seasons
were always "forgetting" to include you in the list—
that sort of thing.
("Cop and Sweater" 22)

          What season would fit its [the earth's] lifestyle
most naturally?
("The Phantom Agents" 18)

               That nothing so compact
as the idea of a season is to be allowed
is the note, for today at least.
(*"Avant de Quitter Ces Lieux"* 50)

                  For there is a key,
and it leads to your door. Yet it is only repetition, something
the seasons like a lot.
("Part of the Superstition" 41)

The opening lines of "Hotel Lautréamont" comment on a specific poetic form (ballads), but they are really a comment on language and particularly on poetry, which is shaped by forces far beyond the talent of an individual poet. The repetitive and interlocking pattern of the pantoum creates a sense of two poems occurring simultaneously: one that has been heard before, and one that is absolutely new. These elaborate repetitions and variations are metonyms for life experience, both repetitive and new at the same time. Each stanza moves the reader deeper into the complexity of the poem as the startling mystery of the Hotel Lautréamont becomes at once both clearer and more bewildering. The clarity has to do with our increasing awareness that language is a closed form, or *trobar clus,* as the Provençal poets called it, that limits our apprehension of a world beyond language itself. Our bewilderment grows out of the concurrent realization that it is the only tool we have to express our conscious understanding of the world. It allows us both to communicate with one another and to produce a common culture, but that culture itself encases us in a dark bubble that prevents us from seeing things as they actually are. As is nearly always the case with Ashbery, however, he asks us not to take this paradox too seriously; after all, it's only the marvelous diversity of life, and even if we can't quite understand the point of it, things *seem* to happen for particular reasons. The poem's playful opening lines underscore this point, and the first and third lines begin the circle that closes at the poem's end:

> Research has shown that ballads were produced by all of society
> working as a team. They didn't just happen. There was no guesswork.
> The people, then, knew what they wanted and how to get it.
> We see the results in works as diverse as "Windsor Forest" and "The Wife of
>   Usher's Well."
>   (14)

The enjambed second line shakes loose its linkage and appears free and unattached as the opening line of the next stanza, which further exemplifies the collaborative creation of art, across both time and media. A "few seconds" of historical time—corresponding to a century or two—produced the ballad form or, using an example from another media, the violin concerto:

> Working as a team, they didn't just happen. There was no guesswork.
> The horns of elfland swing past, and in a few seconds
> We see the results in works as diverse as "Windsor Forest" and "The Wife of
>   Usher's Well,"
> or, on a more modern note, in the finale of the Sibelius violin concerto.
>   (14)

If we think of this repetition and variation as repeated and new musical notes that make the piece fuller and fuller as it progresses, the new "notes" here are "the horns of elfland" swinging past and the music of the Sibelius concerto. These will become the dominant notes of the next stanza, which introduces the idea of the decline of narrative (modernism and postmodernism?) and reiterates, in a new and playful form, the idea of art as the product of collective experience:

The horns of elfland swing past, and in a few seconds
The world, as we know it, sinks into dementia, proving narrative passé,
or in the finale of the Sibelius violin concerto.
Not to worry, many hands are making work light again.
   (14)

So we move from ancient fairy tales ("horns of elfland") through ballads to a world in which the narrative impulse has been shattered, and the future of art seems chaotic and confusing. How sweetly the chummy romantic fatalism of the last line of that stanza reassures us about the continuing collaborative function of art that enables it to uplift the human spirit: "Not to worry, many hands are making work light again." Although the world may seem to be sinking "into dementia," as always, artists are inventing new forms to contain our language, our music, and our art, just as they did in the ancient and medieval worlds. And the reader of this poem is witnessing that very inventiveness.

The final quatrain of the first section becomes even more positive about these developments. The reader is reassured that the end of narrative was inevitable, "long overdue," and that we can now accomplish "indoors" what our ancestors "quested" for in the outer world. In poetic terms, the interior monologue replaces the epic as a truer index of the zeitgeist. Earlier in the collection, in a clear allusion to the opening of *The Cantos*, Ashbery writes, "I need a reason to go down to the sea in ships / again" (HL 4). Unlike Pound, he envisions his work not as a grand epic statement struggling to cohere but more like "chatter" to be passed around among his readers. "Hand me the chatter and I'll fill the plates with cookies," he writes in "And Forgetting," a poem which contrasts epic grandeur with postmodern actualities. And those postmodern actualities enable a poet to "stay indoors" and chronicle his or her own interiority rather than narrating the adventures of heroes:

The world, as we know it, sinks into dementia, proving narrative passé.
In any case the ruling was long overdue.
Not to worry, many hands are making work light again,
so we stay indoors. The quest was only another adventure.
   (14)

I will spare the reader the tedium of explicating the remaining three sections of the poem like this, except to say that the kind of incremental repetition we see in the first section continues to unfold throughout the poem, illustrating a series of paradoxes: on the one hand, "there's nothing new under the sun," and on the other, every artifact produced in our time is utterly new. On the one hand, life is utterly repetitive and boring, and on the other, each day is a new adventure. On the one hand, art is produced by individuals; on the other, it emerges from the collective consciousness of a culture. On the one hand, life's patterns are thoroughly unpredictable, and on the other, everything that is was destined to be what it is. The poem's final lines bring us full circle once again to the first and third lines of the opening stanza:

> You mop your forehead with a rose, recommending its thorns.
> Research has shown that ballads were produced by all of society;
> Only night knows for sure. The secret is safe with her:
> the people, then, knew what they wanted and how to get it.
>   . (16)

The "optimism" of the earlier part of the poem has dissolved into mystery, uncertainty, and loss. The final line tells us that "the people, *then,* knew what they wanted and how to get it," implying that the people, *now,* have hardly the same sense of surety and purpose. Although this is the "end" of the poem, our research has shown that every line in it has occurred twice, and were it to continue, the next stanza would begin with the identical line that began the poem. The cycle of optimism and pessimism, wonder and despair, pleasure and pain, light and darkness, the rose and its thorns, would continue, as of course it does in our daily life experience.

Although that experience is diverse and embodies contraries, there is the further paradox that "Our rooms darken / with every new place of experience" (39). This central fact of life, expressed in a poem called "Part of the Superstition," raises the question of how to retain optimism and purpose in the darkening world we live in. We are getting older, not only as individuals, but as a civilization, and even as a species, and everything that lives contains within itself the seeds of its own demise:

>   All roses
> admit this, and life stays on, fidgeting, their dream
> disappointed, on the run, and it's your fault,
> who never had the courage to know nothing and simultaneously
> be attentive.
>   (39)

That last phrase—"to know nothing and simultaneously / be attentive"—has Keatsian overtones of negative capability, the quality that Keats saw as essential to the poetic temperament. As he put it, it is present when an individual "is capable of being in uncertainties, Mysteries, doubts, without any irritable reaching after fact & reason." It allows an artist to let go of the struggle to "make sense" of the paradoxical and impenetrable world and to substitute instead the primacy of individual experience, even when that experience seems repetitive, mundane, inconclusive. Here's Ashbery's summation of that view:

For there is a key,
and it leads to your door. Yet it is only repetition, something
the seasons like a lot. And as you get up to go you mutter,
and that's it!—the fortunate crisis that was always
going to stave us off, and explain so much
about car wrecks, and postage stamps and the like.
      (41)

Both our knowledge and our lack of knowledge are what charge life with desire and evoke its essential bittersweetness, which has surely been the dominant quality of Ashbery's verse from its beginnings. The conclusion of "Part of the Superstition" gets this state of affairs exactly right:

Farewell in the rain; it is surely lucky to know
as much as we do, and not to know as much
as we do. Or were taught was proper. Papers
will explain it, music it. That's a promise.
      (41)

Like the work of Wallace Stevens, with which it has many affinities, Ashbery's poetry constitutes a harmonious whole and proposes that poetry, music, and art bring us closer to "understanding" the world we live in than science can; these surely are the "papers" that will explain it and turn it to music; but the final phrase of this poem vibrates with irony, as it is a promise that no artist, however encompassing his or her vision, can seriously make. But that, of course, does not stop John Ashbery, who has been a purveyor of paradoxes and oxymorons throughout his career, from making it.

Appendix: "Life" Metaphors in John Ashbery's Poetry

Because life is short
We must remember to keep asking it the same question.
      (TP 6)

No, it had not yet begun, except as a preparatory dream which seemed to have the rough texture of life.
      (TP 7)

To escape in either direction is impossible outside the frost of a dream, and it is just this major enchantment that gave us life to begin with, life for each other. Therefore I hold you. But life holds us, and is unknowable.
      (TP 11)

Little by little
You are the mascot of that time
You have your own life too
But are circumscribed by the time's growing concern
So that your activities are diminished
Or simplified, like a dog's.
　　　(TP 33)

Yet they really existed. For instance a jagged kind of mood that comes at the end of the day, lifting life into the truth of real pain for a few moments before subsiding in the usual irregular way, as things do.
　　　(TP 54)

It was different in those days, though. Men felt things differently and their reactions were different. It was all life, this truth, you forgot about it and it was there.
　　　(TP 55)

Life became a pregnant silence, but it was understood that the silence was to lead nowhere.
　　　(TP 63)

An alternative way would be the "life-as-ritual" concept.
　　　(TP 70)

. . . on this busy thoroughfare that is the great highway of life.
　　　(TP 91)

We can no longer live our lives properly.
　　　(TP 111)

Meanwhile the shape of life has changed definitively for the better for everyone on the outside.
　　　(TP 114)

But it is life englobed.
　　　(SPCM 69)

　　　　　　　　　　　　It wants
To siphon off the life of the studio.
　　　(SPCM 75)

> Its positive side is
> Making you notice life and the stresses
> That only seemed to go away[.]
> (SPCM 75)

> It may be that another life is stocked there
> In recesses no one knew of[.]
> (SPCM 76)

> What is beautiful seems so only in relation to a specific
> Life, experienced or not, channeled into some form.
> (SPCM 77)

> I think it is trying to say it is today
> And we must get out of it even as the public
> Is pushing through the museum now so as to
> Be out by closing time. You can't live there.
> (SPCM 79)

> Parmigianino
> Must have realized this as he worked at his
> Life-obstructing task.
> (SPCM 80)

> Around a drum of living,
> The motion by which a life
> May be known and recognized[.]
> ("Litany," AWK 6)

> *You have*
> *No right to take something out of life*
> *And then put it back, knowingly, beside*
> *Its double.*
> ("Litany" 20)

> *Once given*
> *They can be forgotten in the sad joy of life.*
> ("Litany" 27)

> *It's sad the way they feel about it—*
> *Poetry—*
> *As though it could synchronize our lives*

With our feelings about ourselves,
And form a bridge between them and "life."
    ("Litany" 35)

        But you
Will continue in your own way, will finish
Your novel, and have a life
Full of happy, active surprises.
    ("Litany" 36)

All life
Is as a tale told to one in a dream
In tones never totally audible
Or understandable, and one wakes
Wishing to hear more, asking
For more, but one wakes to death, alas,
Yet one never -
Pays any heed to that, the tale
Is still so magnificent in the telling
That it towers far above life, like some magnificent
Cathedral spire, far above the life
Pullulating around it (what
Does it care for that, after all?).
    ("Litany" 37)

The ending is too happy
For it to be life, and therefore it must
Be the product of some deluded poet's brain: life
Could never be this satisfactory.
    ("Litany" 39)

We travel on, life seems full of promise,
And ambition is so recent as to be almost
Stronger than living, and makes its own
Definitions and pays for them. Surely
Life is meant to be this way, solemn
And joyful as an autumn wood rent by the hunters'
Horns and their dogs.
    ("Litany" 45)

To be consigned to this world
Of life, a sea-world

Which forms, shapes,
Faces probably decorate—
　　　("Litany" 50)

　　　　　　　　　It is, then,
Gigantic, yet life-size. And
Once it has lived, one has lived with it.
　　　("Litany" 56–57)

One idea is enough to organize a life and project it
Into unusual but viable forms.
　　　(W 69)

　　　　　　　　　　　　　　　And as it
Focuses itself, it is the backward part of a life that is
Partially coming into view. It's there, like a limb.
　　　(W 70)

　　　　　　　　　　　I became as a parent
To those scenes lifted from "real life."
　　　(W 71–72)

　　　　　　　　　Life was pleasant there.
And though we made it all up, it could still happen to us again.
　　　(W 75)

In the interests of a bare, strictly patterned life that apparently
Has charms we weren't even conscious of.
　　　(W 76)

　　　　　　　　What is restored
Becomes stronger than the loss as it is remembered;
Is a new, separate life of its own.
　　　(W 77)

Enough to know that I shall have answered for myself soon,
Be led away for further questioning and later returned
To the amazingly quiet room in which all my life has been spent.
　　　(W 89)

　　　　　　　We know life is so busy,
but a larger activity shrouds it, and this is something
we can never feel, except occasionally, in small signs

put up to warn us and as soon expunged, in part
or wholly.
>   (FC 3)

>   Sometimes one's own hopes are realized
and life becomes a description of every second of the time it took.
>   (FC 7)

Conversations are still initiated,
haltingly, under the leaves, around an outdoor table,
but they insist on nothing and are remembered
only as disquieting examples of how life might be
in that other halting yet prosperous time
when games of strength were put away.
>   (FC 11-12)

One lives thus, plucking a mean sort of living from the rubbish heaps
of history, unaware that the parallel daintiness of the lives of the rich,
like fish in an ocean whose bottom is dotted with rusted engines and debris
of long-forgotten wrecks, unfolds.
>   (FC 13)

>   What distractions would be concocted for us
if we had strayed? And who is the baron that manipulates our daily lives
from afar?
>   (FC 19)

>   But—
what is a waiting room for, after all? If not to
live out one's life scarily to the borders of altered lawns
with red leaves nestled on them.
>   (FC 23)

>   Only long after
>   your death
will the life you so busily led be imputed to the cornerstone of rot that was
the secret, driving force in it: something everyone at the time found to be OK.
>   (FC 32-33)

>   Still, life is reasonably
>   absorbing
and there's a lot of nice people around. Most days are well fed

and relaxing, and one can improve one's mind a little
by going out to a film or having a chat with that special friend.
  (FC 35)

         But you see so many
of us are like that bird, that man I mean, that for but a few can life resonate
  with
anything like serious implications. So many were hung out to dry, or, more
  accurately, to rot.
  (FC 37)

         Life is an embroidery-frame,
  and what you put
into it gets left there, there are so many kinds of designs, literally millions
  of them
and the combinations of these—well.
  (FC 50)

         O if only one
  belonged to something,
life would be harder perhaps but we'd have the strength to go along with
  whatever they
wanted us to say.
  (FC 57)

      And yes, life has a way of sidling on in rain-slick
  afternoons
like this as though nothing were amiss, as though we had just
seen each other five minutes ago and that tantrum was all for naught.
  (FC 103)

         In some ways
it's a life, or something you'd have no difficulty recognizing as such, but I
  wonder,
how are they going to fit me in at the end?
  (FC 170)

       But as usual life is a dream
of blackbirds slowly flying, of people who come to your door needing help
  or merely
wanting to attack you so they can go away and say contact was made and it's
your day in the barrel.
  (FC 176)

One of us stays behind.
One of us advances on the bridge
as on a carpet. Life—it's marvelous—
follows and falls behind.
      (HL 3)

The cartoon era of my early life
became the printed sheaves and look:
what's printed on this thing?
Who knows what it's going to be?
         (HL 61)

Because if all of life is just a blip or some kind of exclamation
mark at the bottom of last week's weather . . .
         (HL 71)

Once forgotten you're as good as dead,
anyway. And who would help you now?
You might as well be trapped at the bottom of a well
in the Sahara. They don't know you're alive,
or that your life was anything but exemplary

when it came time for you to live.
         (HL 151)

Notes

1. Helen Vendler, "A Steely Glitter Chasing Shadows," *New Yorker,* August 3,
1992, p. 73.
   2. Alex de Jonge, *Nightmare Culture* (New York: St. Martin's Press, 1973), 15.
   3. Ibid., 1.
   4. Ibid., 2.

4 | John Ashbery's Landscapes

Bonnie Costello

ASHBERY IS MUCH more than the Cheshire cat or the Brer Rabbit of American poetry, though he may be the Piranesi of landscape. His disappearing paths and slippery terrain, his shifts in scale and perspective, and his subversions of narrative sequence all point to his larger interest in the nature of thought and knowledge, the relationship of mind to environment, and the play between temporal and spatial awareness. "Everything is landscape," he writes in *The Double Dream of Spring* (1970), a volume which takes its title from the surrealist landscape painter Georgio de Chirico. And the landscape is never quite transparent—a patina seems always to be forming on it. Consciousness arranges the world which slips away into history. Ashbery accelerates this process so that consciousness becomes itself the landscape, or perhaps the timescape in which he meditates. As we move through the shifting labyrinths we make of the world and of ourselves, renegotiating boundaries at every step, a creative absorption substitutes for the deferred sense of transparence. Like de Chirico, Ashbery offers us decentered landscapes with many perspective lines, which both undercut the ideal of a timeless subjective vision and open new possibilities for revery in temporal extension instead of spatial depth.

In focusing on landscape in Ashbery, I mean to shift attention away somewhat from the predominant view of his work as language centered. The poet's syntactic and rhetorical strategies for resisting conclusion and hierarchy, his polyphonous pronouns, his homonymic play, do invite a notion of the poem as a site of purely linguistic transactions. The relationship between Ashbery's disarming sentences, as syntactic and grammatical units, and his tumultuous landscapes, as mental pictures, is an interesting one, not quite causal or analogical. I don't have time to puzzle out this relationship here, but I want to stress that landscape imagery in Ashbery's poetry cannot be reduced, as Marjorie Perloff has suggested, to the parodic trappings of Romantic discourse.[1] Nor is it evidence of the detached spatiality Fredric Jameson has described as postmodern.[2] Landscape is, rather, a fundamental, generating trope of knowledge in Ashbery's poetry—attractive, I believe, because it insistently invokes an observer and his or her environment and draws out assumptions of knowledge within our everyday accounts of what we know. Ashbery's poetry

sets out to present the feeling of our contemporary landscape of knowledge—
unsteady, even cataclysmic, full of trompe l'oeil and obscurities, but occasionally luminous. His work remains deeply tied to the meditative tradition of
landscape reverie and allegory from Dante to Stevens. But he explores for consciousness uncharted "spaces" in which temporality is dramatized rather than
suppressed.[3]

Mark Johnson and George Lakoff have demonstrated the extent to which
"knowledge is a landscape" is indeed one of the metaphors we live by, just as
"sight" is our Enlightenment term for understanding.[4] There is no obvious necessity in this metaphor: the Maori of New Zealand speak of knowledge as
treasure, food for chiefs, a magic cloak.[5] In speaking of knowledge as a landscape, we both accept perspectivism and claim grounds beyond perspective.
Landscape is our trope of knowledge because it makes the knowledge seem to
be "of" something, not an entirely self-enclosed system.

At the same time, "landscape" in Ashbery displaces "nature" as an epistemological trope and retains a sense of incompleteness and mediation in our
forms of knowledge. Landscape, "a portion of land that the eye can comprehend in a single view" (*Webster's*), is engaged but incommensurate with an
environment in which space is not absolute, a reality of shifting tectonic plates
that can never be mapped, a "ground" that is not stable.

These shaky conditions of landscape do not leave Ashbery in a stance of
skepticism, though certainly skepticism is his starting point and drives his vision. There is more to the world of Ashbery's poetry than shallow irony, blank
parody, corrected banality, commodity fetishism, and decreative emptiness,
though all such qualities can be found there. If knowledge is a landscape, then
landscape is a space for dreaming, epistemology a form of reverie. He approaches "vision in the form of a task" ("Fragment," *DDS*), sometimes even
as a burden or compulsion. If his imagination is spatial, its means of expansion
is to feature "time's way of moving sideways out of the event." If he resists
converting the incomplete or unsaid to a metaphysics of the ineffable, he continues to pursue the charge of unaccommodated thoughts and makes a landscape of that pursuit. And if in retrospect our search for transparence, crashing
through landscape after landscape, itself looks constructed, like a golf course
"with a few natural bonuses left in," the balm of "pale Alpine flowers" lingers
to keep alive the dream, our "chief work" ("A Wave," *W*).

Ashbery's topography is a complex one, shaped not only by rivers, mountains, trees, islands, capes, peninsulas, storms, and clouds but by many a farm
and field of grain, barren plains, lakes, and ruined cities. I cannot undertake
here an iconography of Ashbery's landscapes, which anyway keep changing:
pastoral, sublime, suburban, bureaucratic. In *Some Trees* (1956) he tends to
prefer pastoral landscapes but then moves toward imagery of the sublime in
Rivers and Mountains (1966). In *The Double Dream of Spring* (1970) he in-

troduces the paraphernalia of popular culture and suburban fancy into rural scenery, leading to the abandoned picnic grounds of *As We Know* (1979). *Three Poems* (1972) initiates the trope of the journey. *A Wave* (1984) represents perhaps his most varied terrain, continuing the motif of a journey, starting from "home," lured by an ideal of mindlessness, but driven on through a landscape of deserts, beaches, orchards, and steeply shelving hills in its Sisyphean ascent. *Flow Chart* (1991) abandons vertical tropes, though it clings to geographic ones; the River God presides, and we live in a space of spongy, alluvial mud. But throughout all these volumes and their various topographies, Ashbery's landscapes are dynamic, temporally inscribed, and constantly redirected; they involve dramatic shifts of scale and proportion, so that the trivial or odd rises to become the dominant and monumental, the corner becomes the center. They tend to be multiple as well, so that while we are establishing one perspective line, another is emerging to claim our attention. They collapse into billboards or shrink to postage stamps. But there is always, within them, a principle of ground our cognition cannot fix, a sense of reality which our constructed landscapes may block out but which also drives their creation and de-creation, even if it is "too primitive to understand us." Ashbery is not a poet of the void, though he occasionally passes through an "invisible terrain." Even in *Houseboat Days* (1977), where the poet is like Noah, afloat on a flood brought down by degenerate systems, he can build on a reality of water; eventually the ground presents itself to awaken the Orphean poet. "Data banks," Lyotard has said, are "nature" for post-modern man.[6] Along these lines, Ashbery has been portrayed as a poet of the posttechnological sublime, of information overkill, of discourse speaking to discourse, where the observer and the environment collapse into simulacra. Yet, while the bureaucracies of language set up formidable facades, there are no data banks in Ashbery, no computer networks or videos, and only one warehouse. Throughout Ashbery's poetry, architectural pinnacles spin up in our sight but are mostly seen in ruins, if at all. Landscape in the broadest sense survives its various scene changes. In Ashbery's recent book, *Hotel Lautréamont* (1992), the sycophantic self reports to Control about "earth, our example," but it remains the example we inhabit, even if we can't live like Thoreau. .

It is difficult to say anything very empirical about so abstract and elusive a poet as John Ashbery, but I want to cite a couple of biographical facts that have indirect bearing on my subject. This so-called New York City poet was raised on a farm near Rochester, New York. Memories of this childhood, which surface throughout the poet's career, present a complex antipastoral continually yielding to pastoral yearnings. This "North Farm," this "patchwork of childhood north of here," makes a regular symbolic appearance in his work as the ambivalent homestead in which the prodigal son can never quite settle, which he will not recognize when he finds it. Ashbery is a vigorously homeless poet (like Lautréamont, who lived his brief life hopping hotels). He tracks the mental journey of our search for home, though he is less than confident that such thinking is enough to summon us into dwelling. The middle distance, itself a result of our perceptual and cognitive makeup, never comes into focus, never becomes a location, but recedes as in Zeno's paradox.

This is not a poet who has put aside pastoral, who has banished its pleasures and settled for a completely urban reality. Though Ashbery's book jackets until recently stated that he "lives in New York City," he in fact spends most of his time two hours away in the relatively rural Hudson, New York. He lives just down the road from the former property of the luminist painter Frederick Church, whose house "Olana" was designed so that each window would frame a perfect landscape. (Ashbery, like Baudelaire, whose "Paysage" he translated, is very fond of window views, which mark the negotiation between mental and environmental landscapes.)

The term "landscape" is a deliberately porous one for Ashbery, who can mean by it either environment or painting, or, more often, both at once, since our landscape is etymologically and practically a shaping and framing of the land. Indeed, sometimes it is unclear whether the poet is describing a painting or imagining an actual scene. Ashbery for a long time made his living writing art criticism. Some of his favorite painters have been landscape artists. I will be exploring the dynamics of this term "landscape" in Ashbery, his sense of the mind as an unmappable, metamorphic terrain, his sense of environment as mediated, framed, and proportioned by concepts out of step with it.

"Litany" (from *As We Know*), a long, two-column double monologue which resists dialectic, text, and gloss, or any stable opposition, actually ends up revealing many of Ashbery's predilections. In the passage that I will read, the "author," a kind of aesthete, tells us about paintings, "things that are important to him," while the voice of the other column rambles in a more three-dimensional, moralized landscape. As always, it is hard to tell just what investment Ashbery has in anything he "recommends"—yet it is toward the sentiments to which he is most prone that the poet directs his irony, and the sentiments often survive in an invigorated form:

> Almost all landscapes
> Are generous, well proportioned, hence
> Welcome. We feel we have more in common with a
> Landscape, however shifty and ill-conceived,
> Than with a still-life: those oranges
> And apples, and dishes, what have they to do
> With us? Plenty, but it's a relief
> To turn away from them. Portraits, on the other
> Hand, are a different matter—they have no

Bearing on the human shape, their humanitarian
Concerns are foreign to us, who dream
And know not we are humane, though, as seen
By others, we are. But this is about people.
Right. That's why landscapes are more
Familiar, more what it's all about—we can see
Into them and come out on the other side.
  (AWK 49)

Ashbery is here talking about "pictures," of course, not natural landscapes, thus he can celebrate rather than regret their contrivance, even if he
smirks some at the naive appeal of illusion, the false sense of ownership, the
"other side" as the fiction of the vanishing point. There is of course a wonder-
ful perversity in calling landscapes more "humanitarian" than portraits or
those strange/familiar metonomies of still life that reveal our domestic and
social arrangements. But the dream of self-transcendence, of forgetting our humanity, our existence in time, place, society, is the human appeal of traditional
landscape. Ashbery asks how we might engage this aspect of our humanity
without falling prey to its devices and delusions. In his landscapes we never do
quite come out on the other side, transcendental or otherwise, though he is
always alluding to it; landscape leads into landscape. But there is a great deal
of room for reverie in this method.

    In painting, one-point perspective allows the feeling of "coming out on
the other side," through the vanishing point around which the "well proportioned" landscape arranges itself. As Andrew Ross has pointed out in *The Failure of Modernism* (1986), much of Ashbery's poetry approaches the problem
of the self through a critique of Albertian perspective: a bodiless, metaphysical self contrived for the beholder of isomorphic space is exposed as a fetish.[7]
Ross's emphasis is more on the skeptical side of Ashbery, whom he calls
"doubting John Thomas." I see this skeptical figure as the initiator of further
ventures into environment. In an early long poem, "The Skaters" (RM 34–63),
Ashbery, impatient with the snowfall of memory and association, and the en-
tropic dartings of the skaters—thoughts driven by the need for novelty—invokes the orderly landscapes of art:

(Viz. "Rigg's Farm, near Aysgarth, Wensleydale," or the "Sketch at Norton")
In which we escape ourselves—putrefying mass of prevarications etc.—
In remaining close to the limitations imposed.
  (47)

Ashbery's parodies of the art historian here mock the yearning to escape
our transience and confusion through art, to order life by the principles of art,
but he also shares the susceptibility: "How strange that the narrow perspective

lines / Always seem to meet, although parallel, and that an insane ghost could do this" (36). It is the "insane ghost" of Albertian perspective, who insinuates his way into our desires, that Ashbery addresses: "it is you I am parodying, / [you and] Your invisible denials" (42) of time, of the frame, of the body, of the beholder. We do not escape our constructions, but Ashbery's strategy in "The Skaters" is to subvert the hypnotism of the vanishing point by deranging it into antimimetic "a **bigarrure** of squiggly lines" (36). This is not the end of the story but the beginning of a new effort. Inspiration here is "a great wind" which "lifted these cardboard panels / Horizontal in the air" (36), not to reveal bare reality or expose an abyss but to set the panels down in a new arrangement.

Yet behind all the cardboard panels "The Skaters" retains a sense of fluent, "pre-existing, pre-seeming," prelandscape space, a phenomenological "shapeless entity" in the "evidence of the visual" to which the child, in this surprisingly Wordsworthian poem, is "devoted" but which is "replaced by the great shadow of trees" that makes it a landscape. Perhaps Ashbery is even alluding, in some way in "The Skaters," to Wordsworth's skater in Book 1 of *The Prelude,* who sees the landscape spinning around him, confusing fixed for moving objects. But what in Wordsworth may be read as a mere perceptual experiment of induced motion against the confidence in a stable, substantial landscape and integrated self is in Ashbery a more habitually swirling condition.

Later in "The Skaters" Ashbery in his New York apartment takes on the identity of Crusoe—paradigm of the solitary lyric observer—and tries to order the world around his island as if it were a painting: "One's only form of distraction is really / To climb to the top of the one tall cliff to scan the distances." That mastering prospect, though, remains illusory: the vultures below "look like bees" but will, he knows, be "rending me limb from limb once I have keeled over definitively." The eagles "always seem to manage to turn their backs to you" (55). Nevertheless, he persists in viewing the world as a sublime landscape:

> Sure enough: in the pale gray and orange distances to the left, a
> Waterspout is becoming distinctly visible.
> Beautiful, but terrifying;
> Delicate, transparent, like a watercolor by that nineteenth-century Englishman
>   whose name I forget.
>   (55)

This scene won't stay still, either, of course: "Now the big cloud that was in front of the waterspout / Seems to be lurching forward, so that the waterspout, behind it, looks like a three-dimensional photograph" (56). As the realism and turmoil of the scene and the coming storm drive even the vultures to their nest, Crusoe, tempted as he is to let this landscape turn to environment, to "linger on in the wet" of pure awareness, decides he really "had better be getting back to the tent." Our constructed landscapes don't stay in place, but neither can we do without them. To "linger in the wet" is not really an option, though we may peer out of what he calls in another poem "wet casements."

Ashbery favors scenes which feature hazard, climatic change, or digressions of line ("prolongations of our reluctance to approach"), as if they could resist the patina with their inner dynamism or digression, as he tells us in "Litany":

> Pictures of capes and peninsulas
> With big clouds moving down on them,
> Pressing with a frightening weight—
> And shipwrecks barely seen (sometimes
> Not seen at all) through snow
> In the foreground, and howling, ravenous gales
> In the background.
> (AWK 48–49)

Such pictures, obscure in foreground and background, presenting their elusive middle distance, work at the limits of landscape as fixed space, though all their turmoil is of course framed and controlled, the hazard put at an aesthetic distance.

At one level these are probably tacky imitations of Turner, and Ashbery's pleasure in them has an element of camp. But the poet's way is often to recognize the essential emotion even in kitsch (and vice versa) and to redirect it toward more rigorous forms. Indeed, a double register of the luminous and the homely can be felt throughout the poetry and marks the course he lays between skepticism and reverie. Ashbery commented about a group show at the Whitney Museum: "The urge toward grandeur is there, co-existing with the intent to subvert it, through a dead-pan, no-comment rendering. It is true that just plain solemnity will no longer do, the days of Bierstadt are no more."[8] But if Bierstadt is out, the genre of landscape, Ashbery has shown, is inexhaustible. A great deal of the grandeur of Ashbery's poetry comes from his dreaming in time-space and the allegorical adventure it always seems to carry, even as the dead-pan rendering tends to make the space a shallow one. The decreative, subversive side of Ashbery, the skeptical side, is itself part of what makes him a dreamer, for as he has said of minimalist art, "The dream of escaping from dream is itself a dream" and dreamers "are insatiable expansionists" (RS 12). The major means of expansion—since the Romantics used up natural space and the modernists aesthetic space—is time.

> By that time
> Space will be a jar with no lid, and you can live
> Any way you like out on those vague terraces,
> Verandas, walk-ways—the forms of space combined with time

> We are allowed, and we live them passionately,
> Fortunately, though we can never be described
> And would make lousy characters in a novel.
>   (AWK 85)

Lousy characters presumably because our lives don't obey the rules of plot and point of view.

The most fundamental difference between Ashbery and a Romantic or transcendentalist poet would seem to be the metaphysical basis for topographical reverie. "I no longer have any metaphysical reasons / For doing the things I do," he writes in a poem pointedly titled "The Preludes" (AWK 91). Alluding to Wordsworth, as much as Eliot, Ashbery implies that one prelude will never suffice for the endlessly redirected journey he is on. But Ashbery is not an entirely gratuitous dreamer either, and his poetry is based on the premise that we never really give up "the prospector's hunch": "the reasons though were not all that far away, / In the ultramarine well under the horizon," and in fact the metaphysical is never, it seems, gone for good—"all that we see is penetrated by it," "a present that is elsewhere" ("As We Know," AWK 74). We dwell in our constructed world and are constructed by it ("this space" we call our landscape is a "checkerboard . . . / Trapped in the principle of the great beyond" ["Statuary," AWK 76], and we are its pieces, its "landscapeople," its "staffage"—those tiny brush-stroke figures the apprentice puts in). Those little figures in the landscape often natter insidiously to the poet of his entrapments (landscape, if not language, speaks man, they say), but the poet only half listens. The poet's nonalienated half is already ahead of the game, aware of his part in the production of the "charge," as in "The Picnic Grounds":

> Will the landscape mean anything new now?
> But even if it doesn't, the charge
> Is up ahead somewhere, in the near future,
> Squashing even the allegory of the grass
> Into the mould of its aura, a lush patina.
>   (AWK 98)

Ashbery both invests in and undermines the mythology of presence with such phrases as "the mould of its aura," something we manufacture, then worship. If the "allegory of the grass" told us of mutability ("all flesh is grass"), the "charge" is stronger; it can turn mutability to transport (hence Whitman's *Leaves of Grass*). Ashbery is yet one further step ahead. His creative passions go toward beating that charge, even as it arises in himself, to the horizon of a landscape, anticipating the next illusion, exposing the "lush patina" on the luminous moment. But the effect of such doubling back is as much to intensify as to detonate the charge. So the tortoise of consciousness wins the race with time by hopping on its back.

These usurpations of sequence are not spots of time. Their enunciatory and temporal aspects are retained. In "Song: 'Mostly Places . . . ' " from *April Galleons,* Ashbery preempts our "progressive" impulse to give up the empty "quarry" of imagination (Romanticism) for the more valuable "light" of "out-doors" (modern objectivism). By the time such a formulation has begun to claim our attention, another charge of meaning, submitted before but only now appearing on the landscape, intervenes:

> And why does the humble packet of seeds
> The gardener plants erupt into cold pockets of fire
> On the horizon at night?
> You see there is a more abrupt truth
>
> That preempts whatever this moment is taking,
> The hors d'oeuvres this moment is preparing.
>   (AG 49)

The cozy feast for two we might enjoy with nature in a realist mode is canceled for new engagements with old loves.

While an ironic hum persists throughout Ashbery's poetry, there are, in fact, "pellucid moments." Such moments stand in contrast both to the snow-fall and to the raging gales of the immersed beholder's unorganized awareness and the checkerboards and grids of fixed perspective. They tend to be associated with landscape description and involve a subversion of linear thinking or a "narrative moratorium," as in "A Wave":

> And what to say about those series
> Of infrequent pellucid moments in which
> One reads inscribed as though upon an empty page
> The strangeness of all those contacts from the time they erupt
> Soundlessly on the horizon and in a moment are upon you
> Like a stranger on a snowmobile.
>   (W 81)

Of these contacts "nothing can be known or written, only / That they passed this way." The language here conflates the moment of knowledge or explanation ("in which / one reads inscribed as though upon an empty page"), and the "contacts" with reality supposedly explained (the snow like the empty page, the stranger like the invisible inscription). Such moments tend to be horizontal and self-referential, folding back into the constructed landscape of knowledge, yet they are charged with strangeness, not beyond knowledge, but ahead of it. Thus in "A Wave" Ashbery remarks that knowing (as opposed to knowledge)

                              can have this
Sublime rind of excitement, like the shore of a lake in the desert
Blazing with the sunset.
    (W 70)

Knowledge, that mutable fruit, becomes less important for itself than for its anticipatory effects, its rind. This is barely a landscape, empty and approaching night. The lake is Ashbery's (as it is Auden's and Stevens's) favorite trope of reflection, here in its primary form, before even the trees have been arranged around it to turn reflection into landscape, the pellucid moment into knowledge. Such biblically charged wilderness and desert spaces develop rapidly into abandoned picnic grounds and crumbling cities. Yet

                    if it pleases all my constructions
To collapse, I shall at least have had that satisfaction, and known
That it need not be permanent in order to stay alive.
    (70)

This horizontal charge arising as in a rearview mirror is not sublime and will not jump-start us into eternity (as certain forms of catachresis can do in poets like Hart Crane or Charles Wright). It remains embedded in time, even drawing fuel from time. So Ashbery's "pellucid" moments are often calm rather than ecstatic, registers of transience and appearance that confound narrative logic. They are less epiphanic than telescoped visions, as in the following passage from "A Wave," in which we briefly emerge from an accelerating series of changing landscapes into a glassy moment of meditation.

                    anybody
Will realize that he or she has made those same mistakes,
Memorized those same lists in the due course of the process
Being served on you now. Acres of bushes, treetops;
Orchards where the quince and apple seem to come and go
Mysteriously over long periods of time; waterfalls
And what they conceal, including what come after—roads and roadways
Paved for the gently probing, transient automobile;
Farragoes of flowers; everything, in short,
That makes this explicit earth what it appears to be in our
Glassiest moments when a canoe shoots out from under some foliage
Into the river and finds it calm, not all that exciting but above all
Nothing to be afraid of, celebrates us
And what we have made of it.
    (W 76-77)

The descriptive passage (which almost forgets the allegorical purpose that launched it) collapses together spatial and temporal variation, treating them as one. The trees mark out various landscapes that have meant something—have borne fruit—from time to time. The waterfalls seem natural and also, as in Wordsworth, timeless, though Ashbery would stress that this is the "waterfall effect" in which the eye tires in its gaze on ceaseless motion. Yet they too conceal the social, the transient human arrangements which the flowers of speech aestheticize. All this is both cast off and gathered up in one vision, one temporalized landscape. This time-space gives a qualified feeling of reality ("this explicit earth"), but also of illusion ("what it appears to be"). So in the mirror of our "glassiest moments" the canoe shoots out like an explanation, but one that ultimately "celebrates us" and what we made of the earth, not the earth itself. We pause in such spaces where, as he writes in "Polite Distortions,"

> the laundry
> Of our thinking will be spread out on bushes and not
> Come to tempt us too much.
>   (AG 62)

These are sunny moments when the "vast shadow" of causal logic pulls in momentarily.

One of the absorbing, if frustrating, qualities of Ashbery's meditative poetry is the uncertainty of its representations—part anecdotal, part dream vision, part allegory, depictive, and diagrammatic by unannounced turns. "The flowers don't talk to Ida anymore" and "mirrors fall from trees," yet symbols persist. Ashbery often presents himself as a poet of "paysage moralisé," but the landscape, the moral vision, and the terms of their connection are all in flux. He does not simply map thought and feeling onto unstable, dynamic elements in a landscape (volcanoes, storms, clouds), though he does include these. Such fugitive and cataclysmic images do not by themselves undermine an overall fixed spatial vision. In Ashbery's mapping the levels of reference themselves are unstable, since there is no extratextual system (historical, biblical, or psychological) to fix them. Frost might "have at heart your getting lost" in his journey poem "Directive," but the terrain is easily mapped to certain subtexts and concepts. Ashbery's allegory leads into Scheherazade-like serial reverie which turns back into allegory when we least suspect it. Since knowledge is landscape and landscape is a kind of dreaming, the boundaries between allegory and reverie are naturally open. This is not to say that Ashbery holds any surrealist faith in the truth of the unconscious—he is actually more interested, I believe, in the shapes a conscious, discursive rhetoric can make, following a serial rather than sequential procedure.

While I cannot index the complex iconography of Ashbery's landscapes, I want to look more closely at two of his most obsessive variations on the perpendicular: rivers and mountains, and trees. Not surprisingly, Ashbery shakes

these traditional metaphors by their roots, setting their symbolic structure and
pictorial integrity in question.

    The opening lines from his poem "Rivers and Mountains" have the virtue
of being contained enough to illustrate these points about allegorical levels and
perpendicularity of thought. Throughout the poem, and indeed the volume
which bears its name, Ashbery weaves his way unpredictably among levels and
referents; including map, terrain, nature, city, writing, thinking, land, and sea:

> On the secret map the assassins
> Cloistered, the Moon River was marked
> Near the eighteen peaks and the city
> Of humiliation and defeat—wan ending
> Of the trail among dry, papery leaves
> Gray-brown quills like thoughts
> In the melodious but vast mass of today's
> Writing through fields and swamps
> Marked, on the map, with little bunches of weeds.
> . . . .
> So going around cities
> To get to other places you found
> It all on paper but the land
> Was made of paper processed
> To look like ferns, mud or other
> Whose sea unrolled its magic
> Distances and then rolled them up.
>   (RM 10)

The "assassins" are out, presumably, to get the "president"—that is, the pre-
siding thought or precept which the poet serves. The military maneuvers and
cartographic manipulations throughout *Rivers and Mountains* have to do with
ideas competing for our attention, insights growing conventional and losing
their appeal. Thought is dramatized as a spatial struggle. Later in the poem
their tiny camp, which seems to exist on the map itself,

>   had grown
> To be the mountains and the map
> Carefully peeled away and not torn
> Was the light, a tender but tough bark
> On everything.
>   (RM 11)

    So the landscape on the map undergoes a metamorphosis to the point of
breaking through to another dimension, a dimension itself not "reality" but
its "tough bark." The poem moves along this landscape of thought to various

momentary promising orders and ideals that get usurped, various Romantic and symbolist transports which turn into institutional structures: tax assessment areas, seminaries, and so on, at which point they are "not worth joining," and the ox of desire has pulled the cart away. Ashbery subverts the linear narrative he invokes—here he introduces uncontextualized characters, specific but nonmimetic scenes, seeds of plot that are never resolved. The poem is driven by an overall trope of imagination and writing as a landscape. But no thematic or spatial stability replaces the dissolving narrative.

Throughout the volume *Rivers and Mountains,* the poet undercuts the tendency to the vertical, to raising our camps to the skies until we think they are natural as mountains and believe the prospect they offer to be truth. In the poem I have just discussed, the mountains turn out to be a wet dream, and the phallic analogy is not incidental. The vertical thrust of desire continually falls back into the horizontal in this flexing perpendicular. Ashbery does not simply chart a perpendicular model of thought, permanence against flux, culture against nature, but makes a dynamic, temporally driven axis in which monuments tumble, rivers seem to rise "into the dusk charged air," and lakes become the sites of skyscrapers. This early habit of casting all the features of the landscape into flux and competition for centrality and proportion, and particularly this manipulation of the perpendicular, is a persistent feature of the poet's work.

If knowledge is a landscape, ideas are trees (a landscape consisting of many). The logical sequence of roots, trunk, branch, leaf, and the teleological process of growth are, as Deleuze and Guattari have pointed out, the model of Western thought.[9] Their alternative botanical model of the rhizome—that horizontal, subterranean, nodal stem that sends up shoots—provides an enticing image for Ashbery's poetry. But his own inclination has been to work with the landscape metaphors that already preside over our thought and to reimagine those. Hence from his first volume, *Some Trees,* the tree has been a major iconographic feature of his work. The first idea is, of course, the Tree of Knowledge, and it is under this tree that the pastoral and epistemological traditions of landscape form a partnership. The Tree of Knowledge promises us unity (despite its branching), rootedness, shade and protection, and, above all, ascent toward heaven. But in Ashbery's poetry the tree has dropped so many seedlings, each with its own assertive stem and precarious limbs, that we are now in a forest of symbols so vast that we cannot see it for the trees. (Though we may glimpse the treetops, we cannot escape landscape.) But the point (perhaps of all antipastoral poems) is the inevitability of the desire for home, for innocence, for a retreat from multiplicity. "What a pleasure to lie under the tree, to sit, stand, and get up under the tree!" he says in "Variations, Calypso and Fugue, on a Theme by Ella Wheeler Wilcox" (a poet of the Joyce Kilmer generation and faith). "But all good things must come to an end, and so one must move forward / Into the space left by one's conclusions" (DDS 24).

If the dream of home is one side of the pastoral ideal embodied in the tree, the other is the dream of transport. "Too Happy, Happy Tree" (AG 44–45) is a paradoxical commentary on the history of an apostrophe, how it persists and gets reinvented. The immediate source of the title and several lines in the poem is Keats's "In drear nighted December":

> Too happy, happy tree,
> Thy branches ne'er remember
> Their green felicity.

But all Keats's poems of transport—"Ode to a Nightingale," "Ode to a Grecian Urn," and "On the Sonnet"—are evoked. From Ashbery's late vantage point it all seems as predictable as it is irresistible—what, his poem asks, will the postmodern version of transport be, "cooly meditative, choosing to tour the back lot"—and anyway, "how much branching out can one take?"

This contemporary fatigue with transcendence in its attenuated forms leads to an end-of-the-line moment, marked in climatic change, glacial moraines, hurricanes, shipwrecks. The poet's seismograph registers such cataclysmic moments as if they were the hiccups. These are "fulcrums" "of inevitable voyages to be accomplished or not."

The poem, which began with arborial transport, now focuses on the tree-lined but horizontal ground, on our own condition as involuntary seekers in history: "one lopes along the path / Thinking, forcibly," the very search for versions of transport which will tease us out of thought, an enforced condition, a kind of blindness. "And by evening we have become the eye, / Blind, because it does the seeing." We are back within the problem of the observer, the ideal having evaded us, the self "sloughed off"; "we have become the eye," but one far from transparent.

By retaining the trope of landscape, Ashbery preserves, in however qualified form, a notion of the observer and a notion of what—somewhat tongue in cheek—he calls earth or nature. I have to step lightly here; in Ashbery the plank of reason crosses a swamp. "Nature," he observes, "forces us into odd positions and then sits back to hear us squawk." He seems wryly on nature's side in this matter. The conditions of our perception and cognition (including metaphor) are self-certifying and determine the reality to which they seem to draw attention. Hence, for instance, the rose is "always miming freshness tracked by pathos." Nature is an artist working for certain effects, especially realism, of course. Nell Blaine's landscape paintings are, he says, sensuous but also astringent because "even at its most poetic, nature doesn't kid around" (RS 238). The trouble with environmental art, he writes in a review, is its "tremendous competition from nature" (RS 343). Of Pierre Bonnard he writes: "His paintings are unfinished, in the same way nature is. They seem about to change, just as light is always on the point of changing" (RS xv). To name knowledge after nature, even in this bracketed way of landscape, is to view it as creative, inexhaustible, based on a "ground" that is always changing, that can also be explored, worked and reworked, viewed from many different vantage points, and traversed on an infinite series of pathways.

Ashbery's poetry may be an alternative to the abandoned subjectivity of the lyric observer, but it is not an easy or firm alternative. As he writes in "October at the Window" (AG 33–34),

> In the dim light of the early nineteenth century
> Someone traveled there once, and observed
> Accurately, and became "the observer,"
> But with so much else to do
> This figure too got lost, charged
> In the night to say what had to be said:
>
> "My eyes are bigger than my stomach."

This is Ashbery's starting point. There is an easy wisdom such a starting point might lead to:

> One must always
> Be quite conscious of the edges of things
> And then how they meet will cease
> To be an issue, all other things
> Being equal, as in fact they are.

But such a complacent postmodern relativism will never satisfy the dreamer: "But do these complex attitudes / Compete successfully with the sounds of bedlam," where the dreamers of the past go on "observing" in an effort to bring the world into the imagination?

It is no accident that Ashbery has come back several times in his career to the figure of John Clare. Even as his reflections on Clare take a tone of modern superiority, there is in them a strong empathy for "the observer" seeking to pass out of his or her knowledge into the self-forgetful concentration on nature. Ashbery shows much less patience toward the more famous Romantics with their lofty idea of the self and its transcendent purposes. Clare resisted converting the landscape to a prospect for visionary flight. Writing of his preenclosure home of Helpston, Clare adopts, his critics have argued, a preenclosure poetics which resists fixed perspective and static pictorial or conceptual rendering.[10] As a profoundly postenclosure poet, Ashbery aims, not for Clare's innocence, but for a fluent sense of landscape within the open jar of time space.

Nature continues among several contemporary poets—Robert Bly, the late James Wright, Dave Smith—to be a site of immanence and thus authority for the poet's vision, perhaps not in the Bierstadt tradition but certainly in the Romantic. In its apparent stability and concreteness, landscape is still the most widely available donor of the experience of presence—space is the generous lie told by time. Several critics (Angela Miller and W. T. J. Mitchell, for instance) have implied that landscape as a genre (poetic or painterly) must fade precisely because it suppresses real history and essentializes perspective, supporting an imperialist view of the world. But this seems to me a very narrow and short-sighted view of the genre's appeal and potential for revision. Ashbery invents a landscape we cannot stand in the middle of, that won't stay still within its frame, a frame that keeps slipping. Time and the land are united in a conspiracy that sabotages all other yearnings for oneness but opens up new dimensions of the terrain.

"Haunted Landscape" (AWK 80–81) illustrates this process well, so I will close this chapter with a brief reading of that poem. Thinking here is not dwelling; the would-be settler is always just passing through. Our knowledge, as the title of the volume implies, is figurative, social, presumptuous, and temporal. A close reading of the poem is challenging, since spatial references (here, ahead, behind), temporal references (then, now), and pronoun references (he, she, you) are all shifting and multiplying variables in this pseudojourney without subjective center or linear path that stays in place as the scene keeps changing. Yet Ashbery achieves a serial continuity within this journey through competing specular structures.

> Something brought them here. It was an outcropping of peace
> In the blurred afternoon slope on which so many picnickers
> Had left no trace. The hikers then always passed through
> And greeted you silently. And down in one corner
>
> Where the sweet william grew and a few other cheap plants
> The rhythm became strained, extenuated, as it petered out
> Among pots and watering cans and a trowel. There were no
> People now but everywhere signs of their recent audible passage.
>
> She had preferred to sidle through the cane and he
> To hoe the land in the hope that some day they would grow happy
> Contemplating the result: so much fruitfulness. A legend.
> He came now in the certainty of her braided greeting,
>
> Sunlight and shadow, and a great sense of what had been cast off
> Along the way, to arrive in this notch. Why were the insiders
> Secretly amused at their putting up handbills at night?
> By day hardly anyone came by and saw them.

They were thinking, too, that this was the right way to begin
A farm that would later have to be uprooted to make way
For the new plains and mountains that would follow after
To be extinguished in turn as the ocean takes over

Where the glacier leaves off and in the thundering of surf
And rock, something, some note or other, gets lost,
And we have this to look back on, not much, but a sign
Of the petty ordering of our days as it was created and led us

By the nose through itself, and now it has happened
And we have it to look at, and have to look at it
For the good it now possesses which has shrunk from the
Outline surrounding it to a little heap or handful near the center.

Others call this old age or stupidity, and we, living
In that commodity, know how only it can enchant the dear soul
Building up dreams through the night that are cast down
At the end with a graceful roar, like chimes swaying out over

The phantom village. It is our best chance of passing
Unnoticed into the dream and all that the outside said about it,
Carrying all that back to the source of so much that was precious.
At one of the later performances you asked why they called it a "miracle,"

Since nothing ever happened. That, of course, was the miracle
But you wanted to know why so much action took on so much life
And still managed to remain itself, aloof, smiling and courteous.
Is that the way life is supposed to happen? We'll probably never know

Until its cover turns into us: the eglantine for duress
And long relativity, until it becomes a touch of red under the bridge
At fixed night, and the cries of the wind are viewed as happy, salient.
How could that picture come crashing off the wall when no one was in the room?

At least the glass isn't broken. I like the way the stars
Are painted in this one, and those which are painted out.
The door is opening. A man you have never seen enters the room.
He tells you that it is time to go, but that you may stay,

If you wish. You reply that it is one and the same to you.
It was only later, after the house had materialized elsewhere,
That you remembered you forgot to ask him what form the change would take.
But it is probably better that way. Now time and the land are identical,

Linked forever.

In the mental landscape "the outcropping of peace" is presumably a pastoral respite from cognition, a promise of "presence" (thus an outcropping of what is otherwise submerged)—in the "blurred" afternoon "slope" of vision's mountain. In short, this is Eden, the travelers Adam and Eve, and their story a compressed version of human history. The place is immediately haunted, though, as the complex perspective includes the past and erases it; "so many picnickers had left no trace." There is no original Adam. The narrator's retrospective vision begins to merge with that of his subjects. By the end of the first stanza the haunted feeling has begun to transform the scene itself, so that the "outcropping of peace" becomes a contrivance, a landscape designed to attract by its illusion of naturalness—a picnic ground. This is the logic in Ashbery's task of vision: the blurred slope of vision leads to a promise of transparence, which turns out to be haunted, an arrangement. The attention shifts from a central "here" which forgets the frame to a margin "down in one corner," where the construction of the pastoral landscape becomes most apparent where it dissolves, where "the rhythm became strained, extenuated, as it petered out / Among pots and watering cans and a trowel." But as the seekers approach the edge of the first landscape (as the present becomes the past), they begin constructing another on its site.

The third stanza in this sequence of four-line stanzas, then, seems less a development of the plot from the exposition than a new beginning. The approach is now split, so that in fact two perspectives (in addition to that of the narrator), two landscapes, open up. "She" (sensuous Eve) would "sidle through the cane"—move with a sideways motion, harvesting a "landscape" of existing thoughts, indulging in the pleasures with which she is presented. "He" (sententious Adam) aims at the production of new knowledge, a freshly cultivated landscape, through groundwork. His plan is a "legend," a dream of fruitfulness, and a key to knowledge. His ambitious dream includes an integration of harvesting and planting, a "braided greeting" (a marriage of intentions) achieved by "casting off" old dreams to get to the unifying truth, the "notch" in the mountain range of prospects where they can move through to view the fertile valley of ordered knowledge. This is a rather different point, of course, from the one we began in, "here" and "now" having together shifted without our noting it. And while "they" hand out handbills to announce their new insight, the insiders (the narrator's retrospective vision now enfolded into the scene) smirk because they know it too is haunted, already cliché.

Stanzas 5 and 6 accelerate the rhythm of revision moving, in "Kubla Khan" fashion, from the picturesque to the sublime, then to dwindling memory. This entire movement is registered within one sentence, projected onto one site, as if it were one thought, so that no perspective becomes fixed. In this metamorphic landscape Ashbery casts temporal knowledge in a geologist's spatial vision of history. We enter it expectantly as "they"—the seekers now gleefully embracing process over static purpose—project their landscapes out beyond themselves, farms yielding to plains and mountains, worn down by glaciers where the crumbling rocks meet the ocean's roar. There is certainly intensity here, suspended at the end of the stanza. This exuberant vision of process almost seems to take the place of the pastoral vision at the opening of the poem. But we come out the other side of the thought as a retrospective "we." Having reached the end of the line of the expansive sublime of process which projected broad horizons, we now look back to see the horizon "shrunk from the / Outline surrounding it to a little heap or handful near the center." This is our inevitable retrospective view of our ambitions, but it is not privileged.

Stanzas 8–10 recapitulate stanzas 5–7 in a milder, more sympathetic tone. The little heap or handful at the center, the very idea of a center, may look from the outside like a fetishistic commodity that will "lead us by the nose." Such an ironic perspective might well end another poet's meditation. But the ritual process of "building up dreams . . . that are cast down . . . with a graceful roar" gets affirmed here, for all the sniveling or snickering of the retrospective view. The chimes swaying over the phantom village condense images from Wallace Stevens's "Mrs. Alfred Uruguay," in which the female pilgrim, ascending the mount of vision by the via negativa, passes the man of capable imagination on his way down, "poorly dressed, . . . lost in an integration of the martyr's bones" of creative sacrifice, to find "the ultimate elegance, the imagined land." [11] Unlike "Mrs. Alfred Uruguay," "Haunted Landscape" refuses to stabilize the mountain landscape it begins with; it is more dispersed and temporal, much less dialectical. But the impulse to construct a "dream" in terms of landscape that can absorb the skepticism in "all that the outside said about it" remains Stevensian.

Having emerged from the series of landscapes into this retrospective posture, Ashbery does not end but establishes a new scene, like a Chinese box around the first. The trope of theater now makes the figures from the first part of the poem, including the insiders, characters in an endless series of performances, the journey and ascent to vision a ritual gesture. In stanza 11 we seem to be even further from the dream, looking now at a painting, as life's cover turns into us, or we into it—a painting in which our anxieties themselves become a canvas of fixed night, our apocalyptic feelings decorative, with a "touch of red." But Ashbery will never fix vision in this darkness, or aestheticize the void. The task of vision must continue. If the "duress / And long relativity" which characterize dreaming in stanza 11 now seem fixed as in a frame with "knowledge" something like a book with a cover, the pun on "cover" makes the "eglantine for duress" also a ground cover, and we are back in landscape. The picture promptly falls off the wall, and we are returned to an uncertain dimension of living and knowing. A door is opened to let in an unidentified "man" and a new perspective, rearranging things once again and forcing our engagement through the irrational disturbance of plot.

Ashbery proves, once again, the Houdini of poetry who can escape any box he puts himself in, yet insists on the necessity of the box. Time combined with space is the basis of this magic, as in the last stanza of the poem, in which moving and staying in place, past and future, time and the land become linked in a serial chain even the poem will not undo.

Retrospective vision is, for Ashbery, even more tempting than prospective vision. We want to sum up, to gather history into space, see the Ice-Storm (also I-Storm) which presses into the earth as a crystal text before it melts away. But the creative urge is by its nature more restless than imperial. The desire to end always competes, in Ashbery, with the desire to change. We may long to frame "a landscape stippled by frequent glacial interventions" (W 77), historicized but finally firm. It

> holds so well to its lunette one wants to keep it but we must
> Go on despising it until that day when environment
> Finally reads as a necessary but still vindictive opposition
> To all caring, all explaining.
>   (W 77–78)

That, of course, would not be a day for poetry.

Notes

1. Marjorie Perloff, *Poetic License: Essays on Modernist and Postmodernist Lyric* (Evanston, Ill.: Northwestern University Press, 1990).

2. Fredric Jameson, *Postmodernism; or, The Cultural Logic of Late Capitalism* (Durham, N. C.: Duke University Press, 1991), 154–81.

3. Ashbery explained to Sue Gangel in 1977: "I don't know what my life is, what I want to be escaping *from*. I want to move to some other *space*, I guess, when I write, which perhaps was where I had been but without being fully conscious of it" (Joe David Bellamy, ed., *American Poetry Observed: Poets on Their Work* [Urbana: University of Illinois Press, 1984], 20).

4. Mark Johnson and George Lakoff, *Metaphors We Live By* (Chicago: University of Chicago Press, 1980).

5. Anne Salmond, "Theoretical Landscapes: On Cross-Cultural Conception of Knowledge," in *Semantic Anthropology*, ed. David Parkin (London: Academic Press, 1982), 82–85.

6. Jean-François Lyotard, *The Postmodern Condition: A Report on Knowledge*, trans. Geoff Bennington and Brian Massumi (Minneapolis: University of Minnesota Press, 1984).

7. Andrew Ross, *The Failure of Modernism: Symptoms of American Poetry* (New York: Columbia University Press, 1986), 161–208.

8. John Ashbery, "1976 and All That," quoted in Rob Wilson, *American Sublime: The Genealogy of a Poetic Genre* (Madison: University of Wisconsin Press, 1991).

9. Gilles Deleuze and Felix Guattari, *Capitalism and Schizophrenia,* trans. Robert Hurley et al. (New York: Viking, 1977).

10. See John Barrell, *The Idea of Landscape and the Sense of Place, 1730–1840: An Approach to John Clare* (Cambridge: Cambridge University Press, 1972).

11. Wallace Stevens, *The Palm at the End of the Mind,* ed. Holly Stevens (New York: Vintage, 1972), 186.

PART 2

Explorations of Influence

5 | The Absence of a Noble Presence

John Koethe

> Perhaps you are being kept here
> Only so that somewhere else the peculiar light of someone's
> Purpose can blaze unexpectedly in the acute
> Angles of the rooms.
>
> "Clepsydra" (RM)

THE CHARACTER OF John Ashbery's influence on contemporary poetry has been shaped in large part by the way in which his own reputation has developed. He is acknowledged to be one of the most significant living American poets and one of the genuinely important poets of this century, a consensus that has formed dramatically during the last fifteen years. Yet a passion for his work by a limited, and largely nonacademic, audience—and the influence of his work on a small number of poets—goes back at least twenty years beyond that. It isn't easy to remember, from the accommodating, directionless, and rather passionless perspective of poetry today, that his poetry originated at a time when there really *was* an important distinction to be drawn—and felt—between the Academy and its Other, and that for the most part his work was belittled or ignored by the former and championed all the more fervently for that fact by the latter. One private example: I recall writing an enthusiastic—and, I thought at the time, quite densely argued—review in the campus newspaper of a reading he gave at Princeton in 1966, only to learn that it was regarded with amusement by some of the faculty in the English department as symptomatic of the naïveté of the student literati who'd organized the event. The acceptance of his work by the poetry-reading public—such as it is—only began, I think, with Harold Bloom's recognition of the importance of *The Double Dream of Spring* in the early seventies and was only established in 1976 by the accolades accorded *Self-Portrait in a Convex Mirror*.

I've rehearsed the history of the reception of Ashbery's own work because I think it bears on the question of the nature of its influence, an influence which strikes me as somewhat problematic. Part of it is diffuse, and reflected in its role in the remodeling of what might be thought of as the "generic" poem of the age from what it amounted to thirty years ago. Part of it is the direct effect it has had on the development—but often, alas, the lack of development—of particular poets and schools of poetry. Yet it seems to me that, with a couple of exceptions, neither its diffuse nor its direct influence really reflects or re- sponds to the distinctive aspects of his work that occasioned them in the first place.

My own sense of how other poets have responded to Ashbery's work, and of the respects in which that response has seemed wanting, has been shaped by my own involvement with it; I want to try to describe some of the perceived characteristics of his poetry that originally drew me to it so strongly, since I have the impression that many of these perceptions are not widely shared. When I started writing seriously in the early sixties, the poems that helped form, from a distance, my conception of what poetry could and ought to be were principally the high modernist works of Yeats, Eliot, Pound, and Wil- liams—the last three especially, and especially in the linguistically fragmented modes of "The Waste Land," *The Cantos,* and *Pictures from Brueghel* (along with, from an even greater distance, the poems of Keats, Shelley, and Tenny- son). The contemporary models I tried to emulate were the Black Mountain poets Charles Olson, Robert Creeley, and Robert Duncan, whose writings seemed to me to combine the ambition and seriousness of the high moderns with a compelling theoretical argument for the centrality of language to per- ception and thought. Duncan's work in particular became my first real poetic obsession, for the way it managed to incorporate a Shelleyian lyricism and ro- manticism into the austere and discontinuous linguistic framework of projec- tive verse. In all these poets' works I found a scale of ambition, a conceptual purpose, a concern for the nature and possibilities of the medium of poetry, and a powerful affective element which made the work of more academically acclaimed poets like Robert Lowell, Theodore Roethke, and Richard Wilbur seem tidy and smug by comparison, and that of Beat poets like Allen Ginsberg and Lawerence Ferlinghetti emotionally conventional and unself-conscious in its exploitation of rhetoric.

When, against this background, I came across a copy of *The Tennis Court Oath* in 1965, it completely changed my conception of what poetry could be and, in a real sense, changed my life (for it showed that the relation between poetry and one's life could be much more direct than I'd ever imagined). Here were poems whose linguistic disruptions and conceptual disorientations were far more extreme than anything I'd ever encountered; yet rather than falling apart or simply becoming inert, they seemed permeated by a romantic sensibil- ity purer and more intense than anything I'd experienced in Duncan's work. I know that this is a somewhat idiosyncratic reading of *The Tennis Court Oath,* but I still think of it as an essentially *lyric* book, a powerful expression of philosophical dualism in which the body, and indeed "all that is solid melts into air,"[1] until only a dispersed and decentered subjectivity remains. And pos- sibly because I came to this book just shortly before the publication of *Rivers and Mountains,* I felt a greater sense of continuity between the radically polarized linguistic constructions of the former and the dense, meditative ruminations inaugurated by the seminal poem "Clepsydra" in the latter than many other readers seemed to perceive. True, the conventions of syntax were largely restored, and the poems adopted a tone of logical or narrative progression. Yet the landscape these restorations helped reconstruct wasn't a tangible setting in the external world at all but rather an abstract "region that is no place."[2] And the kind of consciousness arrayed against it—and arrayed, it seemed to me, so furiously—wasn't the familiar subject of the speaking voice, but a diffuse, impersonal, and transcendent subjectivity.

I said earlier that I think that the influence of Ashbery's work takes roughly two forms: first, a broad influence on the character of the kind of poem the literary culture regards as stereotypical, and that young poets in their formative stages—at least young poets without prior theoretical allegiances—try (or get accused of trying) to emulate; and second, its direct influence on particular poets and schools of poetry.

The first of these is largely a product of the celebrity his work has achieved since the midseventies, a period in which he has displaced Robert Lowell as the paradigmatic poetic figure of the day (although I know that similar claims can be made for James Merrill in this regard). The exemplary poem of thirty years ago was characterized by a strong speaking voice, and the criteria of its success were the authenticity of that voice and the force and clarity with which the states of feeling, thought, and perception of the person from whom it originated were conveyed. The relation of the poet to the poem was one of *control* (even when the emotions the poem incorporated were passive), and its style was marked by literalness, a clipped diction, an avoidance of indeterminacy, an insistence on the concrete and the particular, and the calculated refusal of rhetorical effect. It rarely acknowledged its status as writing, and its attitude toward the impulses of romanticism was one of irony and condescension.

The generic poem of today seems quite different (though just as unappealing and, fortunately, just as nonexistent). The tone is liable to be nostalgic, and its motions those of reverie. Its predominant feelings are passive ones like resignation and loss; its language is resonant and suggestive; the use of the narrative past tense invests it with a mythological quality; and its overall effect is one of tenderness. It dissociates itself, especially in its transitions and patterns of inference, from everyday ideas of rationality and control; its awareness of language is informed by a sense of its limitations; and it is likely to incorporate an apology for its status as writing, and for the processes of the imagination which produced it.

This poem is constituted in large part by qualities that have been associated with Ashbery's work since its public reception in the seventies—passivity, an acquiescence in indeterminacy, an avoidance of rationality, and self-reflexivity. Of course other poets have contributed to its constitution as well—W. S. Merwin, Mark Strand, and James Wright come to mind, and there are several others. But what strikes me as problematic about this aspect of Ashbery's influence is its superficiality. The current generic poem is usually deployed as a stylistic variation on the underlying conception of poetry exemplified by its earlier incarnation: that poetry ought to be a vehicle for the expression, formulation, and validation of a self-conception or personality, or of states of mind. Of course the personality and states of mind it is called on to validate today aren't those of thirty years ago, a difference which is reflected in the nature of the poetry which is supposed to accomplish the task. But then clothes, manners, and attitudes aren't what they were thirty years ago either. Yet one thing that can never be said of Ashbery's poetry is that its primary function is to serve as a vehicle of personal self-expression. This is not to say that it lacks a distinctive psychological character—indeed, the most problematic aspect of its influence is a misapprehension of what its psychological (or better, spiritual) character actually is. But to the extent that it has merely furnished a poetic vehicle or style that can be deployed in the service of a conception of poetry which is antithetical to it, its influence has been disappointing.

Ashbery's direct influence on certain schools of poetry has been more interesting, but here too not as fruitful as it might be. This influence developed prior to, or at least independent of, the public vogue for his work and can be seen, I think, in two broad groups of writers: the first might be called the second (or, I suppose by now, the nth) generation New York school poets, while the second comprises poets of a more theoretical orientation, currently typified by the Language poets. The strain in Ashbery's work to which the New York school poets seem most responsive is a domestic and deflationary one: the texture of daily life and the experience of ordinary pleasures, perplexities, and disappointments come to replace, or to be placed on a level with, movements like loss, disillusionment, the passage of time, and death as catalysts for the poetic imagination. At the same time, the imagination itself gets reconceived, not in terms of transcendence, but as a method for recovering the immanence of the everyday. This tendency sometimes issues in a knowing and patronizing antiaestheticism, but at its best it is capable of yielding poems of a refreshing, casual lyricism, reflective of certain moments that are actually present in Ashbery's own work.

The more theoretically inclined poets who have responded to Ashbery's work tend to limit their enthusiasm to *The Tennis Court Oath* and *Three Poems,* often showing little interest in his later books and viewing Bloom's assimilation of his work to the main line of American poetry running through Whitman and Stevens less as a vindication of it than as an act of academic co-optation. Their interest is in the deconstructive aspects of his writing, in which a refusal to conform to or acknowledge poetic conventions and expectations leads to an awareness of their essential arbitrariness and a heightened sense of the palpability of language itself. The main impulse is neither expressive nor lyrical, but philosophical: to argue that the ordinary conception of language as a natural, transparent medium for the communication of prelinguistic feelings and thoughts is a socially constructed one, maintained in part by the aura of linguistic directness with which poetry is commonly endowed.

While there are poets in both of these schools who have produced individual poems of great accomplishment and interest, I must admit that I find the results of Ashbery's influence to date somewhat disappointing on the whole. Though there are exceptions (and I want to turn to this shortly), what seem lacking are substantial bodies of work by individual poets that manifest his influence but have a distinctive character of their own. This isn't the case with other poets of something like Ashbery's stature—with James Merrill, for instance, one can cite examples like Alfred Corn, Richard Kenney, and J. D. McClatchy of poets whose works have been partially shaped by his, but which still manage to exhibit characteristic obsessions and directions of their own. In some ways Ashbery's case resembles Eliot's, another poet of enormous reputation and importance, whose work was a dominant influence on the generic poem of its day, but for whom it is difficult to identify major figures whose works constitute his legacy (though I would argue that in some respects Ashbery himself is such a figure).

Why is this? In what strikes me as an extremely insightful remark, Allen Grossman has observed about Ashbery's poetry that

> it is the sentimentality of his relationship to the past that he seeks to conserve in a structure which has, as he says, the shape, or anti-shape, of falling snow, but which is still a world characterized by snow and by rain and by sentiment: it is still a landscape with the seeds of tragedy inside it, seeds which he does not allow to germinate, but from the promise of which he derives his significance as a writer. Ashbery . . . is fundamentally a manager of traditional resources.[3]

I think that this is correct. And the traditional resources he seeks to conserve are the fundamental impulses of romanticism, which I would characterize as subjectivity's contestation of its objective setting in a world which has no place for it, and which threatens to reduce it to nonexistence. (I also think that much the same can be said of Eliot, though we have only lately begun to read him this way.) But the form that the romantic contestation takes in Ashbery's work is a belated one, differing from its traditional manifestations in several respects. For one thing, it does not attempt to valorize the individual self but rather to assert the claims of the diffuse, impersonal subjectivity I spoke of earlier. Moreover, it is informed throughout by an acknowledgment of its own failure ("I am only a transparent diagram, of manners and / Private words with the certainty of being about to fall"),[4] an awareness that accounts for the passivity that is often wrongly taken to be the central emotional tendency in his work—wrongly, because in Ashbery the contestation isn't less intense for being futile ("But its fierceness was still acquiescence / To the nature of this goodness already past").[5] Traditionally the self seeks to reestablish its claims in the face of the magnitude of the natural, objective world through the Kantian experience of the sublime. And it is mark of our distance from even as recent a formulation of that response as "The Auroras of Autumn" that the possibility of such a resolution is altogether absent from Ashbery's poetry.

Now while the romantic impulse underlying Ashbery's work has been noted by critics like Bloom, it seems to me that the poets most directly influenced by his poetry have not, for the most part, responded to that impulse very strongly. There are of course instances of Ashbery's style being adopted in the service of the poetic enterprise of the validation of the individual self, a stereotypically romantic one—but this is quite different from the abstract version of romantic contestation his poetry enacts. The poets who have been most directly influenced by his work, and whose interest in it largely predates its more public acceptance, have tended to emphasize either its domestic and deflationary aspects or else its deconstructive ones. I consider this unfortunate. These aspects are genuine, but I think of them as merely part of the form the diffuse, decentered version of romantic contestation takes in his poetry, almost as though this whole glittering postmodern contraption were powered by an old-fashioned wood-burning stove.

I think these generalizations about the ways poets have responded to Ashbery's work are roughly correct, but there are important exceptions to them. Of the poets whose writing is marked by Ashbery's influence, yet which has an integrity and substance of its own, the most fully realized is Douglas Crase in *The Revisionist*. He takes over the high meditative style that emerges in Ashbery from "Clepsydra" on: long, fluent lines that unroll in supple movements through unbroken and extended verse paragraphs; a tone of argument that remains poised and abstract, even though couched in terms that are mostly casual and colloquial; and an emotional undercurrent that gathers slowly but insistently, and with great culminative force. Yet his poetry also enacts a distinctive and original version of the romantic contestation central to Ashbery's.

Crase is a more public poet than Ashbery, not so much in terms of his poetry's intended audience, but in the ways in which its subjectivity and its objective setting are conceived. In Ashbery the objective setting is a fragmented personal world constituted by an inaccessible past, disrupted relationships, and communicative indeterminacy; and the subjectivity is an almost solipsistic one. The objective setting of Crase's poetry is a geographic America in which anonymity and collective forgetfulness have become the conditions of mere being, against which he deploys an Emersonian transcendental consciousness which tries to establish itself by reimagining that setting, an act in which the pathetic fallacy gets raised nearly to the power of truth.

One way of characterizing the difference between Ashbery's and Crase's work—one which also helps clarify the sense in which Ashbery's is "private" while Crase's is "public"—is in terms of the structure of the subjective consciousness which informs each of them. Both are enactments of the process whereby the raw materials of an archaic, primary mentality get transformed into conceptualized thought through the activities of interpretation and acknowledgment, a fragile and never-completed process constantly threatened by the possibilities of failure and regression.[6] In Ashbery's work this process is closer to the original Freudian paradigm, with the archaic, primary material being something like the hallucinated objects of wish-fulfillment, constantly on the verge of coalescing into a rational narrative structure which always dissolves just as it is about to be achieved. In Crase, though, the primary raw material, which simply presents itself without explanation, isn't the private phantasmagoria of the hallucination or dream but the common locales and features of the contemporary American landscape, which for us have regressed into a kind of immediate meaninglessness. His poetry enacts the effort to transform (or restore) this material to significance through a process of identification, acceptance, and love—a process which, if successfully completed, would result, not in the mature rationality toward which Ashbery's poetry gestures, but rather in a transcendental vantage point which views our common setting sub specie aeternitatis, from an almost planetary perspective. As with Ashbery, what the poetry presents is the process itself, rather than the completed conceptualization toward which it points (though oddly enough, Crase's work seems somewhat more optimistic about the possibility of achieving its aims than Ashbery's, even though its aims are more grandiose). And also like Ashbery, the interest of the poetry is in the movements of mentality and perception themselves, rather than in any identifiable subject or self to which they may be ascribed (though Crase doesn't hesitate to adopt a declamatory mode of expression when it seems called for by the scale of the poem).

The result is a poetry that bears the unmistakable marks of Ashbery's style and cast of mind, yet which does not seem at all imitative. What Crase does in a way is receive Ashbery into the body of American poetry that is the common property of all poets, rather than let his work remain the private preserve of those who feel a temperamental affinity with it, or have some special relation to it. In particular, he recovers Whitman through Ashbery—or put another way, he enlists the rhetorical and psychological strategies of the poet many castigate as our most private and hermetic in the service of a public, Emersonian project of reclamation of his own—a Bloomian swerve implausible enough to render almost believable the claim that even while "the past / Seems to be level in its place there's room for more / And the ragged additions polish the previous days."[7] And his example is powerful enough to make me think that the full measure of John Ashbery's influence on American poetry has yet to emerge.

Notes

1. Karl Marx and Friedrich Engels, *The Communist Manifesto*, ed. Samuel H. Beer (New York: Appleton-Century-Crofts, 1955), 13.

2. The phrase is from Paavo Haavikko's "Winter Palace," in his *Selected Poems*, trans. Anselm Hollo (New York: Grossman, 1966), a poem which Ashbery has suggested may well be one of the century's great poems.

3. Allen Grossman, *Against Our Vanishing* (Boston: Rowan Tree Press, 1981), 49.

4. "Clepsydra," RM 31.

5. Ibid.

6. My remarks here on the development of subjectivity owe much to Jonathan Lear's *Love and Its Place in Nature* (New York: Farrar, Straus & Giroux, 1990).

7. Douglas Crase, "The Revisionist," in *The Revisionist* (Boston: Little, Brown, 1981).

6 Purists Will Object

Some Meditations on Influence

Donald Revell

THE PRESUMPTION OF self-knowledge endangers a poet by subordinating what is made to a fixed idea of the maker, the Dedalian. Eliot's dictum concerning escape from personality suggests a technique: the making of a poem as a syntactic escape from self-knowledge, from the self as known sum, the product of which escape is an inward revision as well as a sequence of original verbal effects. The poetry of John Ashbery is the most enabling that I know, an uninterrupted and beautifully various series of spurs and permissions. And it follows that I feel myself most enabled by my *un*certainties as to the specifics of his influence on how I think of poems and write them. His work surrounds more than it designates; it animates more than it names. That this is true of all the primary instigators of our avant-gardes—Duchamp, Beckett, Cage, and others—encourages me to describe and avow the influence of Ashbery's poetry without at the same time feeling obliged to assign to it a fixed value or precise dynamic. My purpose in what follows is such an avowal through eight brief meditations on the enabling qualities of eight passages, each from a different Ashbery collection. Along the way, I hope not to define influences but to witness the means by which influence happens. Definition would be a traduction. Influence is exemplary, after all, not metaphoric.

> But she, of course, was only an effigy
> Of indifference, a miracle
>
> Not meant for us, as the leaves are not
> Winter's because it is the end.
>   ("Illustration," SoTr 61)

Influence begins as an incident of disturbance. It continues as a sequence of disturbances in a manner that Robert Lowell described as "stirring and blurring." The sequence proceeds unmethodically between the general and particular. This is how one begins to hear and be changed by Ashbery. The "she," the woman whom I would by habit imagine as any one of a number of idealities (erotic, aesthetic, organic, or abstract), preempts my habitual response by being "only an effigy." Ashbery's poems often practice a preemptive lessness, an unexpected diminishment of figure and image which turns the canonical reflex into a pratfall and leaves the reader gazing bewilderedly up at what has been diminished. Reduced to an effigy, the "she" acquires an imaginative status and power that conventional exaltation could never have provided. By itself, this instance of inversion technique is enough to produce a *vertige*, a disturbance recognizably avant-garde. But the momentum of the passage continues through several instances: the effigy, usually a product of satiric or outraged passions, is of "indifference," a caricature of no tone; and indifference, a state usually deprived of affect, is a "miracle," a liberating disturbance of natural law; and still the liberation is "not meant for us," although the double pause of a line and stanza break allows us plenty of leisure to imagine that it is and to begin to anticipate its precise form. Intention gains force through the denial of intention, just as Ashbery changes the way I understand poetic decorum by abjuring the accumulation of meaning that is decorum's conventional purpose. The phrases "mean" by failing to add up, by congregating possibilities, most of them contradictory, but not synthesizing them. The particular (e.g., the effigy) and the general (e.g., the undetailed miracle) no longer function as categories in such a congregation because Ashbery refuses to allow them to refer to anything beyond themselves. As winter is the literal, intentionless end of nature, this passage represents the literal, unaggressive end of metonymy. The feeling in the passage, simultaneously vivid and nonspecific, exercises passion without imperiousness, reference without attitude.

Where some readers find themselves resenting such indeterminacies as artless and unhelpful, I have, since first reading Ashbery as a student, in the little Carnegie-built library in Binghamton, New York, watching the pigeons homing at sunset to the green dome of the city hall across the plaza from the window at which I read, felt exhilarated and companioned by such unimperiousness. The end of metonymy has meant for me the beginning of an unlimited inclusiveness, an invitation in every passage to enter the poem bringing my own *immediate* circumstances along with me. It seems beautiful to me that when I remember my first reading of almost any Ashbery piece, I remember my own situation at the time intermingled with the figures and gestures of the poem. As the effect is beautiful, it is one I desire for my own poetry. The undeclared intention leaves open the possibilities of new hybrid intentions and makes of saying an escape from what I merely meant to say. Ambition delays meaning in order to mean more largely, more generously, abetted by the necessary cooperation of the reader, who must bring his or her own circumstances to bear in order to read at all. Reading "Illustration," I am entirely free to determine the implications of an "effigy of indifference," just as I am free to judge the distance or nearness of such a Beckettian finality as resonates in "because it is the end." In writing, Ashbery teaches me to desire not an increase in my individual portion of imaginative freedom but an increase in the stock of freedom available to anyone.

> There is nothing to do
> For our liberation, except wait in the horror of it.
>
> And I am lost without you.
> ("They Dream Only of America," TCO 13)

Because freedom is intentionless, its accomplishments, "our liberation," require nothing of us. Yet in a further variation of inversion technique, Ashbery establishes this nothing as neither nugatory nor still. It requires great effort, a redoubling of negative capability, to articulate phrases, lines, and stanzas without resort to the reassurances and little victories of expressed intent. That is why Ashbery poises the line "There is nothing to do" as a positive, proposing absolute indeterminacy as a task—the nothing that somehow *must* be done. Here, as everywhere in *The Tennis Court Oath*, Ashbery reminds me that the imagination is not an inward quality in search of expression but, rather, an event that occurs when perception contacts the world with the force of desire in the form of words or paint or sounds. Imagination defines itself in what it does, participating in liberty *as* liberty. Desire declares the unsatisfactoriness of the present moment (emotion "recollected" is not emotion) and directs the mind toward its liberation from that state. And where can the mind go but to the world, and how can it travel but indeterminately, dissatisfaction being the sum of what has been determined? Just as "nothing" is a task, so waiting is an activity, a pioneering. The imagination happens, poems happen in the time pried open by waiting, time made porous to accidents and to new juxtapositions by the deferral of particularity. There, words contrive new syntaxes and thus new meanings because none has been prescribed. There, the mind moves more ways than one.

This multiplicity is the primary prerequisite of imagination, a "horror" owing to the utter defenselessness it prolongs and prolongs. Where there is no horror, no uninterpreted, there is only the awful and unacceptable condition of certainty: that isolated, final, and feckless utterance "And I am lost without you." If I have no single destination, I cannot be lost, only en route. As long as I am waiting, anything may yet arrive. As America failed in the moment it became an ideality instead of a plurality of discrete, then overlapping, events (a city on a hill instead of an explorer's beautiful misinterpretation), voices and poems fail when they reconcile themselves to a solitary posture. Closure victimizes thought. *Some*thing victimizes the *nothing* in which and by which our liberation persists. Every final word expresses defeat. John Ashbery does not deny that a final word always gets said. The trick is to prolong the dream, the recital, the ice storm, all the unfinished originals. The trick is to write as far into the accidents as one can before collapsing into statement. Poetry stops where nothing cannot be said any longer or in only one way: "And I am lost without you."

> I prefer "you" in the plural, I want "you,"
> You must come to me, all golden and pale
> Like the dew and the air.
> And then I start getting this feeling of exaltation.
>   ("A Blessing in Disguise," RM 26)

The actual implementation of delay and the exercise of desire in the widest time, the broadest space, depend upon a form of stubbornness. ("Virtue is really stubbornness," as Ashbery writes in "The Picture of Little J. A. in a Prospect of Flowers," SoTr 41.) As here the voice insists upon the plurality of its desired object, I have learned to do my best to maintain the variousness of any subject, to be greedy on behalf of my figures, to want them visible and elusive, vivid and imprecise. We are used to thinking of clarity as a kind of focus. Yet in placing desire at the heart of his technique, Ashbery opts for the clarity of expansiveness, a kinetic rather than a pictorial apprehension of whatever the imagination finds or makes desirable. Such stubbornness refuses to privilege the spatial distinctions to which most poems aspire; it slides away from the epiphanic representation, from the brilliant immanence of things such as Lowell's aquarium in its Sahara of snow, preferring instead a presentational restlessness, a sequence not of images but of qualities. Thus, "You must come to me," not in a specific form, but "golden" and "pale." It is the goldenness and the paleness that matter; beside them the simile "like the dew and the air" seems as arbitrary and behindhand as all similes truly are in the context of desire. The presentational has neither time nor appetite for similes. Its feelings and objects rely upon whatever succeeds them or is summoned by them for their measure of clarity. (We all, John Ashbery included, owe much to Frank O'Hara for his courage in displacing traditional simile and metaphor with a distinctive, kinetic next-ness. I don't think he was kidding when, in "Personism: A Manifesto," he expressed the rationale of his technique by saying, "If you're going to buy a pair of pants you want them to be tight enough so everyone will want to go to bed with you." The life of anything in a poem rests not with the thing itself but with what comes next because of it or with what is drawn to it by whatever qualities it exerts.)

If I am, for example, writing about a woman looking at paintings in a gallery, I have learned from Ashbery not to picture her but to follow her from canvas to canvas, taking pleasure and desiring even more pleasure because of her inexpressive momentum, the way she takes the qualities of one painting along with her, momentarily, into her confrontation with the next painting, and so on. And as pleasure always feels itself to be (rightly or wrongly) a beginning rather than an ending, the first in a series of sensations rather than the last, this kinetic technique allows for satisfaction with no concurrent diminishment of appetite, with no loss of momentum or potential for variation.

Ashbery writes, "And then I *start* getting this feeling of exaltation." Until the inevitable final word, the poem's last sensation, the virtue of stubbornness keeps the poem in step with and indistinguishable from everything available to it in time.

> Mixed days, the mindless years, perceived
> With half-parted lips
> The way the breath of spring creeps up on you and floors you.
>   ("The Double Dream of Spring," DDS 41)

The language of stubbornness catalogs more than it defines. This is the use of appetite, for motivation. We have all lived "mixed days," and we can all look back on "mindless years." Yet we cannot literally picture them, and *my* mixed days and mindless years cannot serve as paradigms for anyone else's. Ashbery insists that time is physical, is flavored and textured, that it is more than a site to be occupied or observed. Perception happens in the mouth tasting and speaking simultaneously so as to elide the distortions of reflection and memory. Perception of this kind can never be figurative; poet and reader are simply carried along by it to make of it what they can in each other's company, but individually. What Ashbery recommends is *not* automatic writing. His destination is the entire actual, not the secret cloister of the unconscious. I believe he recommends that the poet write *with* instead of *about* moments of being. (Think of the curtains that keep on billowing in "The System.") Image and symbol translate perception into repeatedly accessible forms. "Mixed days" and "mindless years, perceived / With half-parted lips" arrive purely as themselves, still in flux, not to be consulted but to be completed by every individual reading in countless unprepared ways. As Breton insisted, automatic writing is absolutely unalterable. The writing in "The Double Dream of Spring" changes with every reading because of the inherent incompleteness and stubborn provisionality of its figures. In automatic writing, the unconscious exerts total authority. In an Ashbery poem, authority is conjured in process, in the extent to which an intimate versimilitude arises and is maintained between poet and readers as they continue through the poem, nurturing it with their own appetites, completing it with their own provisional conclusions. It invents a kind of faith: seeing with no evidence of having seen, knowing without any fixed points of reference. When I write with such a faith, I can make a phrase such as "the color of windows" or "the anatomies of the wind" and, without qualifying it further or locating it in any particularized context, poise it in my syntax as a finished statement rather than a phrase. It is what the speaker *is*, not merely what he or she sees. Windows have color, and the wind has a body, but a person must be in their presence or imagine their presence to know them. Thus, to read my phrase is to join me somewhere, not to receive a message

from me. And you will know the place in your own terms, having had no further terms from me.

The language of stubbornness speaks every way at once so as to leave the
invitation of each phrase open. The recognizably poetic diction of "The way
the breath of spring" slides without transition into the slightly vulgar, out-of-
date colloquial of "creeps up on you and floors you." Too many poems have
made an institution out of spring, a trope. Here the season is returned to time
and arrives as it truly always does, as an overwhelming surprise. To try to say
everything, one must be willing to use *all* the words in any truthful combination. In these opening lines of "The Double Dream of Spring," Ashbery invents
my realism.

> At once the weight of the other years and above all the weight of distinguish-
> ing among them slipped away. You found yourself not wanting to care.
> ("The New Spirit," TP 37)

In "Why I Am Not a Painter," Frank O'Hara writes, "It is even in / prose,
I am a real poet." And again, I don't think he was kidding, for surely it is
the prose poem that has done the most to revivify the genres of poetry in our
avant-gardes. Rimbaud, Fargue, and Jacob took the line away from the lyricist
and opened it to unmeasured tempi. This "other tradition," as Ashbery calls it
in his prose *Three Poems,* reaches our own poetry through the innovations of
Williams's *Kora in Hell* and in the collagings of his *Paterson,* thriving and di-
versifying now in the work of Edson, Simic, Berg, Tate, and others. So it is not
really surprising to me that I have, from among all of Ashbery's books, learned
the most and continue to be the most influenced by *Three Poems,* never mind
the fact that I have never written a prose poem. The literal feeling of reading
Three Poems is a shocking education: the eyes move over page after page, slid-
ing coolly over a surface of pronouns without antecedents, imagining nothing
in particular, following no single train of thought; but when those eyes lift
from the page, the room is changed, the world is changed. Ashbery's words
suddenly adhere to the reader's surroundings. In this way, *Three Poems* is nothing *but* influence; the poem happens in the moment when the reader turns
away from the poem. *Three Poems* models an insinuating fluent mundo of delay and stubbornness: the poem as more than object, more even than experience. It models a new means of experiencing, a new head.

The notion that a poem need not address itself to the clarification or elaboration of some property of mind, circumstance, or heart but can instead assume the status of otherness—subjectless and therefore equal to poet and
reader alike—thrills and refreshes me. It has always seemed to me that to read
is to choose to be an other—not necessarily an author or fictional character
but oneself reconfigured by new words and new combinations. In making a
poem, a poet unburdens the language of its "distinguishing" utility, its syntac-

tic atomizing, letting the words cluster as they do in each of us, vagrantly, un-captioned, but with the integrity of selves. Too many poems deteriorate into puzzles, feeling themselves captured at some point by an emerging identity to which they must supply a local habitation and a name, a "solution." But the self, the tourbillon of phrases moving consciously and unconsciously headlong in time, is not restricted by identity in any such mechanical way. It can and does mix its metaphors shamelessly. Its antecedents are rarely certain. To para-phrase Ashbery's "Soonest Mended" (DDS 17–19), a self is, and therefore a poem can be, an "emulsion," a suspension of undissolved, unreconciled parti-cles in unstable relationship one to another. When I write a poem, I find my-self "not wanting to care," urgently desiring the carelessness to say and believe what I need not explain or understand. And if I write to be someone else and not merely someone else's, the writing must be careless lest it be cap-tured by the rhetoric of solution. Think of the beautiful passage from *Paterson* Book 3: "Only one answer: write carelessly so that nothing that is not green will survive."

> It is the lumps and trials
> That tell us whether we shall be known
> And whether our fate can be exemplary, like a star.
>   ("The One Thing That Can Save America," SPCM 45)

Where the technique is carelessness, the medium is recklessness. In an Ashbery poem, time subjects the improvisations of language—selves, desires, attitudes, dreams—to "lumps and trials." The success of any improvisation, its material viability over time, depends on the results of these trials, upon what literally happens to it in the open field of collisions and reorientations that is the poem as a whole. Ashbery's art is thus materialistic in the most fundamental sense: what a poem is made of is what a poem means. Williams calls for such a ma-terialism in *Paterson,* "a poetry / of the movements of cost." Some figures go unresolved or disappear entirely, eroded to irrelevance or nothingness by the exigencies of their "fate"; others survive, not necessarily intact or unchas-tened, but competent to change and still illuminating, "exemplary, like a star" in that a star, even as it dies, offers light and direction and the indeterminate thrill of its unique, remote possibilities. Every poem eventually abandons its figures, either by ending or by taking up new figures in medias res. Value arises from duration or intensity, as it does with stars, and so value evidences itself as a function of materiality, a quality of cost.

    For example, "Syringa" (HD 69–71) sends an Orpheus entirely its own into "the nature of things to be seen only once, / As they happen along, bump-ing into other things." This Orpheus proves most adaptable, shifting and changing his songs to extol and then to exhaust many measures of art, nature, love, and time. And in the end, he is not torn apart; rather, he is simply used

up, burned out like a star, and the poem continues to its finish without its
Orpheus and yet with something of the beauty of his example, his fatal trajectory. Orpheus "is no longer / Material for a poem," and so the poem finds
other material. The reckless economy of poetry teaches that "stellification / Is
for the few," that out of many figures, only a handful resonate with enough
life in enough time to set us the kind of example, that is, an exemplary self, in
search of which we originally resort to the writing and reading of poems. In
order to find these, the imagination tries and squanders a great deal, living
carelessly off its only capital: the real and real time. The compact measures of
bad poetry are niggardly; they refuse to waste words and try to pass off such
parsimony as virtue. Ashbery has taught me that I *must* waste words, lots of
them, trying them against and upon one another, allowing them and their syntaxes to fall apart sometimes in order to find, not the true ones, but the ones
that seem true at the time, the ones whose example I am willing to follow to
their ultimately silent ends. The wasting and the falling apart are the circumstances, the medium of poetry. Goethe's Faust enters history at the moment he
defines *logos* as action. To offer merely the frugal artifact despairs of beauty in
advance.

> You can't say it that way any more.
>   ("And *Ut Pictura Poesis* Is Her Name," HD 45)

Despair acquiesces to repetition and submits the imagination to unacceptable
archetypes. The poetics of despair practices a museum-shop mimesis, producing reproductions of what is no longer reproductive. The vernal influence
of John Ashbery does not traffic in despair, and in the piece closest to an *ars
poetica* of any he has made, the freedoms of the stubbornly careless voice break
the mimetic open at both ends, celebrating the liberty of subject in one direction and object in another. The imagination is no mirror, and the world is no
image. In every passage of "And *Ut Pictura Poesis* Is Her Name," words resonate and combine in more ways than any merely harmonious syntax could
contain. As John Cage has suggested, in the new music every instrument is a
percussion instrument. Thus

>   She approached me
> About buying her desk. Suddenly the street was
> Bananas and the clangor of Japanese instruments.
>   (HD 45)

In the logic of percussion, one sound follows another, and that is all. The effect
created depends entirely upon the intensity and materiality of a collision; the
context is an event of impact, not a prescribed tonality. Mimesis assumes that
understanding is the true end of imagination, that reality can be captured.
Ashbery continually gives evidence to the reverse: imagination is the *literal end*

of understanding ("so that understanding / May begin and in doing so be un-done" [HD 46]), and in poetry, reality escapes capture, accompanied and abet-ted by the percussion of language and thought. The profligate waste of words in an open field of collisions ("an almost empty mind / Colliding with the lush, Rousseau-like foliage" [HD 45–46]) increases the real by unframing it, in-creases the personae of syntax by unsubordinating them to copywork.

But it's all there in that very first line: "You can't say it that way anymore." Whoever you are, whatever it was you wanted to say in whatever way you had wanted to say it, will no longer suffice. Between the intention and the act falls, not a shadow, but the entire world, and it isn't just falling but moving around like crazy. Intentionality (mimesis & co.) is a hollow man's self-mocking iso-lation. The reckless abandonment of intention's mimetic typography closes the gap between the poem and the world, between the desire to make and the de-sire to be remade. Ashbery replaces mimesis with amazement without recourse to Dadaist excess, but via a constant preparedness to be unprepared by the next word, the next phrase, the next situation, however homely or extrava-gant. The courage to write the next word, even and especially when it contra-dicts all the words preceding it, opens a poem to the beautiful by freeing it from the picturesque. "You can't say it that way anymore" resonates for me much as Rilke's "You must change your life" must have resonated for poets earlier in this century. Change is terrible only when it has been prescribed or when its outcome is foreknown. When reckless, when arbitrary, change liber-ates possibility from precedent, and that is the highest purpose of action that I know. I learn from Ashbery that the technique of poetry is an unstyling, the conquest of fidelity by desire.

> What need for purists when the demotic is built to last,
> To outlast us, and no dialect hears us?
>   ("Purists Will Object," W 17)

Poetry works on principles of dispossession, resisting pressures to convert de-sire into acquisitiveness. Ashbery's profoundest influence makes itself felt in the ways in which he discovers motives and momentums of desire in language it-self, the inclination of words and phrases themselves to forsake what is merely available in favor of what might be made available by new expressions, the un-determined sponsors of new selves and new ways of perceiving. If, as Rimbaud avows, life is elsewhere, then desire is our only birth and new expression our only vitality. Ashbery is no enfant terrible; his restless originality feels to me more like tenderness than like the shock of the new, a tenderness inclined to the nurturing of time's timeliness and to an attentive love of the ephemeral, which is, after all, everything. All purists are reductive, enslaved by their ex-clusive versions of a golden age. Theirs is the poetry of reenactment, curiously imperious and irrelevant at one and the same time. But the demotic, the popular songs and show tunes whose ephemera Ashbery's voices remember to love, expresses the unchaste, entirely innocent activity of time whose compounding of more accidents, intentions, and events than any one self or design could possibly comprehend is the supremest fiction, unimperious and not at all fictitious. The demotic is "built to last" because it is never finished, cannot even conceive of finishing. Acknowledging no distinction between being and making, its expressions assume the momentary to be larger than eternity, its reaches wider, its improvisations more compelling than the claustral gestures of any heaven. The momentary demotics "outlast us," and to keep pace with them, poets must dispossess themselves continuously of selves and symbols or else risk the aphasia of pure design.

I've said that influence is disturbance. Writing this sequence of little meditations, I've remembered that disturbance is excitement and that Ashbery excites me most with his insistence that the language is always somewhere ahead of me, that "no dialect hears" me because the endless improvisation of any dialect's existence has no time to reflect upon my reflective self. The word I am looking for, which is of course always the next word, is nowhere to be found. It is, instead, waiting to happen and then happening now.

7 | Nimbus of Sensations

Eros and Reverie in the Poetry of
John Ashbery and Ann Lauterbach

James McCorkle

JOHN ASHBERY IS our great poet of the present and the momentary. The lines
of his poems map thought in a simulacrum of thought's unfolding within a
social context. His poetry, however, is also the work of memory and the labor
and play of recollection. Ann Lauterbach's work similarly is concerned with
the demands made upon memory and its defining narratives. Both poets have
been closely involved with the visual arts, which come to serve as an implicit
metaphor for their poetics of presence and memory, eros and reverie. In Ashbery's poetry, presence and memory depend on each other; no assemblage of
the present, of the very momentum of thought and perception within language, can be void of memory or the force of remembering. Within this doubled condition, excess would seem unavoidable and reveals a plenitude of both
present and past. This excess is not directly a result or symptom of social and
cultural forces, such as consumerism or the concurrent economics of inflation,
recession, underemployment, and overproduction; instead, this excess is a critique of such conditions and a revelation of possibility. In that such excess also
revisions eros, there is a libidinal decentering. For Ashbery, this sense of eros
provides a social context that is in juxtaposition to Lauterbach's much more
phenomenological conditioning of eros. While both poets share similar rhetorical structures and sensibilities aligned with the visual arts, their work di-
verges from each other in their approaches toward the social and the phenomenological.

The intimacy of memory and presence would imply an enforcement of the
self and would reject any form of libidinal decentering—that is, a privileging
of the phenomenological rather than the social. The tradition of the lyric,
which demands an autonomous *voice,* would seem to ensconce the self further
and thus exclude Ashbery's work as lyric, although his thematic concerns are
thoroughly those defining the lyric.[1] Instead, Ashbery's work significantly revisions the lyrical ideals of the self and the voice. His poems reinscribe the property
of melopoeia, that the poem be sung, as central to lyric form. Melopoeia implies an interchange between the space of the poem, the poet/singer, and the
audience. In this configuration, Ashbery's lyric moves toward the social voicing

rather than the hermetic voice usually ascribed to lyric poetry. The textures of sound are the domain of this melopoeia.

Improvisation, interruption, impurities, and the excess of passion—hence the marvelousness of the title *Flow Chart*—are determining features of Ashbery's lyricism. In contrast to contemporary neo-romantic poetry, the epiphanic is folded into the larger movements of sounds and is not the condition to which his poems move. The desire for an epiphanic closure reduces the possibility of impurities, of other sounds or voices, entering into the lyric. The epiphanic as lyric precludes eros, yet eros as lyric always enfolds the possibility of the epiphanic. Thus, Ashbery commences a reconsideration of the relation between eros and the lyric.

The poems of Ashbery and Lauterbach, the texts themselves, have assumed *voice(s)* that suggest both a diaspora and a reconvening of voices. Voice—in speech and writing—is the trace of the fleeting and conditional presence of the self. The equation of voice with authorial control and expression, perhaps the defining condition of the lyric from Sappho to Wordsworth, Yeats, and Rich, for instance, is reformulated with such poets as Stein, Moore, Bishop, Ashbery, and Lauterbach. That these poets have relinquished the privileged position of the narrative "I" has not coincided with a disavowal of identity or responsibility but ironically with a fuller consideration of the self and the voice. A revelatory displacement of the self or voice into the world of phenomena occurs, and such recuperative displacement undercuts our notion of a relentless, heroic "I." Not surprisingly, Stein, Moore, Bishop, Ashbery, and Lauterbach are poets who reside within the world of objects as thoroughly as the collagist Joseph Cornell and who turn writing into explicit objects of collage.

Ashbery's comments on Cornell's collages, from Cornell's 1967 retrospective and contained in Ashbery's *Reported Sightings,* serve as metonymic *ars poeticae:* Cornell "establishes a delicately adjusted dialogue between the narrative and the visual qualities of the work in which neither is allowed to dominate. The result is a completely new kind of realism. . . . Each of his works is an autonomous visual experience, with its own natural laws and its climate: the thing in its thingness; revealed, not commented on; and with its ambience intact" (RS 16). Cornell's collages and box-constructions compel both nostalgia and immediacy, created by the fusion, as Ashbery states, of "the object and its nimbus of sensations, wrapped in one package, thrust at the viewer, here, now, inescapable" (RS 17). Objects containing all varieties of history are assembled in Cornell's work; their particular assemblage and relationships to each other create sets of narratives that are ambiguous yet offer an intimation of recognition. Cornell creates scales of grandeur and intimacy, narratives of the cosmos and of lost childhoods, and dioramas of the intimately sublime. In each of his constructions eros and reverie are present.

As Ashbery notes, "Cornell's art assumes a romantic universe in which inexplicable events can and must occur," a condition which in turn leads to the sensation of the "inevitable," something "marvelous or terrible" (RS 17–18). Ashbery's own work could be described as combining these same elements that he has observed in Cornell's collages. In the poem "Clouds," from *The Double Dream of Spring*, Ashbery suggests the inevitable and fatal:

> He shoots forward like a malignant star.
> The edges of the journey are ragged.
> Only the face of night begins to grow distinct
> As the fainter stars call to each other and are lost.
>
> Day re-creates his image like a snapshot:
> The family and the guests are there,
> The talking over there, only now it will never end.
> And so cities are arranged, and oceans traversed,
>
> And farms tilled with especial care.
> This year again the corn has grown ripe and tall.
> It is a perfect rebuttal of the argument. And Semele
> Moves away, puzzled at the brown light above the fields.
>   (DDS 68–69)

These concluding stanzas draw forth memory and meaning, reifying the drama of Semele through the issuance of her name. Ending and naming, and implicitly death for Semele's sexual consummation with Zeus destroys her (yet also creates Dionysus), define the inevitable and the unstated as well as what was preliminary and possible: "Thus the thing grew heavy with the mere curve of being, / As a fruit ripens through the long summer before falling" (DDS 67). The condition of Semele is emblematic of our condition:

> How do we explain the harm, feeling
> We are always the effortless discoverers of our career,
> With each day digging the grave of tomorrow and at the same time
> Preparing its own redemption, constantly living and dying?
>   (DDS 68)

Though it is one of Ashbery's more traditionally lyrical poems, "Clouds" is both a gathering and a recollecting. A meditation on inevitability, death, and the metaphysical connection between death and sexuality, the poem provides a "nimbus of sensations."

Cornell's work serves as a metaphor for Ashbery's poetry, for it provides a useful model of recollection in regard to Ashbery's poetry. Cornell's constructions are memory theaters, much as Ashbery's poems "Self-Portrait in a Convex Mirror" or *Flow Chart* are fluid mnemonic structures that move from the personal to include the polyphonic social. Moreover, memory is given tangibility, although its referred-to presence is irrecoverable. Memory becomes a phenomenon, objectified in ways parallel to the sense of the realness of dreams: in both memory and dreams, objects are charged with meaning and portent. Consider Ashbery's "Pantoum," from *Some Trees,* where the structure necessitates rearrangement and repetition enforces the possibility or portent of meaning:

> Why, the court, trapped in a silver storm, is dying!
> Some blunt pretense to safety we have
> And that soon gotten over
> For they must have motion.
>
> Some blunt pretense to safety we have:
> Eyes shining without mystery
> For they must have motion
> Through the vague snow of many clay pipes.
>   (SoTr 43)

These concluding stanzas have been shaped by the pantoum's formal demands, but they also operate as vitrines, or viewing chambers, of elements the poet has rearranged, allowing narratives to emerge and recede through the rhythms of juxtaposition. The pantoum offers a version of the dream process, where images and narratives are arbitrary but also metonyms for withheld memories. Cornell's implicit series, such as the window facades, the sandboxes, or the recurrent reproduction of the Medici prince, also reflect the pantoum's procedure of repetition and generation.

The poem "Pantoum" attempts, as Ashbery says of Cornell's collages, "to keep all the stories that art seems to want to cut us off from, without giving up the inspiring asceticism of abstraction" (RS 17). In locating a kinship between Jackson Pollack and Cornell, Ashbery sees in their work "the understanding of a work of art as a phenomenon, a presence, of whatever sort" (RS 17). "Pantoum," of course, is a highly abstract poem, for it has formalized language and distilled it toward the absoluteness of being solely composed of signifiers. Yet in so doing, the poem has allowed the potential for meaning to become almost excessive. That Cornell's art offers the "idea that anything can happen" (RS 18) again parallels Ashbery's own work. The poem is seen then as a phenomenon or a thing, yet it is porous and we must react to it, for our narratives and its stories coincide.

The opening section of the title poem of Ashbery's collection *Houseboat Days* further demonstrates that any self-fulfillment of the poem will be banal—indeed the poem's pleasure is its deferral or dispersal of satisfaction. Indeed all reading would seem to enact this narcissistic condition of pleasure deferred. The rejection or dismemberment of the self in Ashbery's poetry is only a corollary to the complex negotiation between the plural and singular, between the surface and depth of images and the self, and between representation and voice.[2] This porousness or the deferring of completion constitutes the possibility and presence of pleasure:

> "The skin is broken. The hotel breakfast china
> Poking ahead to the last week in August, not really
> Very much at all, found the land where you began . . . "
> The hills smouldered up blue that day, again
> You walk five feet along the shore, and you duck
> As a common heresy sweeps over. We can botanize
> About this for centuries, and the little dazey
> Blooms again in the cities. The mind
> Is so hospitable, taking in everything
> Like boarders, and you don't see until
> It's all over how little there was to learn
> Once the stench of knowledge has dissipated, and the trouvailles
> Of every one of the senses fallen back.
>   (HD 38)

Puns, shifts of tonalities and pronominal identification, hyperbole, and metaphor present in this passage are arguably the most typical and the most influential aspects of Ashbery's work. The opening lines of "Houseboat Days" establishes a wounded, fragmented narrative. Is the wound—the broken skin or the ruptured surface of text and experience—that of the figure of the "you," who may serve as poet, beloved, poem, and reader? The isolation of the figure is quickly mediated by the mock-critical phrase "We can botanize / About this for centuries." The passage also demonstrates a linguistic anamorphosis—that is, a distortion of an image, as in "you duck / As a common heresy sweeps over." Such distortions and substitutions are typical of dreamwork as well as our distracted daily life. Ashbery reiterates his sense of expansiveness throughout the passage: the mind is likened to a hospitable boardinghouse letting in strangers; this image of the house, recalling Gaston Bachelard's poetics of space, returns at the end of the passage to restate that life is both beautiful and various. To argue such a position, however, Ashbery must resort to anamorphosis, otherwise such a statement or sensibility as "Life is beautiful" remains sentimental. Irony and distortion allow such a statement to return to our conversations as a provisional truth.

The porousness of the poem shifts the condition of poetry away from being a container of meaning to suggesting a transmission, flux, or exchanging of meanings. Such a porousness informs social and ethical processes, in that each reader must assume a heightened responsibility for these transmissions the poet initiates. In *Signeponge/Signsponge,* Derrida writes,

> The antidote for an unsaturable subjectivity: spongistic and pharmacopoetic.

It has to do with an overflowing of the signature.

Overflowing with activity, but with an altogether receptive, open, welcoming activity, ready, in its guile, to receive all impressions, the sponge.

Overflowing with activity, between no one, the sponge. Overflowing with activity between the person, the proper name, the name of the thing, a proper name of a thing or a common name of a person, the sponge.

It is an indefatigable mediator, shuttling between the parties of an impossible contract. The parties are impossible to live with, inaccessible, and do not wish, at least as parties, to enter into the contract.

Let the other sign first.

The sponge will then have spent itself, multiplied itself, itself overflowed.[3]

Derrida develops, through his reflections on the prose poetry of Francis Ponge, an anagrammatic and polyphonic poetics. The word, the name, and the poem fills, overflows, and drains in preparation to fill again, thus undermining any notion of a stable, bounded, or lawful language. Poetic language, for both Derrida and Ashbery, would arguably be able to saturate space. Here space is both literal (in which the printed typeface saturates the blank space of the page) and metaphoric (the duration of reading and the immersion of ourselves into the process of reading, whether we are resistant or engaged). To drench or saturate inscribes excess or the possibility of overflowing and invokes a libidinal energy no longer centered upon the self. This saturation and porousness begin a reconsideration of the lyric. The very name or authorship of the poem is set adrift, the possibility of a voice, singular and immutable, is lost. Ashbery's poetry, however, engages multiple readings; thus the dialogues within the poems and between the poems and its readers are constantly attempting to include others.

Saturation, however, also implies the possibility of attaining a full apprehension of the work. Ashbery's poetry overflows, yet in this continuity language is always coming; there is no sense, however, that one will come to a full meaning. Meaning, narrative, and voice are placed in a mise-en-scène. This is not, however, a nihilistic collapse into indeterminacy and finally nonsaturation. The mise-en-scène corresponds to Ashbery's statement that his poetry is about "the experience of experience . . . and the particular experience is of lesser interest to me than the way it filters through to me. I believe this is the way in which it happens with most people, and I'm trying to record a kind of generalized transcript of what's really going on in our minds all day long."[4] As S. P. Mohanty and Jonathan Monroe have argued, Ashbery's work has not emphasized an isolated self, but "a counter-emphasis on the self as an ineluctably social construction."[5] Ashbery's poetry is not a passive register of the world but a recognition of the social "as an internal force that manifests itself above all through the multiple presence of conflicting discourses."[6] These conflicting discourses—ranging from clichés, popular romances, and literary allusions—not only allow for a change of self, but also invoke what Marjorie Perloff calls, borrowing from Roland Barthes, a "corrected banality."[7] By including the commonplace(s), Ashbery's work invokes a social community capable of continual revision and incorporation.

Ashbery's *Flow Chart* exemplifies the porousness of the contemporary poetry—indeed, the very title suggests the processes of saturation and fluidity. Certainly the heterogenous and decentered languages of this long poem are a direct extension of his experiments in *Three Poems*. M. M. Bakhtin's concept of heteroglossia is particularly appropriate, for it extends Derrida's formal sensibility and the implicit sexuality of language into the diverse social contexts and intentions of language.[8] In discussing *Three Poems*, Ashbery stated, "This continuing urge of mine to put things back together resulted in my supposing there was a book where every page, or almost every page, would be totally covered with words and a very long poem completely filling up these pages that give me the same pleasure that the one-word exercise did way back then."[9] In *Three Poems*, Ashbery writes over the page, saturating the blankness with printed words, which is in fact a production of pleasure. In *Three Poems*, Ashbery explicitly refuses, as Margueritte Murphy writes, "the position of the monologic poet whose lyric 'I' controls and anchors the discourse," and indeed to "escape the isolation of the lyric voice in the text."[10] Meaning becomes ephemeral, and what we finally listen for are the voices of the poem.

Ashbery, as the "recording angel" (TP 104) of *Three Poems*, decenters the identities of pronouns not only to put into question the lyric "I" but to create or renew eros. That angel, Ashbery writes, "who was supposed only to copy it all down has joined forces with the misshapen, misfit pieces that were never meant to go into it but at best to stay on the sidelines so as to point up how everything else belonged together." Murphy, in examining this moment of self-reflection, argues that Ashbery attempts to reveal the disadvantages of dialogic discourse but discovers its inevitability.[11] An examination of this revealing moment cannot end here, however, for Ashbery has substituted the polyphonic field for the centering gaze, the collage for the rigid lines of perspective, and sound for sight. Instead of the isolate lyric voice, it is multiple or social voicing that informs the poetry. This is in turn an implicit critique of heterosexuality's cultural exclusivity and centrality. What were located on the sidelines and gave definition to "everything else" or the subject of writing have now come off the sidelines and onto the field. The responsibility of the lyric poet would be, in Ashbery's poetics, to decenter the writing of eros.

The decentering of eros constitutes a profound re-visioning of the social community, one informed by a vision of gaiety or gayness. By disrupting the panoptical narrative "I," Ashbery's poetry disputes the codes of normalcy that restrict some to the sidelines. Under such a normalizing gaze, *otherness* appears "misshapen, misfit." That homosexuality remains outside discourses informing the social community, homosexuality then offers, in Jean-François Lyotard's words, "the unpresentable in presentation itself" or "that which denies itself the solace of good forms." [12] That Ashbery's poems put into question lyricism's subjectivity and its definition of a genre parallels the disruptive quality homosexuality has within the ideological demands of our culture. The correspondences between the disjunctive, polyphonic lyric and homosexuality are best described by Roland Barthes's definition of the text of bliss: "The text that imposes a state of loss, the text that discomforts (perhaps to the point of boredom), unsettles the reader's historical, cultural, psychological assumptions, the consistency of his tastes, values, memories, brings to a crisis his relation to language." [13]

While not creating a homosexual writing—analogous to *l'écriture féminine*—Ashbery's disjunctive poetics offers a parallel and responsive critique of aesthetics and sexuality. Barthes's language of crisis echoes Ashbery's own moments of foreboding, extremity, and even apocalypse. As a counterbalancing vision, Ashbery offers that of a decentered eros, one which is always reinscribing other voices. This recuperative process—that of saturation and excess—seeks to redefine the lyric as well as implicitly redefine the community or those who participate in the generation and transaction of language.

In both *Flow Chart* and *Three Poems,* Ashbery reconfigures the lyric. The doubled voice of traditional lyric poetry—the voice coupled with music, forming a doubled voice, exemplified by "Litany" in *As We Know*—is extended far past the genre's traditional boundaries. The double sestina embedded in *Flow Chart* illustrates the saturated movement of *Flow Chart:*

> We're interested in the language, that you call breath,
> if breath is what we are to become, and we think it is, the southpaw said. Throwing her
> a bone sometimes, sometimes expressing, sometimes expressing something like mild concern, the way
> has been so hollowed out by travelers it has become cavernous. It leads to death.
> We know that, yet for a limited time only we wish to pluck the sunflower,
> transport it from where it stood, proud, erect, under a bungalow-blue sky, grasping at the sun,
> and bring it inside, as all others sink into the common mold. The day
> had begun inauspiciously, yet improved as it went along, until at bed-
> time it was seen that we had prospered, I and thee.
> Our early frustrated attempts at communicating were in any event long since dead.

Yet I had prayed for some civility from the air before setting out, as indeed my
    ancestors had done
and it hadn't hurt them any. And I purposely refrained from consulting *me,*

the *culte du moi* being a dead thing, a shambles. That's what led to me.
Early in the morning, rushing to see what has changed during the night,
    one stops to catch one's breath.
The older the presence, we now see, the more it has turned into thee
    with a candle at thy side.
    (FC 186–87)

In these opening lines of the double sestina, there is a modulation of the
voice between the formal and the conversational. There are no boundaries setting off the double sestina from the rest of *Flow Chart*. The poem accommo-
dates a variety of interruptions and shifts and records them as part of an un-
recoverable whole movement. The "language of breath" is speech as well as
that of inspiration and life. "Breath" serves as a repeated, anchoring word in
the material text and as a limit the lines stretch toward in the spoken text.
These long lines that typify *Flow Chart* further undercut the controlled and
taut lines associated with lyric poetry. The "language of breath," nonetheless,
couples speech, or breath, with lyricism, or the voicing of selfhood. This "language of breath"—perhaps also an ironic reformulation of Allen Ginsberg's
poetics of breath—suggests an amplitude of voicing, which seeks to reestablish
a community that shares various experiences of daily life.

    As Joseph Conte argues in regard to Ashbery's poetry, the repetition and
variation involved in what Conte terms procedural forms, such as the canzone,
pantoum, and sestina, displace both symbolic content and a metaphoric mode
of language.[14] Ashbery's use of these forms is not to restore them or to continue
to evolve their traditional thematics but, as Conte argues, to evade semantic
closure while the form itself reaches closure. Citing an earlier sestina, "Farm
Implements and Rutabagas in a Landscape" (DDS 47–48), Conte states, "The
poet escapes from 'his own astonished becoming' because the sestina is semantically open—no end-word has a single determinate meaning; as addresser or
encoder, he remains unknown, indeterminate."[15] The long lines of the double
sestina in *Flow Chart* seem not to cull out the world's conversations or critique
language other than how it may correspond to the self: hence, the self-reflexive
rejection of "the *culte du moi.*"

    As much as any of Ashbery's poems, *Flow Chart* maps the condition of
poiēsis or making:

                              It seems I was reading something;
I have forgotten the sense of it or what the small
role of the central poem made me want to feel. No matter.
The words, distant now, and mitred, glint. Yet not one
ever escapes the forest of agony and pleasure that keeps them

in a solution that has become permanent through inertia. The force
of meaning never extrudes. And the insects,
of course, don't mind.
    (FC 3–4)

In this passage, the confession that the reader no longer remembers the poem's emotional intention is countered by the recognition of the physicality or thingness of the poem's words—though distant, they "glint." And we have that curious word "extrudes," with its industrial yet also fleetingly biological sound. The force of meaning can neither be thrust or pressed, nor can it be shaped or molded. Not a forest of symbols, but one of "agony and pleasure" that is inevitable and inescapable. The passage's self-revelatory position is undercut by the comment that "insects, / of course, don't mind."

Some thirty-five years separate the publication of "Pantoum" and *Flow Chart,* yet both poems insist on the poem as a presence or phenomenon while also seeking to position the poem within the domain of the social with the implicit ethical demands of the social. In their stark differences—of length, of formal demands—both poems nonetheless demonstrate language's condition of excess. Language cannot be completely controlled, despite authorial intention. Ashbery has long recognized this condition and finds in it, not despair, but the possibilities of creation. Not to control or manage the movement of a poem's meaning implies a recasting of eros: Ashbery's poems ask for a different relationship with its readers, one that does not depend on extruding meaning and form. The complex of revelation, secrecy, intimacy, and desire describe the condition of eros. This complex describes the fluidity of language during *conversation,* a word whose etymology denotes intimacy:

The wheat was the color of old men, the robin . . . Well these are what I had got
to offer you; I suppose it doesn't make any difference now because you have
        something new
that was not in the catalog I have. Something sweet, turning over, something
        unbuttoned.
But now there is no dose you can tolerate, no
sitting in the sun like a chunk of wood or a large broken fungus; it scarcely
matters which. See, I'm like you, a believer. At the same time I want to believe in
        things
that are endless, even though we don't get to see them every day, that are
what color is to a colorless surface, which I believe I have inhabited
        once, or once upon a time.
        (FC 154–55)

This passage reveals the ability that Ashbery has to move to a condition of intimacy that reenforces the understanding or recognition of daily life as well as the fragility of existence. The awareness of mortality, indeed the proximity of death, surfaces throughout the poem as well as in this passage with the lines, "But now there is no dose you can tolerate, no / sitting in the sun like a chunk of wood or a large broken fungus." The "you" may refer to Ashbery's mother, who had died not long before the writing of *Flow Chart;*[16] to an AIDS patient; or to himself in an earlier portrait, "The Picture of Little J. A. in a Prospect of Flowers":

> Yet I cannot escape the picture
> Of my small self in that bank of flowers:
> My head among the blazing phlox
> Seemed a pale and gigantic fungus.
>   (SoTr 40)

The ambiguity of the "you" persists in the passage from *Flow Chart,* but what it offers is not a strict dispersal or indeterminacy of identities but an inclusiveness or community that faces suffering and a crisis of hope: "I want to believe in things / that are endless, even though we don't get to see them every day." The meditation on death, a significant undercurrent throughout Ashbery's work, reflects an abiding concern for the subject that conventional narratives are unable to invoke without trivializing the subject. The subject becomes text, history, voice, and person. It is this multiplicity of subject that is affirmed, rather than a depiction of a constantly slipping series of signifiers plunging into meaninglessness. The lyric, in Ashbery's poetics, becomes choral, in that a range of voices give voice(s) to the survival of the community.[17]

No longer the domain of the self-sufficient self, the lyric reveals the self's reliance upon others in Ashbery's poems. There would be no poem, no phenomena, no presence without the heteroglossiaic interaction of voices. The lyric then is redirected from the personal to a more public space. There is less interiorization; rather, the poems depend upon the rapid flow from voice to voice: each voice marks a threshold, "the beginning, where / We must stay, in motion" (HD 39). The lyric's implicit concern, eros, is then revisioned through the decentering of the voice. In this process, Ashbery de-emphasizes the status of subject and theme—indeed, thematic concerns are implicit and self-evident, to privilege them suddenly opens them to parody, as in these opening lines from poems in *The Double Dream of Spring:* "We hold these truths to be self-evident" (DDS 31) or "The rise of capitalism parallels the advance of romanticism / And the individual is dominant until the close of the nineteenth century" (DDS 53). Nonetheless, the conversations that do go on in Ashbery's poems are about *something,* though the subject is often withdrawn, questioned, or interrupted. In that way, the subject is inseparable from the conversing.

Eros and its function of making, however, do not necessitate the presence of a subject. Ashbery's poetry, especially his longer works, depends upon our inclusion and our willingness to enter this space of the poem—or conversely, allow the poem's space to spread around us, like a painting or a convex mirror, opening various horizons of understanding that overflow the frame. In writing about the painter Fairfield Porter in 1982, in an essay also contained in *Reported Sightings,* Ashbery places Porter among such writers as Wallace Stevens and Marianne Moore, in that "they are intellectual in the classic American tradition . . . because they have no ideas in them, that is no ideas that can be separated from the rest. They *are* idea, or consciousness, or light, or whatever. Ideas surround them, but do not and cannot extrude themselves into the being of the art" (RS 314). Ideas are part of the fabric of the conversation; to "extrude" them is to distort either the idea itself or the phenomena or condition bringing forth ideas—life. Ashbery continues, stating that "beyond the narrow confines of the 'subject' (only one of a number of equally important elements in the work of art, as Porter points out) the secret business of art gets done according to mysterious rules of its own. In this larger context ideology simply doesn't function as it is supposed to, when it isn't directly threatening the work of art by trivializing it, and trivializing as well the importance of the ideas it seeks to dramatize" (RS 315).

Ashbery's work, in many ways, parallels Porter's paintings in that they are habitations that are both familiar but also filled with the sense of the inevitable. Porter's works, in a sense, test the excess of familiarity, yet within them there is always the secreted and the sensation the painting is in the process of revelation. In *Interior with a Dress Pattern* (1969), reproduced for *Reported Sightings,* a child enters from the kitchen bearing what? The child whose back is turned and who faces a fireplace and a frieze contemplates what? On the table the abstracted mosaic dress pattern (whose project is this?) lies next to an open dictionary, but opened to what and by whom? The painting offers a field of conversations and possible narratives as well as suggesting an accumulation of compositions, from Vermeer and Vuillard interiors to the rectilinear abstractions of Matisse. These are not strict allusions but suggestions of what we bring from our horizons to enter the painting. The painting is filled with the processes of making—the dress pattern, the open dictionary, the fire, the child crossing the doorway's threshold.

Considering Cornell's constructions again, they too are habitations, mysterious, anonymous, but clearly created and open, meant to be viewed. Works such as the untitled 1936 construction (Soap Bubble Set), *Cassiopeia #1,* the untitled 1945 construction (Hotel Eden), or the untitled 1948 construction (La Favorite) provide fragments of texts—maps, illustrations, musical scores— that extend the possibilities of a recalled geography. Cornell, the great archivist with his dossiers and folios, begins with the bare object or the real and adds to it mystery and complexity, the world's accretions that lead toward some relation with the inevitable, the unspeakable, that which can never be acceptable. Cornell offers us mysterious plenitude and the illusion of an orderly cosmos, as

Ashbery suggests in the closing lines of "The Skaters," from *Rivers and Mountains*:

> Your knotted hair
> Around your shoulders
> A shawl the color of the spectrum
>
> Like that marvelous thing you haven't learned yet.
>
> To refuse the square hive,
>   postpone the highest . . .
>
> The apples are all getting tinted
> In the cool light of autumn.
>
> The constellations are rising
> In perfect order: Taurus, Leo, Gemini.
>   (RM 63)

John Peto's paintings offer a counterbalancing metaphor to Cornell's work—at least what might be initially perceived as mysteriously celebratory in Cornell's constructions. Ashbery's review of an exhibition of Peto's work at the National Gallery in 1983 provides a mirror to many of Ashbery's concerns: "The ambiguity of the humdrum artifacts he deploys can be agonizing: is there hope for us in their survival or is all his work an extended *vanitas?* Wilmerding [the exhibition's curator] has given his show the title 'Important Information Inside,' from a message on an envelope that appears in several of the rack pictures. And important the information is, though buried so deep inside that one glimpses it only intermittently. But those glimpses are thrilling" (RS 80). Peto's later works—his most important—are extremely realistic depictions of doors and racks with messages, envelopes, tickets, news-clippings attached. These records of daily life, the anonymous transits and transactions of someone, suggest a life that has been cataclysmically interrupted, yet we have only traces, only the detritus of loss.

Cataclysm always threatens eros: at any moment the poem will be interrupted, a final message will be received and conclude the narrative of creating. To assure the persistence of eros would seem the primordial condition and responsibility of a poet. In her essay "On Memory," Ann Lauterbach writes, "it is not possible to write into the unknown, the future, without the known, the past. The past is always there, the setting, the stance: it constitutes us, and we are its constituents."[18] Lauterbach, like Ashbery, suggests a shared past that is an accumulation or recollection of the everyday. The reciprocality between the past and ourselves—as each constitutes the other—establishes an ethical claim, for the past allows for both the positing of our identities and how we may critique our subjectivity.

Following these comments, Lauterbach quotes the closing two stanzas of Ashbery's "Blessing in Disguise," from *Rivers and Mountains:*

Remembering to forgive. Remember to pass beyond you into the day
On the wings of the secret you will never know.
Taking me from myself, in the path
Which the pastel girth of the day has assigned to me.

I prefer "you" in the plural, I want "you,"
You must come to me, all golden and pale
Like the dew and the air.
And then I start getting this feeling of exaltation.
      (RM 26)

Lauterbach's work consistently invokes the tonal range of this passage, where the elegiac, desire, and reverie overlap. That Lauterbach selects one of Ashbery's most conventional lyrics reveals the distinction between her poetics and those of Ashbery. Generally, Lauterbach's work corresponds—or responds—to Ashbery's lyric moments rather than his larger discursive but disjunctive polyphonies. Implicitly, Lauterbach reveals this tension in Ashbery's work and, by extension, re-visions the embedded and perhaps more conventional moments of lyricism in Ashbery's poetry.

Rather than casting this relationship between Ashbery and Lauterbach within the dynamics of Harold Bloom's formulations of influence, Ashbery and Lauterbach share in a concern for the condition of the lyric moment. Within these considerations, however, Ashbery has come to represent a particular poetics that favors a disjunctive sensibility that allows for wit while also signaling warnings to our culture. Thus, Ashbery is part of our horizon of understanding, and any poetry now being written will implicitly respond to the poetics his poetry represents. While there are other poetic sensibilities equally concerned with the lyric, Ashbery's poetry is particularly important in that it reintegrates our mnemonic processes, eros, and the everyday. In contrast, Lauterbach's poetry, on the whole, turns away from Ashbery's mapping of social transmissions (and his implicit creation of a dialogic and ethically *listening* community) to develop a phenomenologically enclosed poetics. Lauterbach, particularly in *Before Recollection,* seizes upon the heightened lyrical *voice* and inscribes it as a phenomenon in itself; this distinguishes her work from Ashbery's lyrical *voicings*.

Lauterbach's poetry tenses itself between recollection and presence, as in the opening stanza of "Approaching the Panorama," from *Before Recollection:*

Maples, reticent, in a hush of russet and rose
Attracting their opposites, and the ice coast
Recedes along a curve coded below the surface
And robins are back working the pervious

And the wild cherry grapples:
A blind drawing, animated, nervous.
    (BR 31)

The thaw, the return of spring, and the returning migrations are present in this moment. Yet presence is tenuous, the poem's final line is cast as an apostrophe and as a singular lyric voice: "O flock of wild blue birds descending!" This final cry is a re-visioning of the lyric in that it counters the previous "A false provision inspiring truths / Lyrically applied: O bold storm! O myriad sky!" The lyric recomposes itself authentically not as an act of positivist mimesis but as simultaneously an expression of the dream, the absent, and the real that is outside disclosure.

    "Beauty is a way of meriting surprise," Lauterbach writes in the poem "Still Life with Apricots." While Ashbery seeks a socially defined ethic—the interconnectiveness of eros—Lauterbach seeks an aesthetically conditioned ethics. Beauty, merit, and surprise are the functioning elements of this poetic equation; importantly, beauty does not equal surprise, as in a Dadaist work, but beauty and surprise merit each other or give each other value. Recalling Ashbery's concerns of self-reflection, memory, and the idea of order in "Self-Portrait in a Convex Mirror," Lauterbach observes, "Each topic is a surface / Ingrained and potential," that becomes "a reverie emptied, / A breach drawn easily, singularly" (BR 33). The condition of reverie further develops the process of decentering the lyric voice and the re-visioning of eros. Gaston Bachelard, in his *Poetics of Reverie*, states that "the night dream (*rêve*) does not belong to us. It is not our possession. With regard to us, it is an abductor, the most disconcerting of abductors: it abducts our being from us."[19] Further, he writes, "Great dreamers are masters of the glittering consciousness. A sort of multiple *cogito* renews itself in the closed world of the poem."[20] Reverie describes the condition of the reader and the poet, both of whom, in their different acts, are enfolded in the space of the poem.

    The pleasure of the surface, the erotic surface that drew Narcissus, describes Ashbery's poetry. Reverie, however, is as much a metaphor of experience, the condition of overlapping and in-between spaces. Reverie, in Lauterbach's poetry, develops series of syntactic openings, a poetics of unfolding spaces that lead to "potentially, a revelation" (BR 3). Eros is envisioned as exploratory movements, in language, toward "unknowable places" and "startling new chambers" (BR 3). If a spatial construction of eros for Ashbery's work is the excess of surface, then Lauterbach's spatial metaphors of eros are also movements through chambers. Without recognizing the possibilities of reverie, Lauterbach speculates in "Still" that

    The sleeping urgencies are perhaps ruined now
    In the soul's haphazard sanctuary,
    Ignored like a household

>	Dormant in the landscape, a backwoods dump
>	Where the last care has worn through its last
>	Memory. We might think of this as a blessing
>	As we thrash in the nocturnal waste:
>	Rubble of doors, fat layers of fiber
>	Drooping under eaves, weeds
>	Leaning in lassitude after heavy rain
>	Has surged from a whitened sky.
>	Thunder blooms unevenly in unknowable places
>	Breaking distance into startling new chambers
>	We cannot enter; potentially, a revelation.
>		(BR 3)

Bachelard argues that poetry gives us a document for a "phenomenology of the soul"[21] and provides witness to the soul's discovering the world. The soul might be said to be lyricism's drawing together of conversant voices rather than the singular voice of the self. Directionality and temporality then are diffuse but aroused; reverie composes "startling new chambers" housing "potentially, a revelation."

Nonetheless, Lauterbach is less willing than Ashbery to give up the "I" as a signaling mark of the lyric. Lauterbach locates herself in a drama of reverie, observing the condition of liminality itself. The poems maintain a traditional lyric's sense of the self while also seeing that self dissolve in dream, writing, and the world:

>	The sky was something else, massive
>	But kind, leaving nothing in its wake.
>	Often I have thought the linear
>	Duplicitous, mapping outer and inner,
>	Showing us core and enclosure
>	As it helps itself over destiny's rail.
>		(BR 64)

The title of this poem, "Subject to Change," puns on the slippage of meanings: subjects change, or the very condition the poem expresses is mutable, or we as readers will subject the poem to revisionary readings, or something undisclosed in the poem may change. These final lines of "Subject to Change" describe a condition of almost mythic inevitability and seeming fatalism that echoes the conclusion of Ashbery's "Clouds."

Lauterbach writes in "Of Memory": "Language recasts the past into the future. Syntax is the privileged map of this excursion: a subject finds its object, the past finds its future: they couple in pleasant annihilation. When I write, as I am writing, I lose all sense of clock-time. I feel as if I had entered another layer or strata, and I have the sensation that I am actually stealing time from

itself" (OM 522). By decentering time in the space of writing—or reading—
the self loosens its hold on the world and commences to enter the world. Thus,
Lauterbach's recasting of language limns the movements of desire:

> Over the years I've come to realize
> And then drift back, as if a sweet scent
> Was worth the trip. She'll go anywhere for a kiss
> And so she will. I like the feel of no comparison.
> I like the invisible pressure of some other time on time.
> (BR 45)

These lines to "Some Other Time" follow a set of "garbled messages" that
appear as a hybrid of telegrams and tabloid headlines. The poem begins with
the question "Where was I," which evokes location in terms of locale and emotion as well as a sense of resuming a narrative after an interruption. Set in
autumn, the poem suggests and rejects the sentimentalizing of the season: "after the explosion and fame of leaves / Comes this tawdry mess that augurs a
month of tasks" (BR 44). The concluding lines invoke loss whose memory
ironically is sensuous. The final line translates Wallace Stevens's argument that
the "imagination press[es] back against the pressure of reality";[22] Lauterbach
suggests that reverie, in its full sensuousness, occurs through the pressure of
time against time.

   The sensuousness of reverie is located in sound, which Stevens notes in his
statement "A poet's words are of things that do not exist without the words."[23]
Ashbery and Lauterbach share in this sensibility, yet it is in Lauterbach's poetry
that lyricism becomes most acutely linked with the double actions of naming
and desire:

> And now I wonder if intimacy is tonal,
> Some agreement of parts along the surface
> Weather, refusing to rest, narrates
> With all the clarity words might articulate to us.
> (BR 22)

As the title of this poem, "As Far as the Eye Can See," suggests, the visual
representation is paradoxical: the title proposes simultaneously limitlessness
and restriction. With these closing lines, Lauterbach turns away from strictly
visual representation and toward "the clarity words might articulate to us."
Lauterbach continues this meditation in "Poem for Margrit, for Frida":

> In rare instances, the iconic
> Is translated precisely:
> Vocal, serene, if layered.
> I write this way for mystery and need,
> The images endeavoring to fold

Around a central nerve,
And to salvage what is worn from wear.
   (BR 50)

The iconic—in its fullest sense a devotional image that is a substitution for the divine or revelatory—is Lauterbach's desired expression. The iconic is never solely visual mimesis, for it is motivated and constituted by "mystery and need."

The iconic is a manifesting of reverie. The constructions of Joseph Cornell or the photographs of Jan Groover (with whom Lauterbach has collaborated) exemplify the iconic nature of reverie. Cornell and Groover share in the use of overlapping and juxtaposed images whose interplay creates an intimacy of time and space. Reverie puts into question the notion of the lyric as a single voice, for it is a condition one enters into:

I wear a wardrobe of birds, heirloom wings, talons.
Now the heron tempts me to believe
All things named are immanent. These leaves
Swirl upward from the simple task of water;
The river is fastened by the radiance of a shield.
A margin of dread meets a margin of wonder,

A scaffold of terror and allure.
Layers of rain will age the view.
Some days there are no sails and some sail by
Inhabited, but the column of sky is
Architectural, burdened with its air.
Later, encrusted on either side, towering stars.
   (BR 30)

In manifesting reverie, Lauterbach relies upon accumulation. Whereas Ashbery's accumulative process is procedural, to use Conte's term, and composed of heteroglossiaic movements, Lauterbach's accumulative process is composed of the pressure of juxtaposed objects, each with its own "terror and allure." This poem, charged with allusions to marriage and disenchantment, concludes with scene of metamorphosis: "I wear a wardrobe of birds, heirloom wings, talons." Outside the world of ballroom, garden, and apse, the poem's speaker encounters an Ovidian world of transformation and terrifying radiance: "Now the heron tempts me to believe / All things named are immanent."

In "Mountain Roads," the opening poem of *Clamor,* the narrator describes the mountains in terms of Burkean sublimity: "The great rims, upwardly dark and darkly elongated, / Are boundaries we must, like it not, accept" (C 4). We must face and are drawn to the overwhelming and terrifying. The mountains' rims denote both female and male sexuality, suggesting again an Ovidian moment of transformation. This terrain of desire is the subject of our "chronic scouting / . . . not as mild tourists / . . . but as ourselves" (C 3). There is a shift between these two collections; in *Clamor*, Lauterbach has become far more social; the poems tend to enter into dialogue and conversation, approaching the apparently arbitrary surface play of Ashbery's poetry. In *Before Recollection*, however, self-enclosed and transformational poems created a series of liminal moments that while being plumbed, enfolded recollection into reverie:

Night water is a smudge of timing
Surrounded by small illusions
Lifted into the visible.
What is it to find these valuables
Just as everything is about to sleep?
A remnant blue rips and flies dreamward
Onto satin wrapped around my father
Whose sleeve was last seen bound to a wing.
    (BR 68)

In lifting the unrecollected into the "visible" or "immanent," Lauterbach evokes dreamwork and the work of icons: to make the sacred or mysterious visible. Again, as in Ashbery's work, Joseph Cornell's constructions come to mind when reading Lauterbach's poetry; indeed her work with the photographer Jan Groover indicates a shared fascination with the accumulation of objects set into mnemonic theaters that recall Cornell's work. That there is an undisclosed narrative, a withheld secret, or an idea of order that has become obscured is part of Cornell's and Groover's visual engagement. The visible is mysterious in their work, constructed from everyday objects set into new configurations.

The mysterious made visible also defines Lauterbach's conjoining of reverie and the erotic, as in the closing lines of "Sacred Weather":

I myself long to refrain
But would bleed and bless
Robe opening on slowly mounted stair.
    (BR 72)

The erotic remains central, but remote, as in "Psyche's Dream": "So that within each dream is another, remote / And mocking and a version of his mouth on her mouth" (BR 43). The erotic is displaced and always across some threshold of dream, behind robes, or reached, perhaps, after climbing stairs. As Lauterbach notes in a discussion of "Psyche's Dream," the poem stretches "the syntax to break-point, holding back the linguistically inevitable."[24] The language of the poem thus stretches to syntactic thresholds that are synonymous with desire.

In "Mountain Roads," Lauterbach, however, retreats from the ecstatic.

Such a retreat implicitly rejects her previous manipulation of the subject and the subjugation of the reader to the ecstatic demands of the poem:

> From the edge of the wood, a hermit thrush
> Begins to memorize the tentative
> And to seduce us directly.
> Pretty soon we'll start remembering
> All over again, but there were no weddings.
> There were no weddings that June. Instead,
> Numbers of us left for Maine and Italy.
> Maine was an old standby, a place
> Where you could paint the air.
> Italy? The land there tilts
> So that you are forced to look up
> Searching the skies for something beyond nature
> But still contained by it. It was, as I recall,
> A summer decisive for its impact.
> Everything tasted fresh and nothing much was sacrificed.
>   (C 4)

The twilight appearance of the hermit thrush at the edge of the woods suggests a moment of lyric ecstasy, but it is quickly undercut by the colloquial deadpan, "Pretty soon we'll start remembering." The narrator's voice commences a layered conversation between herself, the reader, and the others included in the poem. The conversation, however, undercuts itself and retreats to a position that recognizes the banal—"we were cosmetic" or "nothing much was sacrificed"—and deflates the ecstatic. Thus Lauterbach may be revealing a criticism of her own previous ecstatic poetry, thereby entering into an intermural ethical debate.

Further examination of Lauterbach's narratives reveals that they consistently construct liminal moments where the construction of conversational or banal language is examined and invoked:

> The same *if* presents itself
> As conclusively abandoned
> Sounds like shores
> But is music after all, temper or bridge
> Talismanic, virtual, or stilled
>   & another thing
> Could come as an explosion out of thin air
> Ripple of screen, conversation at lunch
> Fires running on into the night
> & looked away from as a child might

In the parade's deft narration
Anyone could join the party

Fun is dialectical but who rules the roles
& to give the little guy stature
Rained out among the multitudes
Margins to be occupied
The donkey's tail in the eye.
        (C 73)

Language is made more radically material in *Clamor* than in the earlier work *Before Recollection*. This is especially true of the third section of *Clamor*, titled "The Elaborate Absence." The poems form artifacts rather than traces or the simulacra of thought, as in Ashbery's poetry. As in this passage from "Broken Skylight," in "The Elaborate Absence," Lauterbach argues for "a self as a vacancy with language schemes." Each fragment occupies a position comparable to the provisional condition of *if*: *if* is a proposed but incomplete history; *if* is also the *broken skylight* in that both provide a threshold or boundary to pass through; and *if* is the result of a slippage from *is,* and thus a re-visioning the condition of the self.

"Broken Skylight" simultaneously both flattens the lucidity of conversational language and interrupts the possibility of a lyrical extension. For example, the brief line "Sounds like shores" exhibits a sibilance that recollects a lyric moment. The alliteration suggests organic continuity and the continual breaking of forms. It also poses a symbolic image: the shore as a conventional image of liminality or a place of arrival and departure. The line further offers itself as an *ars poetica* in that it argues that sounds are always a place of change and mutability. The line suddenly turns conversational—"sounds like" what? we might ask.

The poems in *Clamor* also provide a counterbalancing formulation of the distinction between period and sentence. The grammatical sentence insists on completion. The period, instead, is contoured, for it traces a movement or essaying that occurs in speech.[25] The poem "A Documentary" suggests one version of the period where the syntax avoids completion as long as possible:

And that is what we are
When our sayings float back
Like the shadow of loose kites
Rising over the field, reminding us
Of an event that has perished
And goes on perishing while we build
Against the foraging wind, whose agent
Is disguised in our folly, its indifference
Flapping down on our habits
        (

The way the long-beaked stork flaps onto nests
And tweezes out fledglings.
   (C 13)

This passage exemplifies the period's sense of duration and extension. Syntax, as a means of connecting moments of time, and implicitly the corresponding traces of thought, is disrupted. Instead, time is considered as durational, a site that fills up without any necessary connection to other textual or mnemonic sites. What couples with the initial "And" is left suspended in or as the entire previous period. The second period of "A Documentary" extends and metamorphoses the phrase "our sayings float back" into "loose kites" and then into a "foraging wind" that turns into a "long-beaked stork." These images accumulate as a way of staving off the completion of the meditation on recollection.

The centrality of the "I" is dispersed in such a period. Lauterbach also subverts the authorial control by refusing completion. This is most readily apparent in "Prom in Toledo Night." Speech is in ruins, as are the space and relationships one encounters in daily life. Silence presses upon speech as does reality against the imagination. "Is this a form of exaltation or despair?" (C 62) asks one of the few completed statements in "Prom in Toledo Night." Directed toward the poem itself, the question implies that the poem has attained a coherent and meaningful form. Indeed, the poem adheres to a strict pattern of couplets alternating with single lines as well as a loose syllabic consistency, despite the constant syntactic rupture. The form is constantly a dialogic recognition, "Of course you, as both / Occasion and witness, pull me through" (C 63), where the words and the reader become inseparable in the formation or *poiēsis* of the *poem*.

Ashbery and Lauterbach, and such artists as Cornell or Porter, provide the habitations and the records of inhabiting reverie, as Ashbery affirms in the concluding lines of *Flow Chart:*

> What a city this is! In what rich though tepid layers
>   you can
> almost detect the outline of your head and then
> you know it's time to read on. When crisis comes, with embraceable side-effects,
> let's put a roof on the thing before it sidles, world-bound,
> toward an unconvincing other world. I'm more someone else, taking dictation
> from on high, in a purgatory of words, but I still think I shall be the same
>   person when I get up
> to leave, and then repeat the formulas that have come to us so many times
> in the past ("It's softer"), so faithfully that we extend them
> like a sill, and they have an end, though a potentially hazardous one,

though that's about all we can do about it. Every film is an abidance. We are
merely agents, so
that if something wants to improve on us, that's fine, but we are always the last
to find out about it, and live up to that image of ourselves as it gets
projected on trees and vine-coated walls and vapors in the night sky: a distant
noise of celebration, forever off-limits. By evening the traffic has begun
again in earnest, color-coded. It's open: the bridge, that way.
    (FC 216)

Ashbery's poems suggest a way, an opening, a revelation of the phenomenology of the coursing of a life. The poem insists on acts of speech and writing
always opening onto others; thus Ashbery's poems generate and affirm continuity. Lauterbach's poems seek revelation, as in the closing line of the collection *Before Recollection:* "bleed and bless / Robe opening on slowly mounted
stairs." While this line prefigures Ashbery's closing line of *Flow Chart*,[26] Lauterbach's poetry remains that of the self in reverie. The reverie is without a
doubt driven by powerful desires:

Stare into the lagoon of the beloved, open
Another file, abjure
                    sometimes, after all, emptied.
My girl,
Be not furtive even as the truck is lessened of its burden
And the floor, again, is clean.
The lake is aflame.
And lest you, of all, forget,
Keep it in mind with or without its target, its tune.
    (C 83–84)

Lauterbach's lyricism is iconic in that it opens to rapture. Ashbery's work,
however, moves against the impulses of the iconic and opens to a fully dialogic poetics. The libidinal decentering of the poem revisions our conditions of
pleasure. By seeking an excess (yet also critically observing an excess that is
ideologically driven) of voices and connections in the phenomenal world, the
poem and the poem's soul leave behind the self—the one "always the last /
to find out about it" and always desirous to "live up to that image of ourselves as it gets / projected" everywhere. Ashbery's poetry finds in the tracing
of thoughts voicings of a phenomenology that necessitates and inscribes a social world. Lauterbach, while pursing a parallel critique of the atomistic self,
maintains a phenomenologically enclosed world of objects and, by extension,
poems. Ashbery's poems allow for eros—the pleasure of creating—to be extensive; Lauterbach's poetry, finally, pursues the possibilities of rapture and
thereby risks enthrallment.

Notes

1. For discussions about the lyric and how that term is used interchangeably with "poetry," see Marjorie Perloff's essay "Postmodernism and the Impasse of Lyric" in her *Dance of the Intellect: Studies in the Poetry of the Pound Tradition* (Cambridge: Cambridge University Press, 1985), 172–81.

2. For a discussion of the myth of Narcissus and its relation to the self exemplified in John Ashbery's "Self-Portrait in a Convex Mirror," see Anita Sokolsky, " 'A Commission That Never Materialized': Narcissism and Lucidity in Ashbery's 'Self-Portrait in a Convex Mirror,' " in *John Ashbery,* ed. Harold Bloom (New York: Chelsea House, 1985), 233–50.

3. Jacques Derrida, *Signeponge/Signsponge,* trans. Richard Rand (New York: Columbia University Press, 1984), 80.

4. A. Poulin, Jr., *Contemporary American Poetry,* 4th ed. (Boston: Houghton Mifflin, 1985), 596–97.

5. S. P. Mohanty and Jonathan Monroe, "John Ashbery and the Articulation of the Social," *diacritics* 17, no. 2 (1987): 44.

6. Ibid., 45.

7. Marjorie Perloff, *Poetic License: Essays on Modernist and Postmodernist Lyric* (Evanston, Ill.: Northwestern University Press, 1990), 283.

8. For a discussion of Bakhtin's concepts and Ashbery's *Three Poems,* see Margueritte S. Murphy, "John Ashbery's *Three Poems:* Heteroglossia in the American Prose Poem," *American Poetry* 7, no. 2 (1990): 50–63.

9. John Ashbery, "An Interview in Warsaw," with Piotr Sommer, in *Code of Signals: Writings on Poetics,* ed. Michael Palmer (Berkeley, Calif.: North Atlantic Books, 1983), 302.

10. Murphy, "John Ashbery's *Three Poems,*" 57–58.

11. Ibid., 55.

12. Jean-François Lyotard, *The Postmodern Condition: A Report on Knowledge,* trans. Geoff Bennington and Brian Massumi (Minneapolis: University of Minnesota Press, 1984), 81.

13. Roland Barthes, *The Pleasure of the Text,* trans. Richard Miller (New York: Hill & Wang, 1975), 14.

14. Joseph M. Conte, *Unending Design: The Forms of Postmodern Poetry* (Ithaca: Cornell University Press, 1991), 182.

15. Ibid., 178.

16. In "Paying Attention," a review of *Flow Chart* in the *Economist* 320, no. 7724 (September 14, 1991): 108, Ashbery responded to the question of what had driven him to write such a long poem, by stating, "A friend of mine said to me one day: 'What are you writing?' I'd just been writing some very short poems. And he said: 'Why don't you write a hundred-page poem about your mother?' My mother had died quite recently—as had his—so I suppose that was on his mind. So I said, 'Well, why not? A hundred-page poem . . . I'll do it.' "

17. See W. R. Johnson, *The Idea of the Lyric: Lyric Modes in Ancient and Modern Poetry* (Berkeley: University of California Press, 1982), 178. Johnson writes: "What

matters, for literary choral, is that the agent and the object of choral mimesis be present: the universal representative of the community singing for and to the community about the hopes and passion for order, survival, and continuity that they all share." Johnson sees Whitman and Pound as the prime examples of modern choral poets. Ashbery, I would argue, belongs to this group, except that he dismantles the position of *chorēgos,* or the "universal representative," and develops a fully dialogic community of singers. Also see Mohanty and Monroe, "John Ashbery and the Articulation of the Social," for a discussion of Ashbery's poetry and community; the authors state that Ashbery's poetry is "a form of postmodernism that recognizes the need to reverse what *Habits of the Heart: Individualism and Commitment in American Life* calls 'modernity's tendency to obliterate all previous culture' and forge a social memory which can accommodate revision, interrogation, and indeed radical self-contestation as part of its own existence" (61).

18. Ann Lauterbach, "On Memory," in *Conversant Essays: Contemporary Poets on Poetry,* ed. James McCorkle (Detroit: Wayne State University Press, 1990), 519-20. All further references to this essay will be incorporated in the text and abbreviated as OM. References to Ann Lauterbach's poetry will be abbreviated and noted within the text as follows: BR—*Before Recollection* (Princeton: Princeton University Press, 1987); C—*Clamor* (New York: Viking, 1991).

19. Gaston Bachelard, *The Poetics of Reverie: Childhood, Language, and the Cosmos,* trans. David Russell (Boston: Beacon Press, 1971), 145.

20. Ibid., 153.

21. Ibid., 14.

22. Wallace Stevens, "The Noble Rider and the Sound of Words," in *The Necessary Angel: Essays on Reality and the Imagination* (New York: Vintage, 1951), 36.

23. Ibid., 32.

24. Ann Lauterbach, "Ann Lauterbach," in *Ecstatic Occasions, Expedient Forms,* ed. David Lehman (New York: Collier Macmillan, 1987), 121.

25. See Charles Bernstein, "Socialist Realism or Real Socialism?" in his *Content's Dream: Essays, 1975-1984* (Los Angeles: Sun & Moon, 1986), 413-14, for a brief formulation of the dichotomy of period and sentence. Also Michael Palmer, "Period (senses of duration)," in *Code of Signals: Writings on Poetics,* ed. Michael Palmer (Berkeley, Calif.: North Atlantic Books, 1983), 243-65.

26. I am grateful to Susan Schultz for pointing out the similarity of the closing lines of these two poems to me.

8 | Ashbery's Menagerie and the Anxiety of Affluence

John Gery

Is THERE A *wrong* way to interpret a poem by John Ashbery? At their best, his poems seem to have the tensile strength of the bamboo shoot in the children's tale, where, because of its flexibility, the shoot survives the wind that eventually splits the oak tree. Yet Ashbery's detractors complain of this seeming lack of definition in his work, in what Robert Richman has called "Ashbery's poetry of non-production—involving endless linguistic copulation with no creation [that] threatens to destroy the enterprise of art altogether."[1] His poetry seems to be either all things to all people (which, as he once remarked, is how he likes to think of it himself)[2] or nothing but a casual amalgamation of words and phrases. Either it imitates art, music, and life, or it assaults those dimensions of experience by assaulting the ways in which we might speak about or understand them. His is either an encompassing vision, finely worked out in the tradition of the Romantics, Yeats, and Stevens, or a vision of disruption, dislocation, disjunction, and disarray, like that of a Breton or a Beckett. More in the manner of Whitman than of Stevens or Breton, though, the idiosyncrasies of Ashbery's poetry have so far created not a "school" of followers (a phrase which would suggest a rigorous discipline, a marked similarity in style, and shared themes) but a menagerie of post-Ashberians. Like the animals in a zoo, the poets associated with him tend to differ so remarkably from each other, really, that except for the fact of their relationship to Ashbery, as often as not each belongs to an entirely different species of poet.

What distinguishes Ashbery from the Moderns before him, among other things, is not *that* his style is peculiar (an important first principle with Pound, Eliot, Stevens, Moore, Williams, Stein, and H. D.) but, from a postmodern perspective, *how* it is so. Where we might find the Moderns difficult to understand because of the complexity of their poetics, Ashbery's poetry is marked by such a fluid expression that, taken for itself, it often invites us not to bother to try to understand him any better than we understand ourselves or our environment (in the ordinary sense of knowledge)—that is, to let the meaning go, finally, with a kind of shrug, "as though meaning could be cast aside some day / When it had been outgrown" (SPs 88). In this way, reading him can free us from an orthodox responsibility to "truth" so that everything, from the arch to the ludicrous, from the quotidian to the sublime, becomes fair game.

Subsequently, the anxiety for a younger poet reading Ashbery is not one of influence, as in Harold Bloom's argument for the struggle poets have with their grander predecessors, but one of "affluence." For Bloom, the process of becoming a poet involves "the dialectic of influence," a dialectic that "governs the relations between poets *as poets*" and that originally occurs when a poet "discovers poetry as being both external and internal to himself."[3] The contingent danger in such a discovery, of course, is that "the poet is condemned to learn his profoundest yearnings through an awareness of other selves," to experience "the shame and splendor of *being found by* poems—great poems— *outside* him," and "to learn the dread of threatened autonomy forever" (26). Given such powerful predecessors, "strong" poets can only distinguish themselves, Bloom argues, by way of "revisionary swerves" (44) based on a "misprision," or misreading of the past that will somehow divide from and improve on it.

Rooting the filial relationship (or "sonship") of poets in the age of Homer, Bloom traces the historical lineage of "poetic influence" through "Cartesian dualism" up to "our sense" of the phrase as it was first used by Coleridge. In the course of that development, he suggests, the term has lost its original meaning of influx or "inflow," in which "to be influenced meant to receive an ethereal fluid flowing in upon one from the stars, a fluid that affected one's character and destiny, and that altered all sublunary things" (26–27). Regardless of Bloom's insistently (and oppressively) patriarchal reading of the nature of poetic influence, it is precisely this sense of "inflow" that the idiosyncratic character of Ashbery's poetry subverts. Rather than "flowing in" with the authority and certainty we associate with modernism, it "flows out" abundantly, copiously, always in search of a meaning it can never reassure us has been uncovered. Though by 1973 Bloom may have appropriated Ashbery as an example of a poet who "has achieved one of the mysteries of poetic style, but only through the individuation of misprision" (146), Ashbery has done so primarily, in effect, by deconstructing the very tradition Bloom describes, thereby opening up the field of language for those poets who follow.[4] Rather than asserting an influence over his menagerie as might a Wordsworth, a Yeats, or a Stevens, and rather than deciding what a poem should be, Ashbery prefers only to make suggestions or gestures, as he does in "What Is Poetry," for instance, a poem "trying to avoid / / Ideas," which closes with a question instead of a definition:

In school
All the thought got combed out:

What was left was like a field.
Shut your eyes, and you can feel it for miles around.

Now open them on a thin vertical path.
It might give us—what?—some flowers soon?
     (SPs 236)

Such a release from the anxiety of influence, however, does not particularly make the writing of poetry after Ashbery any easier, just different from
before. With the current bracketing of the Western tradition, a result of the
broad questioning of the canon as well as of the outpouring of multicultural
and interdisciplinary readings of "texts," the project of developing a poetic
voice is arguably more difficult than even Bloom thinks, since a poet has not
one or two "strong" fathers to worry about but an undetermined genealogy of
aunts and uncles with whom to contend. Yet putting that larger issue aside, we
might still ask how, in the case of Ashbery's oeuvre, a younger poet attends to
Ashbery's expansive voice, the many levels and the leveling of his diction, the
multiplicitous yet complicitous layers of his irony, his grand reveries, and his
self-conscious, sometimes self-deprecating, diffusive humor, and then begin to
turn what is found there into discriminate art? In other words, to rephrase
my first question, What, if any, is the wrong way to *write* a poem after the
"affluence" of Ashbery? Such a question is further complicated by the problem
that, as Ashbery's fans and critics agree, his poems often do not seem to be
about anything, so the post-Ashberian cannot even take solace in the fact that
he or she is writing on an Ashberian subject, even if badly.

One way to overcome this anxiety of affluence relating to Ashbery (an "affluence" promulgated in yet another sense of the word by his own prolific output, the wide distribution of his books, the number of awards he continues to
receive, and the industry of investigative scholarship that has grown up around
him) has been to try, usually unsuccessfully, to ignore him. Many of the "New
Formalists," for example, as well as poets of the "deep image" school, prefer
to dismiss his work as anarchic or pointlessly chaotic. Dana Gioia, a leading
spokesperson for New Formalism, has labeled Ashbery "a marvelous minor
poet but an uncomfortable major one,"[5] as a way of minimalizing his impact.
Others consider him tedious or simply impenetrable, while still others mock
his literary "success" as an elaborate joke he has perpetrated on contemporary
readers.

A surprising variety of noteworthy younger poets, however, have chosen to
dip freely into Ashbery's aesthetic as it suits their own purposes and otherwise
to leave him alone. By responding to him selectively, these poets, in their implied critiques of Ashbery, inevitably tend to highlight one or another aspect
of his work without necessarily attending to the whole, therein risking the mis-
appropriation or even corruption of his vision. In Bloomian terms, to exploit

Ashbery this way ideally sets the stage for the "corrective movement" (14) needed to establish these poets within the same continuum of poetry where Bloom places Ashbery himself. But a more recent critic, John Koethe, considers the evidence of these poets' responses "disappointing" and severely limited in its understanding of Ashbery's significance. Koethe argues that, with few exceptions, the qualities of Ashbery's verse now employed by younger poets—his "passivity, an acquiescence in indeterminacy, an avoidance of rationality, and self-reflexivity"—have been adapted only superficially in service of a narcissistic style of "personal self-expression" that is "antithetical" to Ashbery's deconstructive vision.[6] On the one hand, observes Koethe, the "domestic and deflationary" tone that later New York school poets have adopted from Ashbery, though it can contribute to "a refreshing, casual lyricism," only rarely displays his resonant gesturing toward transcendence, loss, or the passage of time. On the other hand, the Language poets' preoccupation with "neither expressive nor lyrical, but philosophical" qualities in Ashbery's work confines itself in Koethe's view too narrowly to his early poetic experiments, while it too often ignores his work of the mid-1970s. While acknowledging the existence of some strong post-Ashberian poems, Koethe laments the dearth of "substantial bodies of work by individual poets that manifest his influence but have a distinctive character of their own."[7]

Despite the force of Koethe's argument for the need to investigate the complete Ashbery in order to comprehend "the form the diffuse, decentered version of romantic contestation takes in his poetry,"[8] critical factors relating, first, to the context of Ashbery's menagerie and, second, to the multiplicitous character of his work mitigate Koethe's criticism and encourage a closer look at the evidence of Ashbery's impact on younger poets than he suggests. To begin with, as Koethe acknowledges, given that Ashbery in his sixties is still producing at the same pace or better than he has been for some thirty years, it is premature to reach more than tentative conclusions about the scope of his work. Furthermore, if the precedents of Whitman or Pound (or even Robert Frost) mean anything, history teaches us, I think, that a poet's tendency (deliberately or not) to "manage" the reception of his or her work plays a central role in how younger poets absorb that work at first, but eventually the nature of that influence will change. In Ashbery's case, the initial mystique emanating from his experimentation and inaccessibility may slowly diminish, especially as more is written about and out of his aesthetic. In truth, the very breadth of his voice as Koethe outlines it, consisting of multiple, "decentered" layers, may mean that not all Ashberians are so readily recognizable as we think they are, especially when we compare them with each other, as I want to demonstrate here.

Second, in recalling the distinction between Ashbery and the Moderns in their relationship to "truth," it is essential to regard the "acquiescence in in-

determinacy" in Ashbery's work not only as characteristic of his poetic method
but as inherent in his vision of experience, a vision that allows for a multiplicity of readings, so that what may not currently appear as a "distinctive aspect"
of his poetry may later be substantiated, after it has been realized in the work
of someone else. In other words, Koethe's "disappointment" in the evidence
of Ashbery's influence is undoubtedly tied to what he believes that influence
should be, rather than to what, in its affluence, it is actually coming to be. The
very diversity of poets' responses to Ashbery in fact embodies the same deconstruction of Bloom's depiction of the Western tradition that Ashbery himself
has achieved, in that the poets in his menagerie constitute neither a "swerve"
nor a "corrective movement" in the end but, as at the close of "And *Ut Pictura
Poesis* Is Her Name," a *desertion* "for other centers of communication, so that
understanding / May begin, and in doing so be undone" (SPs 235). It is along
the lines of this continuum (or "discontinuum," as it were) that Ashbery's poetry locates itself—consistently, even comfortably, given his deep engagement
with the aleatory. Concerning Bloom's Western hierarchy of poets, when Ashbery was asked once to comment on the long list of poets who have supposedly
influenced his work, he sardonically referred to what he calls "the insouciance
of influence," therein undermining the question.[9]

So in taking from him according to their own predilections, rather than in
wrestling with him in order to swerve away from him, younger poets, in fact,
paradoxically reenact Ashbery's own liberating response to the Bloomian man-
date that poets *must* misread their mentors. For them, regardless of the desire
for unity, it is not a matter of cultivating a line in the Zeitgeist. Instead, because "we too are somehow impossible, formed of so many different things, /
Too many to make sense to anybody," as Ashbery says in "The Wrong Kind of
Insurance," what matters is how "we straggle on as quotients, hard-to-com-
bine / Ingredients," in order that "what continues / Does so with our partici-
pation and consent" (SPs 239). And as post-Ashberian Marjorie Welish adds,
in her poem "The Diaries Began,"

> We are now in the middle of a similar bulk,
> as birds sway across this violet planet
> and banter with this cardboard. We live the way we do.
>
> The diaries began so that the inconceivable might be said
> with no hint or substitute.[10]

Once we open up the Ashberian field, then, evidence of diverse readings of
his work by younger poets is not hard to find. Poets as different from each
other as Clark Coolidge and Anne Waldman, Donald Revell and Susan Howe,
have consistently remarked on their early enthusiasm for the poems of *Some
Trees* and *The Tennis Court Oath*, finding in them the kind of liberation that

also excited them about the painting and music being done in New York in the first two decades after World War II. For Coolidge, a major early proponent of Language poetry, Ashbery provided a license to disrupt ordinary tropes in English and to experiment with the interrelationship between the juxtaposition of words on a page and their disembodied suggestiveness. As he himself has noted, "A lot of the work in *Space* was influenced by what was going on in Ashbery's *Tennis Court Oath,* and what that led to in the New York School around the early to mid-sixties. In my case, that meant an interest in single words to generate a larger structure. From there, it's kind of funny. In some ways my syntax got more 'normal,' while in other ways more complicated."[11] As an example, this passage from "Echo & Mildew" in *Space* seems a deliberate recapitulation of early Ashbery:

> the window rips & the curtains in your hand
> so moldy the tools near the captain's
> mike hook-up tipped calcium into the stem
> "Believe . . . " much Tuesday yellow cellophane
>
> too much steam, whine rules dope
> applied in sedimentary bog lay
> sod under the blue & saw the roof
> bagged him a little left of the copper rod.[12]

Though he dispenses with Ashbery's habitual allegiance to standardized punctuation, Coolidge creates the same sense of sustained frustration and variation based on interrupted syntactic patterns that Ashbery does, as in these lines from "Errors" in *Some Trees:*

>   Promises,
> We thought then of your dry portals,
> Bright cornices of eavesdropping palaces,
> You were painfully stitched to hours
> The moon now tears up, scoffing at the unrinsed portions.
> And loves adopted realm. Flees to water,
> The coach dissolving in mists.
>   (SPs 16)

No more than this passage renders decipherable whether "promises" is an appositive or an apostrophe, or whether the "coach" in the last line is one pulled by horses or one standing on the sidelines, does Coolidge's poem allow us to determine whether "whine rules dope" is to be taken as a clause or a series of nouns. Both passages demonstrate a cleaving of language, in the double sense of splitting apart and gluing together. And even in the remarkable early Coolidge pieces, "the a these but   then for" and "On Once," poems not visually like anything Ashbery has done but which, like others in *Space,* read as though portions of words have literally been torn from the page, the same dynamic in Ashbery's neosurrealist work of verbal expectation played against syntactic rupture is clearly present.

However, Coolidge shows little interest in Ashbery's later obsession with time, for instance, nor does he incorporate into these earlier poems the conversational idioms or the peculiar yet readily accessible imagery that are all hallmarks of Ashbery. These qualities tend to resurface in a dramatically different style of poetry, such as David Lehman's. Although Lehman rarely practices Ashbery's (and in a more extreme manner, Coolidge's) delicate incoherence and free play with phrasing, his poetry is informed with Ashberian humor, or what he elsewhere calls "Ashbery's flamboyance . . . of a quieter sort,"[13] notably in its consistent variations on the mannerisms of daily discourse. Many of the poems in his collection *Operation Memory,* such as his sequence "Mythologies" and the Jamesian comedy "Cambridge, 1972," recall Ashbery not just by expressing humor through the odd juxtaposition of imagery and commentary but by using the mock-narrative technique of such poems as "The Instruction Manual" (SoTr 26–30), "It Was Raining in the Capital" (DDS 21–33), and "Hop o' My Thumb" (SPCM 32–34). Even more explicitly, Lehman's parody "One Size Fits All: A Critical Essay," in exploiting typically Ashberian copulatives, includes nothing but strategically placed transitional phrases, as in these two strophes:

Which is to say,
In fictional terms,
For reasons that are never made clear,
Not without meaning,
Though (as is far from usual)
Perhaps too late.

The first thing that must be said is
Perhaps, because
And, not least of all,
Certainly more,
Which is to say
In every other respect
Meanwhile.[14]

Like so many Ashbery poems, this poem, to be sure, does not finally "mean" anything, nor does it have an identifiable subject. However, because it operates according to its own internal logic, as a parody, neither does it enact any of the elusive resistance to reductive thinking in the Ashbery of "The System," for example.[15] In fact, though camp humor is everywhere present in Lehman's poems, his method is more deeply rooted in Frank O'Hara's poetry, with its emphasis on the concrete and its comfortable reliance on meaningful pronouns (especially "I") than in Ashbery's, whose use of the concrete wavers and whose pronouns are often without discernible antecedents.

Concerning yet another marked characteristic of Ashbery, first prominent in *Self-Portrait in a Convex Mirror,* neither Coolidge's nor Lehman's poems usually build on themselves incrementally through a network of self-generating or self-reflexive syntax the way Ashbery's do. For better evidence of this technique, we need to look at Jorie Graham, a poet as different from Coolidge and Lehman in tone and focus as they are from each other.[16] Her poem "Pollack and Canvas" in *The End of Beauty* (1987), for example, begins with a sentence that is thirty-six lines long. Elsewhere, as in this short passage from "Eschatological Prayer" describing a bird singing on a hillside in Montefalco, Italy, Graham blends the self-conscious interruptions of both literary and literal thought into one sentence as it unwinds, creating a sense of equivocation even during the most transcendent of moments:

> Snow gleamed in the margins, originless.
> Snow gleamed in the miles of birdcry and birdsong,
>
> yellow birdsong in the yellow light.
>   And the things of this world were everywhere happy
> to be so grazed
>   on only one side
> by the fierce clean light
>
> and by us
>   sifting the minutes from the dust from those three
> almost repeatable
>   notes
> on which the whole unhearable song
>
> depends.
>   This is what time
> as we knew it
>   was.[17]

The isolation of phrases here through the intertwining of line breaks ("on only one side," "almost repeatable," and "as we knew it," especially) introduces a qualified self-reflexivity into the poem with the same kind of subtlety and insinuation as in these three sentences from Ashbery's "Self-Portrait in a Convex Mirror," one of several descriptions in the poem of Parmigianino's painting:

>   Today enough of a cover burnishes
> To keep the supposition of promises together
> In one piece of surface, letting one ramble
> Back home from them so that these

Even stronger possibilities can remain
Whole without being tested. Actually
The skin of the bubble-chamber's as tough as
Reptile eggs; everything gets "programmed" there
In due course: more keeps getting included
Without adding to the sum, and just as one
Gets accustomed to a noise that
Kept one awake but now no longer does,
So the room contains this flow like an hourglass
Without varying in climate or quality
(Except perhaps to brighten bleakly and almost
Invisibly, in a focus of sharpening toward death—more
Of this later).
    (SPs 192–93)

While Graham practices Ashbery's (and Stevens's) control of the well-wrought syntactic qualification, in her work there is little of Ashbery's self-deprecating irony ("Even stronger," "everything gets 'programmed' there / In due course," "Without varying in climate or quality," or the extratextual signifier "more / Of this later"), the characteristic which Keith Cohen has pointed to as evidence of Ashbery's "structured dysfunctioning of bourgeois discourse"[18] and which Lehman considers "an indispensable part of the most significant and attractive aesthetic strategy available to an American poet today."[19] Instead, The End of Beauty usually relies on irony for more serious effects and, ultimately, for illumination, creating in Graham's work a faith in the truth of things which Ashbery's poetry generally brackets, undercuts, or merely eschews. Nevertheless, the intricate self-reflexivity of her work (including, no doubt, the deliberate use of "Self-Portrait" in five of her poems' titles) carries within it Ashbery's meditative quality, as well as that deconstructive bent that has made him the darling of American Derrideans, even though Graham has substantive connections neither to Language theory nor to the New York school.

Beyond matters of technique, other intrinsic dimensions of Ashbery's sensibility can be found in the lyricism and visual play in John Yau's poetry. Yau, who has studied under Ashbery and collaborated with him on several projects involving painters, is (like Graham) just enough younger than Coolidge or Koethe to have discovered Ashbery in the 1970s rather than the sixties. Unlike Coolidge, in his early work Yau shows little interest in imitating Ashbery's rupture of ordinary sentence structure. Rather, as a representative of what critics refer to as the second generation of New York poets, he employs idiomatic speech in the style of such Ashbery poems as "Forties Flick" (SPCM 5), "Mixed Feelings" (SPCM 42–43), and "Tapestry" (AWK 90), less for its deconstructive effects than for its visual evocativeness and its diffusion of the arcane or the consummate. At the opening of Ashbery's "Forties Flick," for example, in what reads like the start of a screenplay (though we quickly discover this is the *end* of the "flick"), Ashbery provides the vivid imagery of a film-noir set. Yet it requires a careful reading of the first four lines, in fact, to discern the subject of the first sentence: that "the shadow of the Venetian blind on the painted wall, / Shadows of the snake-plant and cacti, [and] the plaster animals" all "focus the tragic melancholy of the bright stare [*Whose* stare? we might ask] / Into nowhere." But as abruptly as the diction then shifts in the next three lines from the loftiness of "tragic melancholy" to the levity of "bra," "panties," "Zip!" and "wafer-thin pedestrians," the point of view also shifts:

> In bra and panties she sidles to the window:
> Zip! Up with the blind. A fragile street scene offers itself,
> With wafer-thin pedestrians who know where they are going.
> The blind comes down slowly, the slats are slowly tilted up.
>   (SPCM 5)

By complicating the texture of this image, Ashbery sets up the poem's later meditation on the paradoxical nature of stylization, that is, on

> The 'art' part—knowing what important details to leave out
> And the way character is developed. Things too real
> To be of much concern, hence artificial, yet now all over the page,
> The indoors with the outside becoming part of you.

In other words, by juxtaposing idioms as well as images, the poem embodies the very conflict between presence and imagination it is discussing.

Several poems in Yau's 1979 book *Sometimes,* including "After Moving," "A Bottle," "Sometimes," "Hatteras," and "Arden," take up this same theme of the uncertainty of being, yet Yau seems to have imitated or absorbed little of Ashbery's multilayered tropology, resulting in a more readily accessible poetry, as in "After Moving":

> Even as the street becomes familiar to you
>   almost incidental
> the way details in novels can add
>   their unblendable color
> to the overall scheme; and faces pass
>   from strangers to companions
> without the intervention of touch;
>   and the traffic

no longer sounds harsh, but grows muted
        as the gray afternoons
that occasionally fill the sky with a festering sun
        behind clouds rubbed smooth;
you feel removed from the surrounding scenery,
        though if you were asked,
you would not deny you have a place
        in this circumstance
and partake of events, though they rarely,
        if ever,
seemed connected as the streets do. . . . [20]

Although Yau's imagery (the faces, the traffic, the "sky with a festering sun / behind clouds rubbed smooth," and so on) is neither as surprising nor as visually stunning as Ashbery's, the poem still manages to focus on the space between experience and thought, between observation and interpretation, a space that wavers even as he isolates it. Like Graham, he adds qualifying clauses in lines 14 and 17, but whereas Graham manipulates her syntax in order to express precisely what it is she sees or means, Yau more frequently heaves an Ashberian sigh, as he backs off from "meaning" in favor of indeterminacy.

In recent years, however, Yau has increasingly turned away from the kind of cerebral poetry that leaves readers "wiser without knowing it, and none the worse for wear," as Ashbery remarks in his blurb on the back cover of *Sometimes*. Instead, his poems have become more self-consciously visual in their surrealism and are more often composed in a narrative voice using litanies of imagery, either because he is devising variations on a theme, as he does in *Corpse and Mirror* (1983), or because he is actually collaborating with painters, as in his "Radiant Silhouette" sequence. In another sequence "Genghis Chan: Private Eye," the virtual cataloging of sentences such as "I was floating through a cross section / with my dusty wine glass," "I would be entering the hyena zone," "I too was stymied by the animal of music," "I wanted to tell you / about the gizmo pit and kinds of sludge / I have catalogued during my investigation," and "I prefer rat back flames to diplomatic curls"[21] begins to reveal a Yau who echoes the Ashbery of *Some Trees*. Nonetheless, while whatever new directions he may take remain to be realized, and while he has yet to match Ashbery's linguistic range and exuberance, the stamp of the elder poet's urbanity informs his work even as it grows more experimental.

More broadly speaking, John Ash's sanguine observations of urban life demonstrate an exuberant fluctuation that unquestionably bears the mark of Ashbery's discursiveness, as the following examples indicate:

The idea was to be at the centre of things,—
but where was the centre?[22]

I regard the world as a TV
on which I change channels at will,
never moving from the bed.[23]

               These are foils and diversions,
though essential ones, and as this is written or read—
nearly identical activities really—we are inhabited
like an embassy by ghosts programmed to repeat us,

helplessly and at random, god knows how many
years in the future: the result must be embarrassment.[24]

Despite his British background, Ash's poems, especially when he writes about music, art, architecture, or film, articulate what Rob Wilson has described as "Ashbery's Postindustrial Sublime," that is, a "post-Whitmanic sublime, with its zany reversals of tone and 'seeming' unions which the half-parodic language undercuts," where a poem can comprise "a bric-a-brac landscape, a storage place of rapture and junk, a destabilized collage of possibility."[25] In "Nympheas," for instance, a poem dedicated to Roland Barthes, Ash writes about the "nightmare rituals of the dining table," intermingling indiscriminately questions about food with highfalutin intellectual terms, in order to savage the hyprocrisy of the kind of sophisticated talk in a "babble of civilised voices" which occurs over "the glazed, gilded, garnished, rococo-pink dishes / / of an ideal Romantic and Classic cuisine," a meal meant more to be seen than to be eaten. In such a context, "to mention the word hunger is an obscenity!" he remarks. But the poem then turns from the table to the wall, where a "predominantly mauve" print shows "the victim of a recent bombing / dissolved into luscious water-lights and lilies," about which Ash concludes, "it looks / / good enough to eat."[26] The satire here cuts more sharply and is more telegraphed than in Ashbery's poems, which themselves tend to equivocate, as at the end of "A Last World" (TCO 56–58), for example, or in the opening lines of "Decoy" (DDS 41–42), where he parodies the *Declaration of Independence* but then parodies the parodists. More important, besides adopting a deflated tone, Ash at his most lucid shares Ashbery's fundamentally egalitarian impulse, one that (for all his expansiveness) "diminishes the scope of the American self," as Douglas Crase has observed, and so frees us from the psychic baggage of Emersonian transcendentalism.[27] Ironically, it may be Ash's British origins that have nurtured his receptivity to Ashbery's democratic impulse, according to which, as Ash asserts in "Advanced Choreography for Beginners," the point is:

> to establish a new lyricism in which all these things will find their place
> equally like buildings on the loop of a promenade
> doors and windows open towards a calm sea that reminds us
> inevitably of a sheet of cellophane that has been crumpled up
> and smoothed out again, but not completely—[28]

In a final striking example of how poets after Ashbery can be so various while still echoing Ashbery, the poems of Marjorie Welish demonstrate not only the same visual juxtapositioning learned from Ashbery by Yau and not only the aleatory play of the Language poets, but the same impassioned vision of desire, presence, loss, and possibility that Koethe characterizes as Ashbery's (a vision, incidentally, also evident in Koethe's own poetry).[29] In fact, as is often the case with a poetry as sophisticated as Ashbery's, it is only after it has been reinterpreted in the work of younger poets like Welish, I believe, that we will be able to understand more deeply the full extent of his vision. In her first collection, *Handwritten,* Welish displays a poignant sense of precision, but she does so with a languid lyricism characteristic of Ashbery's voice in the 1970s and perhaps more completely realized in *A Wave* and *April Galleons,* books written *after* Welish's. In the following poems in *Handwritten,* for instance, Welish shifts her focus with apparent spontaneity, yet each poem builds on its own conceits and uses abstract, self-reflexive commentary almost to excess.

> A beautiful picture has come of picturing it,
> but I have shifted away from my original intention
> like a country without mineral resources
> that goes on indefinitely.
>   ("The Moon")[30]

> Have you noticed that when the reversal occurs
> permanence occurs?
>   ("The Spring Comes, Popular as Ever")[31]

>   A few people
> are stepping onto a Down escalator, a dance consisting of—
> there could be a dance
> consisting of bunches of people stepping
> onto and riding the banks of escalators
> into fresh water. . . .
>   ("An Emptiness Disturbed")[32]

Regardless of such usage, there is rarely any indication that the poet has lost sight of her subject or of her reader, with whom she assumes she is on intimate terms. Although most of the poems in *Handwritten* are less than a page long, overall Welish displays an intense concentration on individual experience, in the way Ashbery does. In her poem "Lure," for instance, Welish weaves philosophical reflection into her imagery with a delicacy reminiscent of *The Double Dream of Spring* and *Houseboat Days*, thereby revealing how the poems in those books actually cohere:

> Home is unexpectedly deep
> as I step into it: how will that help them now?
> Where nothing is disturbed
> and no small sound is made,
> whatever is sore comes through the tiny daisies
> that live untried. I have not escaped
> being more than sad,
> 　　　　　　　early,
> paneled in light, the sea entirely shiny
> and flat, disappearing into the sky
> as the thought: out there is my imagination.
>
> These mornings are doing
> what they always do for my eyes, providing a modern story
> that deals in particulars
> —a particular yellow baseboard—
> but also the lyrical side,
> which is the side overheard or caught unawares
> in the filial language
> of pleasure boats
> and those who rent them for the summer.[33]

As in "Forties Flick," Welish's poem locates us "indoors with the outside becoming part of you," risking sentimentality ("I have not escaped / being more than sad, / early") and suggesting a Romantic metaphor for the imagination in its image of the "sea entirely shiny / and flat, disappearing into the sky." Yet Welish remains circumspect about the "lure" such a comfortable way of seeing holds over the self, recognizing that "these mornings are doing / what they always do for my eyes," namely, attracting them to particulars on which the imagination can work its wonders, while the "lyrical side" remains separate, albeit intertwined "in the filial language" she is likely to misread because of her feelings. The balance she strikes here between beauty and the self-conscious mind results in a poem that celebrates our disposition for wonder while it leaves intact the postmodern deflation of subjectivity. With this mediation in its tone and its treatment of its subject, "Lure" recalls lines such as these from Ashbery's "Crazy Weather," where the desire for "this poetry of mud" is associated with

> A simple unconscious dignity we can never hope to
> Approximate now except in narrow ravines nobody

Will inspect where some late sample of the rare,
Uninteresting specimen might still be putting out shoots, for all we know.
      (SPs 221)

The poet here affirms his yearning but without portentousness or self-aggran-
dizement. "Lure" also reasserts what Ashbery concludes in "The Gazing
Grain," namely, that

              That which is given to see
      At any moment is the residue, shadowed

      In gold or emerging into the clear bluish haze
      Of uncertainty. We come back to ourselves
      Through the rubbish of cloud and tree-spattered pavement.
      These days stand like vapor under the trees.
            (SPs 215)

    While less Ashberian in their particular mode of discourse, Welish's more
recent poems have become increasingly cryptic, yet they still carry the marks
of his oscillating voice and his uncompromising resilience against the easy image or "truth." Many of the sentences in Welish's collection *The Windows
Flew Open* lack the accessibility of *Handwritten,* and as her subject matter
has broadened to become more spiritual in nature, she resorts less often to extended conceits than before, favoring instead a denser language, a more ruptured syntax, and more frequent patterns of repetition, as well as what might
be called her "flammable enthusiasms."[34] This is not to suggest that her poems
lack an Ashberian sense of levity, evident in the book's opening lines:

      In the long run we must fix our compass,
      and implore our compass,
      and arraign our shadow play in heaven, among the pantheon
      where all the plea-bargaining takes place.
                              Within the proscenium arch,
      the gods negotiate ceaselessly,
      and the words he chooses to express the baleful phrase
            dare to be obsessed
      with their instrumentality. Please send for our complete catalogue.[35]

    Not only does the last sentence here undermine any inkling of pretension
that precedes it, but Welish uses the indeterminate pronoun "he," mixes her
diction to open up the field of play, and suggests a meaningfulness we can take
stock in without having to root it in objectivity. Permeated with these and
other Ashberian techniques, her poems nevertheless reconfigure them in order
to express a vision belonging not to Ashbery but to Welish. That vision so far

finds its fullest expression, as it does with Yau, in her sequences: "The Seasons Change," "And Now Such a Shore," and "Carpet Within the Figure," poems not easily explicated. But even a glimpse at her short poem "Skin," as an illustration of her range, suggests how the affluence of Ashbery finds a home in a younger poet without dominating her furniture:

> Our skin, strenuously tutored to appreciate the vernacular
> body a feeling might have. Companies
> of hands, legs, cigarettes, a whip, the sea
> tangle in the mutilated lamplight,
>
> and wrap an intelligent enterprise in a gang of approaches.
> I think that black into pink is devastating. A bitter winter,
> the whip, the sea—all familiar rubble that comes around nightly,
> but so familiar, the feeling need only mention surrender and we surrender.
>
> In the postwar victory, lamplight is harsher, categorical.
> Pink is devastating, a stone lawn.
> A great part of the American pavilion
> has been given over to an iron blue and magnificent écorché—
>
> the spirit, when the spirit is flayed and forbidden
> to talk about itself. It feels normal
> to live in the present amid musculature
> of beautiful early work propped against an uphill sea.[36]

Framed in quatrains like the poems in *Shadow Train*, the language here seems to be discretely undoing, even parodying, its form, while at the same time it establishes its own internal patterns through the repetition of "the whip," "the sea," "black," "pink," "the lamplight," "familiar," "surrender," and so on. Similarly, though Welish deliberately contrasts the "tutored" with the "vernacular," "black" with "pink," "tangle" with "wrap," and other terms, these juxtapositions both suspend the signification of any particular line and create the central contrast between skin and spirit on which the poem rests. Beginning with a fragmented sentence, the poet is marveling at purely physical experience, at how the skin learns to appreciate the variety of textures it touches. It then lists representative objects which simultaneously "tangle" themselves and "wrap an intelligent enterprise," namely, the self, in their "gang of approaches." But as in other poems, Welish follows where her thinking takes her, in what seems an abrupt shift in the second stanza: "I think that black into pink is devastating." The rest of the stanza explains this shift not only in thought but in feeling, when she explains how the very familiarity of a feeling induces our "surrender" to it. The third stanza broadens this observation when, as Ashbery does so often, Welish courts the very edges of meaning: By introducing "the postwar victory," she reduces the "mutilated lamplight" of line 4 (in which feelings are at odds with one another) to a starker condition, imagined paradoxically now as a "stone lawn," a phrase reminiscent of Emily Dickinson's "Quartz contentment, like a stone" which follows great pain, or those "Valves of her attention" which the soul closes "Like Stone."[37]

Finally, the figurative suggestiveness of "lawn" then expands into the poem's oddest statement:

A great part of the American pavilion
has been given over to an iron blue and magnificent écorché—

the spirit.

As opposed to the "pink," "stone," and "lawn" associated with the skin, the spirit is cast as "blue," "iron," and "écorché" (or bark, as though to reverse our usual associations with skin as external and spirit as internal). Whether we imagine "pavilion" as a tent or as the polished surface of a cut gem, we get the sense of a covering consistent with "écorché,"[38] leading to the idea that the spirit "surfaces," as it were, amid the plethora of feelings when, through physical sensation, it is "skinned" and deprived of language by that sensation. What emerges is a fairly complex impression of the spirit. Through her unorthodox presentation and nearly meaningless signification, Welish renews for us the intricate relationship of touch to soul, concluding the poem again with an Ashberian understatement about the dailiness of spirituality, despite the desperation in its struggle to survive:

It feels normal
to live in the present amid musculature
of beautiful early work propped against an uphill sea.

This is not to say that Welish's poetry scales the melodic heights of a Shelley or even a Stevens; indeed, if we accept "postmodernism" as Ashbery seems to, for her to do so would be anathema to her endeavor to situate the "poetic" within contemporary experience. But as with others in his menagerie, while she has neither immersed herself in his influence nor "swerved" from him, quite, the qualities her poems share with his, both in style and in substance, are finally more than superficial.

The diversity of all these poets in Ashbery's wake, it seems to me, serves not only as testimony to the legacy of his art but as proof of his accessibility. That his influence is not reducible to a single style or group of poets only further argues for how his careful undoing of how we understand ourselves can be liberating. In the same way that his best poems dismantle linguistic tropes, "normal" discursive patterns, time, conventional perspectives, and common images of the world, thereby opening that world up to his readers without pre-ordained determinacy, he leaves for poets after him a wealth of alternatives without granting privileges to any of them. The anxiety that accompanies this rich inheritance, paradoxically, is that such wealth ultimately provides younger poets with nothing but themselves, their own worlds (imagined or otherwise), and their own language with which to work. Given the impression of having everything to choose from, they can become successfully Ashberian only by becoming themselves, not "Ashberian." Any less disarming an attempt to own his voice or embody his poetics is, in reply to my initial question, to misinterpret him.

Notes

1. Robert Richman, "Our 'Most Important' Living Poet," *Commentary* 74, no. 1 (July 1982): 68.
2. In one interview, Ashbery remarks that he hopes readers will see his poetry "as trying to become the openest possible form, something in which anybody can see reflected his own private experiences without them having to be defined or set up for him" (A. Poulin, Jr., "The Experience of Experience: A Conversation with John Ashbery," *Michigan Quarterly Review* 20, no. 3 [Summer 1981]: 251). In another interview he reiterates this idea: "A book is going to be interpreted or misinterpreted in as many ways as there are readers, so why not give them the maximum number of options to misinterpret you, for these are all only interpretations. This seems part of the nature of any kind of interpretation" (Richard Jackson, "The Imminence of a Revelation," in *Acts of Mind: Conversations with Contemporary Poets* [University: University of Alabama Press, 1983], 72).
3. Harold Bloom, *The Anxiety of Influence: A Theory of Poetry* (New York: Oxford University Press, 1973), 25. All further references to this book are cited by page numbers in parentheses in the text.
4. David Lehman credits Ashbery, together with the other New York poets, for having made possible "an influence without angst" through his cultivation of "the other tradition" outside of the canon of Western poets, that is, the avant-garde tradition of such poets as Pierre Reverdy, Henry Green, Raymond Roussel, Gertrude Stein, and others (David Lehman, "The Shield of a Greeting: The Function of Irony in John Ashbery's Poetry," in *Beyond Amazement: New Essays on John Ashbery*, ed. David Lehman [Ithaca: Cornell University Press, 1980], 113–14).
5. Dana Gioia, "Poetry Chronicle," *Hudson Review* 34, no. 4 (Winter 1981–82): 588.
6. John Koethe, "The Absence of a Noble Presence," *Verse* 8, no. 1 (Spring 1991): 25.
7. Ibid., 25–26. Koethe goes on to cite Douglas Crase's *Revisionist* as an exception to his own claims.
8. For a fuller account of Koethe's own theory of what constitutes this "romantic

contestation" in contemporary poetry, see his essay "Contrary Impulses: The Tension between Poetry and Theory," *Critical Inquiry* 18 (Autumn 1991): 64–75.

9. Ashbery made this remark at a poetry reading in New Orleans on March 6, 1987, after I introduced him by quoting, among other comments, Helen Vendler's comment, "He comes from Wordsworth, Keats, Tennyson, Stevens, Eliot. His poems are about love, or time, or age" (Helen Vendler, "Understanding Ashbery," *New Yorker,* March 16, 1981, p. 120).

10. Marjorie Welish, *The Windows Flew Open* (Providence: Burning Deck, 1991), 51.

11. Lee Bartlett, *Talking Poetry: Conversations in the Workshop with Contemporary Poets* (Albuquerque: University of New Mexico Press, 1987), 11. For Waldman's comments, see ibid., 267. For those by Revell, see Donald Revell, "Purists Will Object: Some Meditations on Influence," *Verse* 8, no. 1 (Spring 1991): 16–17. For those by Howe and others, as well as for a full discussion of the influence of Ashbery's early work on the Language poets, see John Shoptaw, "Investigating *The Tennis Court Oath,"* *Verse* 8, no. 1 (Spring 1991): 61–72.

12. Clark Coolidge, *Space* (New York: Harper & Row, 1970), 7.

13. Lehman, "Shield of a Greeting," 101.

14. David Lehman, *Operation Memory* (Princeton: Princeton University Press, 1990), 53–54.

15. At a reading of this poem at Wesleyan University in 1989, Lehman introduced it as a parody of the typical college freshman essay, which uses the terms of logical discourse but says nothing. Nevertheless, for comparison, extract the transitions and the logical phrases from the paragraph in Ashbery's "System" which begins "That's the way it goes" (TP 90) to see a contextual paradigm of Lehman's joke.

16. While Coolidge and Lehman might use a word or a repeated series of phrases on which to build a poem *structurally* (as in Lehman's sestina "Operation Memory," for example), self-reflexivity itself is neither the focus nor the theme of their poems as it often is for Graham.

17. Jorie Graham, *The End of Beauty* (New York: Ecco, 1987), 35–36.

18. Keith Cohen, "Ashbery's Dismantling of Bourgeois Discourse," in *Beyond Amazement,* ed. David Lehman (Ithaca: Cornell University Press, 1980), p. 147.

19. Lehman, "Shield of a Greeting," 103.

20. John Yau, *Radiant Silhouette: New and Selected Work, 1974–1988* (Santa Rosa, Calif.: Black Sparrow, 1989), 17. The poem appears in its original version with different line breaks but mostly the same words in *Sometimes* (New York: Sheep Meadow, 1979), 15.

21. Ibid., 189–95.

22. John Ash, *The Branching Stairs* (Manchester: Carcanet, 1984), 56.

23. John Ash, *Disbelief* (Manchester: Carcanet, 1987), 16.

24. Ibid., 50.

25. Rob Wilson, *American Sublime: The Genealogy of a Poetic Genre* (Madison: University of Wisconsin Press, 1991), 221.

26. Ash, *Branching Stairs,* 39.

27. Douglas Crase, "The Prophetic Ashbery," in *Beyond Amazement,* ed. David Lehman (Ithaca: Cornell University Press, 1980), 64–65.

28. Ash, *Branching Stairs,* 40.

29. See Koethe, "Contrary Impulses," 73, where he writes, "The contestation that poetry enacts is almost bound to embody such characteristic movements as desire, expansiveness, regret, disappointment, despondency, consolation, and resignation: for it is in terms like these that subjectivity defines itself against its objective setting." For Koethe's Ashberian poems, see his book *The Late Wisconsin Spring* (Princeton: Princeton University Press, 1984).

30. Marjorie Welish, *Handwritten* (New York: SUN, 1979), 6.

31. Ibid., 7.

32. Ibid., 18.

33. Ibid., 34.

34. Welish, *Windows Flew Open,* 31. Concerning her ruptured syntax and difficult language, in a comment on the role of vision in poetry, Welish notes that contemporary poetry "is incorrigible relative to the norms of prose. Yet this sort of poetry acknowledges the norm of the prose sentence by transgressing its linguistic conventions with knowing precision," because "poetry tests its vision of knowledge or of being through a language of indirection and ungrammaticality." For Welish, "vision emerges from the potentiality of language to renovate sense," not just from deconstructing it ("Symposium Responses," *Mississippi Review* 19, no. 3 [1991]: 122).

35. Welish, *Windows Flew Open,* 13.

36. Ibid., 53.

37. Emily Dickinson, *Final Harvest: Emily Dickinson's Poems,* ed. Thomas H. Johnson (Boston: Little, Brown, 1961), poems no. 122 (341) and no. 95 (303), respectively, 73, 55.

38. Literally, "American pavilion" can refer either to a tent or enclosure, as at a world's fair, or, in gemcutter's terms, to the bottom surface of a gem cut in the particular prism shape known as the "American cut." I tend to favor the latter reading, in which the spirit is "flayed" or stripped of its surface, as might be a gem.

9 | Periodizing Ashbery and His Influence

Stephen Paul Miller

"SELF-PORTRAIT IN a Convex Mirror" and Watergate are doubles. Just as the Nixon administration intertwines efforts to imperialize the presidency and unite all of the nation's surveillance operations under it, so Ashbery's poem creates a mirror world that traps its subject in his own surveillance or self-portraiture. Just as Nixon's efforts lead his administration to self-destruction through a series of surveillance mishaps that highlight America's ambivalence toward presidential authority, so Ashbery's poem leads a fictive character to destroy himself, his round mirror world, and his and the poem's expected subject matter.

Both the poem and the political scandal undermine the strong and, indeed, monolithic configurations they posit. Ashbery uses the second half of "Self-Portrait in a Convex Mirror" to shatter the first half of the poem's self-replenishing and all-encompassing vision of a subjectivity ensnared by the "surveillance mechanism" of the convex mirror. Similarly, Nixon himself, in the Watergate affair, is ultimately the chief target of his own surveillance mechanism.

Ashbery's poem is first published in the August 1974 issue of *Poetry,* the same month that Richard Nixon resigns his office, and correspondences between the poem and the Watergate drama are as rife as they are obvious. "Self-Portrait in a Convex Mirror" is written in the guise of a meditation that overthrows its object of meditation, and during the midseventies, Nixon serves as an "object of meditation" that is banished.

A discussion of Ashbery's use of the convex mirror trope can shed light on the workings of both phenomena. Put simply, a convex mirror is a perfect surveillance mechanism. An ordinary, flat mirror and a convex mirror of the same size are quite different. The sixteenth-century painter Francesco Parmigianino uses a convex mirror to capture the image of everything in his studio in one view so that he can transmute this likeness appearing on his protruding three-dimensional mirror into one on a two-dimensional curved wooden surface. The result is Parmigianino's famed 1524 *Self-Portrait in a Convex Mirror,* which Ashbery describes in his major long poem of the same name. Parmigianino cannot achieve the all-encompassing effect of his round painting with a flat, conventional mirror. Although a convex mirror creates images that are

obviously distorted and that therefore cannot render the same kind of mimeti-
cally "correct" images that a flat mirror does, nonetheless a convex mirror
must capture everything before it. No one can stand at an angle too oblique
from a convex mirror's perimeter to avoid being observed by another occupant
of the same room.

The convex mirror therefore conveys a notion of supreme surveillance.
Any extensive discussion of Ashbery's "Self-Portrait in a Convex Mirror" must
account for this major feature of convex mirrors. As Ashbery organizes "Self-
Portrait in a Convex Mirror" around the central trope of a surveillance mechanism, so one can also organize a consideration of the Watergate affair around
the central trope of another surveillance mechanism: undisclosed audiotaping.
Furthermore, Parmigianino—in Ashbery's characterization, Richard Nixon—
is undone by his own surveillance systems. Ashbery revives poetic topos in his
poetry, and the Nixon administration seeks to apply almost monarchical presidential powers. What is the connection? Perhaps American culture ends an era
of expansion by constructing surveillance devices that serve to monitor and
delimit American culture through the agency of traditional organizing principles like subject matter and the presidency.

"It seems appropriate to mark the definitive end of the '60's,' in the general
area of 1972–74," says Fredric Jameson.[1] This kind of precise periodization,
however, does not concern me here so much as the wider contention that contemporaneous cultural productions as significant as the ones considered here
should, at some point in the critical literature of each phenomenon, be discussed in relation to one another.

One might easily postulate direct influence. After all, even as referentially
evasive a poet as Ashbery could hardly have avoided the Watergate narrative
that was in the air during this period. One could imagine the Watergate Senate
hearings on Ashbery's television while he was writing "Self-Portrait in a Convex Mirror." However, this avenue of inquiry holds limited promise. First, a
problem of verifiability seems insurmountable. How could one ever be sure
what part of the poem Ashbery was writing when Alexander Butterfield pub-
licly revealed the existence of Nixon's self-espionage? Indeed, in terms of "influence," how crucial was this moment of July 16, 1973? Did not John Dean
earlier, during his televised testimony before the Ervin Senate Committee, note
his suspicion that he was being taped in the Oval Office? Did not Dean's Senate
testimony describe the Nixon administration's proclivity toward surveillance
and its attempts to control all federal surveillance agencies and use them for
base political ends? Was not surveillance and self-surveillance embedded in the
logic of the affair?

Even if Ashbery could be trusted to divulge accurate, day-by-day records
of his progress in the writing of "Self-Portrait in a Convex Mirror," a task
fraught with much room for error in itself, how could we ever be sure how the

poem reflects the poet's responses to the unfolding scandal? How could the poet himself be sure? When I first told Ashbery about my parallel between Watergate and "Self-Portrait in a Convex Mirror," he responded with incredulous humor. "You're comparing me to Nixon," he said jocularly. "Someday you'll get yours. . . . Oh, Nixon was a great president. I wish he was still president." Years later, Ashbery himself cited Oliver North's Iran-contra arms and money flow-chart placard as an inspiration for *Flow Chart* (1990).

John Ashbery is indeed one of our most political poets. His customary evasions of logical and thematic closure allow his poetry to register cultural nuances and patterns that poetries of more overt narrative or thematic intent might overlook. The paradox here of course is that strong partisan and referential designs can limit a literary work's political expressiveness.

By the term "political," I mean here the "political unconscious" as articulated by Fredric Jameson, a concept which has much in common with Louis Althusser's notions of ideological state apparatuses, Jacques Lacan's "real," and Michel Foucault's epistemes. The political unconscious, according to Fredric Jameson, is the ideological limitation embedded in a society's cultural mindset. Because of these limits, or, as Jameson calls them, horizons, all literature is ideological and political. Additionally, all literature is primarily political because it is only through the language of culture, in its broadest sense, that the contradictions of economic and political power and inequity can be dynamically yet unconsciously reconciled. Put simply, culture is a cover-up. However, this does not necessarily involve a conspiracy or even a cause-and-effect relationship as much as a kind of "structural causality."[2] Althusser's term, cited by Jameson, refers to a system of causality in which the whole of a culture expresses itself in its parts as cultural phenomena. For both Jameson and Althusser, the totality of a culture is found everywhere in that culture. However, a critic requires "interpretive master code[s]" to unlock these cultural codes, making clear that culture is indeed cultural and historical, not naturally, divinely, or otherwise transcendentally given.[3]

Jameson maintains that Althusser facilitated an interpretive mode that is not reductive. Since everything that can be interpreted is political, nothing is excluded from a political interpretation. In a radical departure for a Marxist, economic considerations are no longer chief determinants. Theories of how culture produces itself must help account for any given part of the whole. Jameson argues that it is no longer possible to understand cultural and literary phenomena distinct from a theory of the cultural and the social powers that hold them in place. This is not to say that close and specific observation and reading are not necessary, but rather to say that one must not renounce the responsibility to theorize associations within the cultural whole. When one energetically enters this general and theoretical realm, one inevitably opens oneself to criticisms of overgeneralizing and of ignoring laws of causality. Causality does constitute our most comfortable mode of accountability. It allows us to identify those who are "outside" of an effect or a result. But causal analysis also allows us to evade total cultural responsibility and, by extension, ourselves. For too long, literary critics have been too conveniently comfortable with their limitations. We must dare to be general in a manner that does not close and reduce our readings of texts and phenomena but rather sharpens our powers of specificity.

Althusser lists every conceivable manner of culture as "ideological state apparatuses."[4] Every function that it is possible for culture to fulfill, such as education and entertainment, is an ideological state apparatus because cultural phenomena serve the limits of conceivable reality so that this reality does not threaten the existing social hierarchy. This hierarchy is deeply entrenched, protecting the most essential workings of social division, inequity, and repression. Althusser bases his notion of culture as an aggregate of ideological state apparatuses on Lacan's category of the "real order." For Lacan, the real is the unknowable limit on our imaginations and symbolic workings.

According to Althusser, even "revolutionary" art assists these limits. Yet it does so in a way that betrays the political realities that it is based upon. What virtue is there for art in a culture wherein all cultural phenomena serve repressive ends? Art works, Althusser posits, because it "accounts" for modes of cultural production. To perceive art is to distance oneself from the ideological horizons of reality so as to make that reality visible. Althusser elaborates upon the relationship between art and ideologically determined reality:

> This relationship is not one of identity but one of difference. I believe that the peculiarity of art is to "make us see" [*nous donner à voir*], "make us perceive," "make us feel," something which alludes to reality. . . . What art makes us *see,* and therefore gives to us in the form of *"seeing,"* *"perceiving,"* and *"feeling"* (which is not the form of *knowing*) is the *ideology* from which it is born, in which it bathes, from which it detaches itself as art, and to which it *alludes.* . . . They make us "perceive" (but not know) in some sense *from the inside,* by an *internal distance,* the very ideology in which they are held.[5]

Successful art, even abstract art, offers its audience the opportunity to note the workings of culture. Thus art can be a kind of spy. Indeed, since art is inescapably political, overt content is not necessary, and abstract art, better camouflaged, can be a more successful double agent.

I am thus not arguing that Ashbery's poetry is rawly realistic. More significantly, I contend that a typical Ashbery poem is effective as a poem and cultural product because it clarifies the workings of that poem's historical period and our present understanding of that period. As Harold Bloom notes, Ashbery's poetry is often organized by the evocation of an Emersonian "Beautiful Necessity."[6] By surrendering to a given reality with abandon, the opposition between determinism and freedom is bypassed. The achievement of "Soonest Mended," Bloom says of one of Ashbery's great poems of the sixties, "is to have told a reductive truth, yet to have raised it out of reductiveness by a persistence masked as the commonal."[7] "Soonest Mended" achieves a liberated and liberating complexity by accepting simplicity, yet seeing through it.

Bloom attributes this freedom within limitations to an acceptance of approaching middle age. Undeniably, "Soonest Mended" concludes upon a tone of acceptance. The speaker, however, accepts a planned regression within his middle-aged years. He accepts and even welcomes "the charity of the hard moments as they are doled out" (DDS 19).

> To reduce all this to a small variant,
> To step free at last, minuscule on the gigantic plateau—
> This was our ambition: to be small and clear and free.
>   (17)

But the speaker also implements "fantasy" and "loose" (18) imprecision into his limitations:

>   this is action, this not being sure, this careless
> Preparing, sowing the seeds crooked in the furrow,
> Making ready to forget, and always coming back
> To the mooring of starting out, that day so long ago.
>   (19)

The speaker associates wisdom, in addition to "action," with youth:

>   probably thinking not to grow up
> Is the brightest kind of maturity for us, right now at any rate.
>   (19)

The "right now" of "Soonest Mended" is the midsixties. The poem negotiates with the romantic imperative of its era. It begins by alluding to life outside mainstream culture: "Barely tolerated, living on the margin / In our technological society, we were always having to be rescued" (17). Within this framework, pseudoreassurance recurrently arrives in the form of a comic-book-like hero:

>   there always came a time when
> Happy Hooligan in his rusted green automobile
> Came plowing down the course, just to make sure everything was O.K.,
> Only by that time we were in another chapter and confused
> About how to receive this latest piece of information.
> *Was* it information?
>   (17)

Conventional, industrial ("a rustling of coils," "rusted, green automobile") re-assurances are no longer credible in the sixties. "We" are in the context of "an-other chapter." What the previous age has to tell us is not applicable and in-deed may not even be "information." We are little served by our former selves: "Weren't we rather acting this out / For someone else's benefit?" (17). Accus-tomed reconciliations lose their bases.

As "summer's energy wanes," so does the desire to simplify:

> no longer
> May we make the necessary arrangements, simple as they are.
> Our star was brighter perhaps when it had water in it.
> Now there is no question even of that, but only
> Of holding on to the hard earth so as not to get thrown off.
> (17)

Glamorous stars no longer hold "water." The speaker reconciles himself to his crisis of disillusionment by noting a psychic opening that is to be the poem's turning point. At the end of the first of two verse paragraphs, the speaker owns up to the limits of his discourse:

> We are all talkers
> It is true, but underneath the talk lies
> The moving and not wanting to be moved, the loose
> Meaning, untidy and simple like a threshing floor.
> (18)

After this "untidy and simple" observation, "the clarity of the rules dawn[s]" "for the first time." The speaker is "shock[ed]" by his alienation: "*They* were the players, and we who had struggled at the game / Were merely spectators." This realization comes "almost a quarter of a century later" (18). Since "Soon-est Mended" is a midsixties poem, this alienation begins with the cold war. What we think of as the heart of the sixties lies at the chronological center of the cold-war era. In the sixties, realities put forward by the military-industrial complex are severely doubted. Appropriately, the speaker appeals to "fantasy."

We live in a fantasy with very real applications, a "fantasy [that] makes it ours, a kind of fence-sitting / Raised to the level of an esthetic ideal" (18). One thinks of Ashbery's poetic development. Bloom maintains that *The Dou-ble Dream of Spring* is Ashbery's first mature collection of poetry not to rely on ellipses, or the apparent omission of subject matter. The critic attributes this to Ashbery's more open confrontation with the American Romantic tradi-tion. I would explain this observation in a manner that does not contradict Bloom's explanation but rather accounts for it in a more encompassing and political context. The sixties is a moment when the American Romantic tradi-tion seemed pervasive in counterculture America. Ashbery's native tradition approaches him from the "outside." His poems can talk more directly to his audience. With *The Double Dream of Spring*, Ashbery's poetry becomes more openly Romantic and less disjunctively modernist. We are reminded of the difficulties inherent in Trilling's dubbing of the sixties as a "modernism on the streets." Modernism can so easily be linked with an elitism that is counter to sixties ideals, if not realities.

As "solid" "reality" fades, the speaker no longer needs to hide his uncertainty. In the sixties, it becomes more positive not to define one's identity or be very certain of what one knows:

> These were moments, years,
> Solid with reality, faces, nameable events, kisses, heroic acts,
> But like the friendly beginning of a geometrical progression
> Not too reassuring, as though meaning could be cast aside some day
> When it had been outgrown. Better, you said, to stay cowering
> Like this in the early lessons, since the promise of learning
> Is a delusion, and I agreed, adding that
> Tomorrow would alter the sense of what had already been learned,
> That the learning process is extended in this way, so that from this standpoint
> None of us ever graduates from college,
> For time is an emulsion.
>   (18–19)

The speaker coyly identifies himself with college-aged baby boomers. Time and age are, after all, liquid. Conformity to a fantastic reality is no conformity at all. We have learned the arts of "conforming to the rules and living / Around the home" from "avatars" (19), suggesting spiritual leaders, such as Meher Baba, who were relatively popular in America during the sixties for their appeals to an admixture of the everyday and the apocalyptic. Similarly, "Soonest Mended" achieves a "hazardous" romanticism by positing the incredible as a given. After all, if the sixties were as an age of the antihero, it follows that heroism could be found everywhere.

It is difficult to say that "Soonest Mended" could only have been written in the sixties. Much of what we identify as the sixties is of course filtered through other decades. However, "Soonest Mended" uniquely synthesizes motifs and tropes that are particularly strong in the mid and late sixties. It attains a kind of originality by accepting and focusing on its historical material. The more the poem accepts its affinities to the wider cultural text, the freer and more unique it seems.

I do not claim to be able to determine what Ashbery intends to signify. In terms of influence, it would be possible to engage in such source findings, since three of the younger poets that I discuss—David Shapiro, David Lehman, and

Thomas Fink—have written about Ashbery. However, I do not claim that Ashbery directly influenced another poet that I discuss, Cherríe Moraga. I claim a wider cultural connection among all of these poets.

As may be apparent by now, the writings of Michel Foucault establish a theoretical basis for relating my close readings of poetry to cultural conditions. Foucault meticulously studies textual details to construe the code of a hidden but prevailing epistemological framework that allows a text to function within its respective time and culture. Foucault terms these epistemological systems epistemes.

Epistemes form the rules and limits through which a culture's modes of knowledge and culture are made possible. Hence, epistemes are detectable in all cultural phenomena. But since, according to Foucault, we discover epistemes through a close textual scrutiny that is attentive to tropological regularities and configurations, epistemes are particularly observable in poetry when we juxtapose poetic texts with contexts that are perhaps unrelated to any authorial intentions. Foucault was aware that epistemes can be used as an overly reductive tool. He thus pointed out that epistemes are in constant flux. Since the historian must be sensitive to small distinctions, close reading is essential. As Ashbery's "Fragment" puts it:

> It would not be good to examine these ages
> Except for sun flecks, little, on the golden sand
> And coming to reappraisal of the distance.
>   (DDS 81)

The analysis of epistemes within relatively small units of time is an antidote to the uncritical synopses of post–World War II American culture prevalent in the press and the media today. Perhaps our most important political work is to render ourselves members of a community who are critically helpful and accountable to one another in all facets of our public discourse. What do we as critics, aesthetic issues aside, really do if we do not build communicative bridges about all manner of cultural phenomena among ourselves, students, and the larger public?

It is not my intention to pin poems too neatly to a decade. Of course, decades do overlap. However, it would be more misleading to avoid what they represent than to grasp them within a problematized framework. How can a critic ignore the tropes and mind-sets prevailing in an era? It is the critic's job to bring the political unconscious to consciousness in a manner that must be unique and seemingly fictional because it has never existed as consciousness before. According to Jameson, history is text. Yet history is not a text until it is made so by those who interpret it. A critic acting on this premise will always be

faulted when a creative reading is equated to a false reading. Jameson's words
in this regard bear citation:

> I happen to feel that no interpretation can be effectively disqualified on its
> own terms by a simple enumeration of inaccuracies or omissions, or by a
> list of unanswered questions. Interpretation is not an isolated act, but takes
> place within a Homeric battlefield, on which a host of interpretive options
> are either openly or implicitly in conflict. If the positivistic conception of
> philological accuracy be the only alternative, then I would much prefer
> to endorse the current provocative celebration of strong misreadings over
> weak ones. As the Chinese proverb has it, you use one ax handle to hew
> another: in our context, only another, stronger interpretation can overthrow
> and practically refute an interpretation already in place.[8]

It is too easy to discount history by saying that its application is too obvious. It sometimes seems that we must strenuously labor to keep recent history
and Ashbery's poetry from shedding light on one another. For example, few
long poems emblematize and explain the sixties as well as "Fragment," another Ashbery poem of the midsixties. One might apply this passage to both
the poem and its era:

> That coming together of masses coincides
> With that stable emptiness . . .
> . . . .
>   winking with it
> To tablelands of disadumbrated feeling
> Treetops whose mysterious hegemony concerns
> Merely, by opening around factors of accident
> So as to install miscellaneous control.
>   (DDS 79)

Ashbery's "Fragment" describes its own "mysterious hegemony," based in large
part upon avoiding a too explicit hegemony and continuity or "coming together of masses coincid[ing] / With that stable emptiness" (79). The sixties
would not have been possible without general prosperity. This prosperity, however, is met with ambivalence. In "Fragment," the articulation of an unspeci-
fied, empty merger is perhaps a product of "disadumbrat[ing] feeling," which
is affected by the paradoxical mix of order and disorder in the "install[ation]"
of "miscellaneous control." Indeed, fifteen pages later, when the poem says
"Anomaly had spoken" (94), there is no doubt but that the poem has demonstrated this.

    This anomaly is also an irreconcilable distance between lovers. The speaker
often addresses a beloved that he seems destined to lose. He takes solace, however, in the notion that an impending reality will bring his love back to him.
The poem, however, sometimes loses faith in the power of wish fulfillment.

"Fragment" exposes the inherent contradictions of a sixties counterculture that questions the surplus production of the Western consumerist culture that it relies on. An inability to transcend consumerist values was never more acutely felt than in the sixties. Apocalyptic prospects cannot fructify. We are separated from the day's "flame-colored phenomena." "Expressions of hope" are "too late." The poem foresees the sixties to be like a love affair that goes nowhere: "This information was like a road no one ever took." Millionaires are "bent on turning everyday affairs into something tragic" (88).

Jameson speculates that during the sixties our economy was stuck in a prolonged transition from industrial to postindustrial, service, and multinational modes. Economic systems lost regulatory power. A sense of economic reality was thus suspended, and all things appeared possible. By the midseventies, however, reality had irrefutably returned.

Jameson's premise, whether it is correct or not, speaks to our mythology of the late sixties and following periods. Each era can be described by its relationship to "reality." We seemed to move from the suspended reality of the sixties, to a return to and ambivalence toward reality in the seventies, to an apparent eighties' affirmation of reality and a contradictory denial of its responsibilities, and to the severe disappointment and anger of the nineties. We have not yet adjusted to the promises and the conflicts of the sixties. It sometimes seems that everything was thrown up in the air then and has not yet fallen. Clint Eastwood's film *In the Line of Fire* (1993), for instance, plays upon this cultural suspicion. Playing the character of a secret service agent who had been President Kennedy's favorite protector, Eastwood claims that Kennedy was "different" from the fictional president he is now defending. Indeed, he claims that everything was different then. Now there is nothing but game-playing. He wonders if the world would still hold definitive meaning if he had been able to prevent Kennedy's assassination. The agent's alienation is so great that he attaches little import in itself to protecting the president. More important, he feels that he must do his job as if it had tangible meaning. He and the would-be assassin played by John Malkovich differentiate themselves from one another in this respect. The professional assassin, trained by the CIA after Kennedy's death, sees what he is trying to do as a mere game. Eastwood's character insists to him that doing a job is not the same as playing a game. Reacting against sixties and postsixties ruptures with reality, he elegantly expresses nostalgia for presixties reality.

The sixties can be described as an unguarded gap between two dominant capitalistic modes, before capitalism coheres into a multinational system that more seamlessly and less obviously engulfs the world. In the words of "Fragment," the sixties are a "multicolored / Parentheses." It is "love in short periods" that "puts everything out of focus" (81).

"Fragment" begins with a simple description of the end of an order that occurs near the start of spring: "The last block is closed in April." "Intrusions" come between the speaker and the object of his address, his apparent former lover. His lover's seeming permission will elude him. He will attain only "sympathy." The poem's remorse is here reminiscent of Ashbery's poetry of the early and mid fifties, collected in *Some Trees* (1956). Much of this poetry seems to mourn the irreconcilability of society's ever coming to terms with gay identity in McCarthyite America. One thinks of "the men" in "*Le livre est sur la table*" who "live in boxes. / The sea protects them like a wall" (SPs 28). In "Fragment," however, the speaker finds powerful solace in a supposition that is similar to the aesthetic "fence-sitting" (DDS 18) of "Soonest Mended" yet also maneuvers against a closeted affection and identity. "Fragment" posits a "moment's commandment" that does not allow any room for the decision to "withdraw" (78) love.

The second of the poem's fifty ten-line stanzas posits a new and happier "reality," in which his lover's face is "the only real beginning." The speaker moves "beyond the gray." He escapes the closed system of "friendship / With self alone." He "open[s] out." What seems like "fiction" sustains him. By the beginning of the third stanza, he turns another "page." "Other sounds are heard." "Propositions hitherto omitted" (78) are entertained. It is possible to "look at it all / Inside out." The solidity of a "statue" is made of an "emblem" (79) foreshadowing the seventies phenomenon of T-shirts with logos.

In the next stanza, the speaker extols his "inability to accept" the "fact" of his lover's absence. He has "power" over his lover, whom he "reflect[s]." In the face of this willful denial of hard and fast reality, "the imagination creates / A claim" virtually to everything. "Factors of accident" assist the imagination to maintain a fantastic "control." "Best to break off / All further choice" (79), says the speaker, who is radicalized around his recognition of an incredible reality. After the "cold collapse" of outmoded reality, we can "water" "into the past with its religious / Messages and burials." With this appreciation of ancient rituals, "A warm and near unpolished entity could begin" (80).

By the seventh stanza, we have clearly moved beyond a "cut-and-dried symposium way of seeing things." However, the speaker must account for the abundance that enables his discourse, his stance, and the economy. There is a "hollow" at the core of the poem's "distribution center." In this hollow are the "ghosts of the streets." Alluding to the Vietnam War, the poem touches on "death in its various forms" and then mentions "the wars abroad" that spoil "the peace / At home." We have nothing to "bear" outside the "surrounding neighborhood" (80). Wars of expansion are debilitating, and the speaker takes comfort in his powerlessness. The "only world is an inside one" that is "fashioned out of external phenomena." "New kinds of fun" assure us of a "certain future." "Satisfaction," however, can only be "phantom." There is nothing but the "active memorial." "Commas are dropped," and "convention gapes"

(81). The poem talks of the outward romanticism of being "all heart and all skin." "Change" is "around us" (82). "Our habits" are confused and "ask us for instructions" (83).

In the nineteenth stanza, "reserves of anxiety and restlessness" become more prominent in the poem. The American "Empire" encounters "hesitation" in its pattern of "possession and possessiveness." There is "so much air of change, but always and nowhere / A cave" (84). By the twenty-fifth stanza "The apotheosis had sunk away." In the twenty-sixth stanza, "The change is more complete than ever before," but it is a "pessimistic lighting up" that is "demanding more than ever to be considered for full / Substance" (86). The poem foresees a return to reality. Curiously, we have learned asceticism from the sixties: "You see, it is / Not wrong to have nothing" (89). Yet this reductivism only facilitates an imaginative life that, in the forty-second stanza, is "consumed" by more ominous future organization in "A surprise dragging the signs / Of no peace after it" (92). Near the end of the poem, the speaker acknowledges his inability to control the love that controls him: "The words sung in the next room are unavoidable" (94).

"Fragment" is Ashbery's most penetrating analysis of the sixties. It is a particularly difficult poem to read when one ignores its periodicity. "The stance," the poem announces to those outside it, "to you / Is a fiction, to me a whole." The poem wrestles between two aspects of sixties expansion. On the one hand, a booming economy makes it possible to denounce an industrial work ethos. "Permissiveness" now has a mainstream currency and no longer "fall[s] back toward recondite ends." "Reality" is "providential." There are "new options" (78), "new kinds of fun" (81), "much air of change" (84), "new experience" (86), and "new passages of being among the correctness / Of familiar patterns" (78). On the other hand, expansion "instantaneously" produces the escalation of an imperialist war. Consumerist "possession" and "possessiveness" create an uncritical "empire." "The grave of authority / Matches wits with upward-spinning lemon spirals" (84).

> Our daily imaginings are swiftly tilted down to
> Death in its various forms. We cannot keep the peace
> At home, and at the same time be winning wars abroad.
>   (80)

"Fragment," like America of the sixties, is never able to reconcile this conflict. However, it manages "to isolate the kernel of / Our imbalance" (82).

The "moment" of the sixties—recalling the crucial introductory phrase of "Fragment" ("a moment's commandment")—produces a sense of unlimited expansion because, metaphorically speaking, the hard-and-fast laws of standards of economics are temporarily suspended. As "A Fragment" puts it, the "day" is "oblong" (78). Limitation is defied, reality is irrelevant, and an exhilarating furlough from it is granted. Indefinite romantic ideals seem more authentic than the eroding realities of industrialism and the cold war.

We associate the sixties with wild expansion. However, the seventies are considered a period of consolidation and codification in which the contradictions of the sixties and reality must be faced. Appropriately, until the midseventies, Ashbery easily can be characterized as an abstract poet whose poems eschew definitive topics. I use the term "abstract" to describe a poem that does not clearly contain reference and subject matter. In this sense, it does not matter whether the topic of an "unabstract" poem is philosophical or unphilosophical and concrete.

Abstraction, in the manner that I use it, and referentiality and subject matter may be considered to be on a spectrum and not opposites that exclude one another. Furthermore, abstraction and topos are perhaps produced more by readings than by texts. Nevertheless, it is my intention here to discuss our tendencies to attribute qualities of abstraction and subject matter when reading the poems that this essay concerns. I am not in these pages preoccupied with whether the site of the dialectic of abstraction and topos is primarily situated within the text or the reader.

I set up the implications of abstraction and the connotations of referentiality and topos as binary oppositions. Abstraction, here, suggests the absence of an agreed-upon reality and an emphasis upon process over product, and subject matter contrastingly suggests a consensus reality and the presence of a set-external reality that is not dependent upon any process or play of language. True, the problematizing of topos is a constant in Ashbery's poetry. However, until the infinitely reproductive mirror play of "Self-Portrait in a Convex Mirror," a definite theme does not provide an obvious focus that can be sustained throughout Ashbery's earlier long poems. Of course, Ashbery's poetry before "Self-Portrait in a Convex Mirror" is not without content. However, the subject matter in almost all of his major poetry before his famed 1974 poem is extremely difficult to trace. (The few exceptions, such as "The Instruction Manual" [SoTr 26–30] are short poems.) Even "Fragment" notably lacks a consistent unifying emblem. Indeed, "Fragment" often alludes to its inability to see a totality outside itself: "Seen from inside all is / Abruptness" (DDS 80). But the subject matter of "Self-Portrait in a Convex Mirror" is ostensibly clearly discernible and visible—in large part helping to account for its popularity. Although "Self-Portrait in a Convex Mirror" is not limited to a consideration of Francesco Parmigianino's *Self-Portrait in a Convex Mirror,* it is nonetheless a meditation upon Parmigianino's painting.

In "Self-Portrait in a Convex Mirror," Parmigianino is trapped within his own mirror creation, which must eventually be destroyed. This is strikingly similar to the manner in which Nixon's espionage systems eventually undo his presidency. I have here examined similarities between Ashbery's Parmigianino and the Richard Nixon of the Watergate affair, as well as the broader cultural context of the midseventies.[9] I argue that just as "Self-Portrait in a Convex Mirror" revives poetic subject matter only to discredit it, the Watergate affair has its roots in the Nixon administration's efforts to exert vast and unchecked presidential powers. Nixon attempts to bypass the "credibility gap" only eventually to magnify and fall prey to it. Nixon is not a villain of history so much as a cultural production that reflects us all. Even if we determine him to be a villain, it still behooves us to understand him in terms of our culture.

Similarly, Ashbery presents his most coherent topos and subsequently undermines it. After all, if the midseventies can be said to codify unaccounted-for aspects of the sixties, the midseventies could then be said to use organizational and surveillance mechanisms to account for what is previously unexplained. However, these organizing instruments of surveillance must themselves be accounted for; as Nixon is undone by his own surveillance mechanisms, so is Parmigianino in Ashbery's poem.

Ashbery's poem about the surveillance tool of the convex mirror initially argues that the human condition is a closed one of self-imprisonment:

> The soul establishes itself.
> But how far can it swim out through the eyes
> And still return safely to its nest? The surface
> Of the mirror being convex, the distance increases
> Significantly; that is enough to make the point
> That the soul is a captive, treated humanely, kept
> In suspension, unable to advance.
>   (SPs 188)

Given this midseventies emphasis on limitation, it is not surprising that the mirror's backing serves as transformative trope. A mirror is, after all, a dynamic antithesis between a transparent window and an opaque "wall." After the round backing of the mirror, which is said to "island" the static scene, is mentioned, it is accounted for and breaks. This displacement of a limiting presence is the ground for "dreams and inspirations on an unassigned / Frequency" (202).

This presence can be likened to the "wall" or barrier aspect of the backing that enables the mirror world of Ashbery's poem. "Dreams and inspirations" suggest the "window" that the poem both refutes and affirms. If we think of referentiality as a kind of wall or horizon of possibility, we can see "Self-Portrait in a Convex Mirror" as a strong precursor of a mideighties poem from Shapiro's *House (Blown Apart)*. (My segue between "Self-Portrait in a Convex Mirror" and "A Wall" is deliberately textual. The mideighties poems that I treat are a somewhat arbitrary selection, since any mideighties poem will be culturally linked to any midseventies poem. This is not to say that I do not positively value the poems that I discuss as culturally illuminating.)

"A Wall"

I have the right not to represent it.

Though every brick is clear as a doubt
Clear as a tear and a mistranslation
Through the window as through December fourth
The clarity of the facts like light snow
After bad dreams forgotten partly whole
And of the whole a part
One may forget so intently you might write

"I cannot now respond to this abstraction
Unshareable satire, courtly dream, and so forth
Sorry, not sorry" But try as I shall not to bump
Or bash it or lift a camera to a sill
To penetrate a copy or to think I have invented it

A banal impossibility as night is written
In pages splitting into analogies like walls
I see in this quiet sunlit stylization
Holding forth onto a garden enclosed and yet at times
Open in a melancholy necessary morning:

A wall I neither restored nor could destroy.[10]

The speaker in "A Wall" confronts a wall of agreement and naive realism. Ironically, in this confrontation, the poem finds a topic, ultimately arguing that it is in the resistance to topos that poetry discovers its subject matter.

The poem opens with a strongly reflexive comment that is set off from the rest of the poem as if it were a topic sentence: "I have the right not to represent it." This "right" is apparently derived from the necessities of poetry's means of production. The speaker points out that every "brick" that can be represented is clear as a "doubt" or "mistranslation," even though some may "write" "intently" and call for such "banal" intent and originality by dismissing "abstraction."

Shapiro characterizes reality as one of many "analogies like walls" that are "written / In pages splitting." However, Shapiro's poem is not a simple valorization of the poetic powers—a "quiet sunlit stylization / Holding forth onto a garden enclosed." Instead, Shapiro ends "A Wall" by positing another wall more necessary than the previously described walls of metaphor that can be said to be built of "brick[s] of doubt." The poem concludes with a single line that seems to respond to the poem's demarcated opening line: "I have the right not to represent it." "A wall I neither restored nor could destroy" significantly modifies the impact of the first line of "A Wall." The speaker does not now appear to master what is valuable, although we know this by the speaker's own admission. Nonetheless, the poem seems to reach its enabling limits. These limits make possible the poet's apparent "invention." Shapiro's wall functions like Ashbery's backing of the mirror.

However, Shapiro's "Wall" sketches a clearer and more intensely poignant reconciliation than Ashbery's "Self-Portrait in a Convex Mirror" of the overlapping functions of abstraction and realism. Shapiro's poem suggests a period that consciously needs to integrate the necessities of epistemological agreement with the seeming authenticity of the poet's play of linguistic experiences and imaginings.

Shapiro rigorously clips his phrases—each phrase taking on the quality of a light "brick." A paradoxically spiritual materiality is emphasized. The problematic of abstraction and realism is given a place of extreme value. Reality must be met as a tropological limit. "A Wall" exists in, and makes visible, the modes of cultural production in the age of Reagan (who, like Nixon, I do not conceptualize as a favorite bad guy of history but rather a production of our culture), wherein ideology is seen as "reality" and the tropological underpinnings of reality are repressed. Wish fulfillment and surplus spending abound.

Taking a route that can be termed the reverse of the more theoretically inclined Shapiro, David Lehman's "New York City, 1974" mixes poetic abstraction with realism by employing the latter rather than the former as a base.[11] However, this Lehman poem analyzes, practices, and parodies the role of memory in constructing an "objective" reality.

"New York City, 1974" can be said to be a revised memory of "Self-Portrait in a Convex Mirror." Of course, cultural productions tend to revise the cultural productions of preceding eras. The obviousness of this fact sometimes causes us not to apply it.

Ashbery's 1974 poem equates a secretive and powerful, yet declining, New York City of the midseventies with a mirror backing that eventually collapses. In Ashbery's poem, New York depicts a crumbling basis for a reality principle in crisis:

> The shadow of the city injects its own
> Urgency: . . .
> . . . .
>   . . . New York
> Where I am now, which is a logarithm
> Of other cities. Our landscape
> Is alive with filiations, shuttlings;
> Business is carried on by look, gesture,

> Hearsay. It is another life to the city,
> The backing of the looking glass.
>   (SPs 195)

As the third of five poems in the last section of Lehman's most recent book, *Operation Memory* (1990), "New York City, 1974" extends Ashbery's trope.

The volume's title poem concludes both its suite of poems and the book. "Operation Memory" presents memory as an arduous task.[12] In a Kafkaesque metaphor, the production of our memory of the last twenty years becomes the primary enterprise of that twenty-year period. This enterprise uncannily is depicted as both a military operation and an academic lifestyle. They are combined in a kind of "intelligence work":

>   To his separate bed
> Each soldier went . . .
>   And there I was, in the middle
> Of a recession, in the middle of a strange city, between jobs
> And apartments and wives. Nobody told me the gun was loaded.
>
>   All my friends had jobs
> As professional liars, and most had partners who were good in bed.
> What did I have? Just this feeling of always being in the middle
> Of things, and the luck of looking younger than fifty.
>
> At dawn I returned to draft headquarters. I was eighteen
> And counting backwards. The interviewer asked one loaded
> Question after another, such as why I often read the middle
> Of novels, ignoring their beginnings and their ends. When
> Had I decided to volunteer for intelligence work?

The speaker often alludes to being a writer and a poet. This metaphoric fusion of the lives of the soldier and the writer responds to the first poem of this sequence: "Vietnam Memorial,"[13] wherein the speaker states that his life had been predicated upon an evasion of fighting in the Vietnam War:

> We who didn't go to Vietnam
> Planned our lives around it just the same.

The poem suggests that life still concerns a complex sense of absence from and presence in the Vietnam War:

> Some numbers never came up.
> We were the lucky ones. The ones who went
> Were forgotten. And I am thinking of them today,
> Thinking of death in Vietnam, and the dead bodies
> That might have been ours.

"Operation Memory," wherein the dubious reality of a life of evasion must be made to cohere, is a logical outcome of, for the speaker, the surrogate basis of the Vietnam War and the post–Vietnam War culture evoked by "Vietnam Memorial."

New York appears in a narrative about the project of remembrance, New York, in "New York City, 1974," as the crossroads of a trip through a void— the midpoint or "backing of the mirror" between the intangible realities of the sixties and the necessary fictions of the eighties. This middle poem in the poetic sequence that concludes *Operation Memory* chronicles a completely open and poetic approach to life:

> Whatever worked: that was the principle
> Behind our cryptic aphorisms, haikus that refused
> To be epigrams.

And yet, in an uncanny allusion to Watergate, Lehman suggests an underpinning that contradicts this kind of operational open-endedness. After all, must there not be some objective standard, some sense of "evidence" that renders interesting an infinite set of particulars:

> If everything is evidence, everything is admissible,
> And my tape recorder proves it.
>
> I wrote
> Everything down, as though it would otherwise disappear,
> As though everything was meant to end up in a book.

The romps of a group of literary acquaintances in "New York City, 1974" are contextualized by the speaker's comment about himself and a friend: "Neither of us knew what he wanted to do with his life." Ultimately, these strong doubts cannot be separated from poetry and its possibilities, and they are reflected in the ingeniously coherent narrative that Lehman constructs by means of thematically disjunctive poetic sequencing. Lehman's narrative navigates the limits of narration, at times seeming to be stranded yet eventually finding new streams on its beaches.

Lehman, like Shapiro, dynamically uses the ambivalent bifurcation between abstraction and realism that "Self-Portrait in a Convex Mirror" powerfully formulates, and the two younger poets find grounds for the rapprochement of these opposing terms. Indeed, Ashbery's poem itself goes far in explicating and defetishizing the false opposition between the referential and the nonreferential. Shapiro and Lehman react to "Self-Portrait in a Convex Mirror" with rich and startling admixtures of the "real" and the "abstract." Speaking broadly, one might hypothesize that serious art and healthy approaches to living must now integrate the lessons of disjunctive modernism with an awareness that the realistic imperative of recognizability requires abstraction. However, this kind of postmodern poetry, unlike modernism, makes no implicit claim that art is an antenna. For better or worse, modernism has been distributed throughout society, and cultural authority is necessarily in a tenuous position.

There are a multitude of fine mideighties poets who should be represented in this regard. I will discuss only two more of them here by focusing briefly on "And Then There's Us" by Cherríe Moraga and "Minimalist" by Thomas Fink.

Moraga's "And Then There's Us" is a short poetic explanation of its title:

> for LaRue and Elvira
>
> Nobody would believe it
> to look at us
> how our families'
> histories
> converge.
>
> > Two women on opposite south
> > ends of the continent
> > working cotton
> > for some man
>
> > > Nobody would believe it.
>
> > Their backs
> > > and this country
> > collapsing
> > to make room for us together.[14]

The poem's speaker addresses two women. She observes that because they look so different, probably racially, that "Nobody would believe" their convergent familial lineage. It is implied that ancestors of the two women whom the speaker addresses are from the pre–Civil War South and prerevolutionary Mexico. The exploitation of their labor, as depicted by a prototypical female ancestor, has paradoxically contributed to the "collapse" of their countries. This collapse engenders an enchanted though actual "room for us together" for the three women.

The construction of race is confronted more frankly and easefully than would have been customary in the midseventies. The race consciousness promoted by "And Then There's Us" is too complicated to be called merely interracial. "Self-Portrait in a Convex Mirror" points toward a "burn[ing] up" of convention[s] for the constructed but "necessary" "roles we have to play." In Moraga, group identification is paradoxically crucial yet acknowledged to be a cultural construct.

Thomas Fink's "Minimalist" is an elegant, syntactically experimental poetic statement upon the many within the one:

handwriting like blush odor
you demand stringent marble

think edge—
square enough empire—
platform atom limn

again tenant shirks
contract—
guess edit perennial—
unsnared equation predicament

swarm interstices.[15]

The poem's opening couplet sets up an impersonal surface reality that makes one think of the marble of a tombstone. From this wish for the death of the personality and the ego, the absent subject is a "think[ing] edge" that through the construction of a "platform atom," or provisional ego, is able to sketch or "limn" an "empire" for itself that is securely if provisionally "square enough." However, there is an inevitable lapse in the unstated "contract" and this always already "again tenant." The contract must be "perennial[ly]" edited through "guess[es]." This constantly unpredictable "unsnared equation predicament" implies a wild metaphorizing force. The multiplicity of the effects of this force "swarm" the small spaces between our writerly and our mental processes.

The first stanza can be read as a relatively conventional sentence, with the subject "handwriting." The second stanza starts with an imperative that implies the subject "you." The imperative voice dominates the rest of the poem, charging the seemingly unsyntactic poem and equating the second person to "handwriting." In effect, "Minimalist" writes with an implied directness of address. Fink weaves a poem from the exquisite confusions between speaker and addressee in "Self-Portrait in a Convex Mirror."

"Self-Portrait in a Convex Mirror" works aesthetically because it is "true" to its era. This is of course not a truth of naive realism. Its authenticity can rather be attributed to the strength with which it "sounds like" or "makes visible" how culture works. "Self-Portrait in a Convex Mirror" may indeed alternatively be understood as a poet's attempt simultaneously to create and articulate his contemporary voice, pertinence, subject, and self. Those projects inevitably entail a clarification of the cultural moment. "Self-Portrait in a Convex Mirror" clarifies the dynamic tensions of the midseventies, and perhaps of the last quarter of a century, more strongly than any other poem. It is therefore appropriate to consider poets as diverse as Shapiro, Lehman, Moraga, and

Fink in the light of Ashbery. Although direct influence is not as likely between Ashbery and Moraga as between Ashbery and the three other younger poets, Moraga subtly uses poetic disjunctions of contexts and line breaks to disseminate her words.

Moraga's speaker, nonetheless, uses a kind of face-to-face conversation with her audience as a powerful tool, and unlike the four other poets discussed, she does not overtly both allude to the poem's self-reflexiveness and shatter its discursive and fictive illusions. These pursuits, and their problematizations, link Ashbery, Shapiro, and Fink, who constantly call the reader's attention to the reading process by writing skillfully nuanced poetries that are balanced between mimesis and antimimesis, thematic representation and sharp disjunction. Such border poetries require more than not making sense. These poets produce a rich language (with a small *l*) poetry that keeps its edge by owning up to an implicit responsiveness to and responsibility for its poetic effects and connotations. They stay close to both a sense of language as a material and language as a promise to represent objects of desire. However, these representations and desires are always adjuncts to what one might consider "good" writing—that is, writing which is ingeniously true to its medium. In this manner, our understandings, feelings, and emotions are trued through poetry. In brief, they dynamically use the ambivalent bifurcation between abstraction and realism that "Self-Portrait in a Convex Mirror" powerfully formulates, and they find grounds for the rapprochement of these opposing terms. Indeed, Ashbery's poem itself goes far in explicating and defetishizing the false opposition between the referential and the nonreferential that some of the more seemingly progressive poets of the seventies and the eighties valorized, wishing to repeat without acknowledgment what Ashbery and others accomplished before the midseventies. Poets like Shapiro, Lehman, Moraga, and Fink, however, react to the poetic and cultural significance of "Self-Portrait in a Convex Mirror" with rich and startling admixtures of the "real" and the "abstract."

Notes

1. Fredric Jameson, *The Ideologies of Theory,* vol. 2, *Syntax of History* (Minneapolis: University of Minnesota Press, 1988), 205.

2. Fredric Jameson, *The Political Unconscious: Narrative as a Socially Symbolic Act* (Ithaca: Cornell University Press, 1981), 31.

3. Ibid., 10.

4. Louis Althusser, *Lenin and Philosophy,* trans. Ben Brewster (New York: Monthly Review Press, 1971), 42.

5. Ibid., 222–23.

6. Harold Bloom, *Figures of Capable Imagination* (New York: Seabury Press, 1976), 189.

7. Ibid., 187.

8. Jameson, *Political Unconscious*, 13.

9. Stephen Paul Miller, " 'Self-Portrait in a Convex Mirror,' the Watergate Affair, and John's Crosshatch Paintings: Surveillance and Reality-Testing in the Mid-Seventies," *boundary* 2 20, no. 2 (Summer 1993): 84–115.

10. David Shapiro, *House (Blown Apart)* (Woodstock, N.Y.: Overlook Press, 1988), 24.

11. David Lehman, *Operation Memory* (Princeton: Princeton University Press, 1990), 77–81.

12. Ibid., 85–86.

13. Ibid., 71–72.

14. Cherríe Moraga, *Loving in the War Years, lo que nunca pasó por sus labios* (Boston: South End Press, 1983), 148.

15. Thomas Fink, *Surprise Visit* (New York: Domestic Press, 1993), 12.

10 | Fossilized Fish and the World of Unknowing
John Ashbery and William Bronk
John Ernest

R ESPONDING TO AN essay that placed his work within the context of twentieth-century poetry, William Bronk said that he felt "as though I were a previously unknown fish whose fossil had been discovered"; on another occasion, seeing his work arranged in display cases surrounded by "related works" reminded Bronk of "Darwin's birds in the Galapagos. I was surprised to note some of my claimed cousins whom I would not have thought of claiming."[1] No doubt, Bronk's response is similar to that of any poet when his or her work begins to be claimed or otherwise appropriated by the academy; the pleasure of being read must inevitably include the displeasure of being "located," misread, and renamed. Bronk, though, is particularly cantankerous in his relationship to what might be called the institution (and critical industry) of poetry; he stands rather deliberately as an outsider, and his response to the idea of influence is less anxiety than annoyance. Responding to the Poetry Society of America Survey on the ten "best" individual books by American poets published in the United States since 1945, Bronk responded characteristically: "Don't ask me. I believe the arts are not competitive. Competition implies a league, a conference, an academy of sorts. But the arts are private and solitary, not communal, and are concerned neither with prizes nor with other people's work."[2] Certainly, tensions between the scholarly (even in its quasi-popular manifestations) and the poetic modes of vision are unavoidable, and one is tempted to see a certain cracker-barrel wisdom in Harold Bloom's assertion that "poets, who congenitally lie about so many matters, *never* tell the truth about poetic influence."[3] Still, I think there is reason to attend to poets' distinctions between, as John Ashbery has put it, "poetry as something living" and "an academic parlor game,"[4] and to question not only the utility but the cognitive character of attempts to locate lines of poetic influence. This I will try to do by discussing two of the most important poets writing today—John Ashbery and William Bronk, on one of whom Ashbery has had no influence.

There are many reasons for considering these two poets together, not the least of which is one's sense that they are speaking to one another from across separate rooms, or at least speaking to an inaccessible reality by way of a heightened awareness of an inescapably fictive world. Both poets have been traced to Stevens, and beyond Stevens to Auden. Both have been located finally in the world of the American Transcendentalists—and, in both cases, one step removed from Emerson: Whitman for Ashbery and Thoreau for Bronk.[5] Both have said that all their poems are love poems.[6] Each has been described as an intensely private poet—private to the extent that each seems to speak for a shared privacy and therefore seems, as Douglas Crase has said of Ashbery, not "our most private poet, but . . . our most public one."[7] Both poets have drawn critics to write about their embodiment of a kind of postmodern *desire* (a key word in criticism on each), to address the contingencies of postmodern mysticism and spirituality, and to announce the arrival of prophets of, in Ashbery's words, "the imminence of a revelation not yet produced."[8] Finding one of the few critical essays on Bronk cozily next to one on Ashbery, in *Contemporary Literature,* with Thomas Gardner making explicit connections in his preface to the issue, one is not surprised; nor is one surprised to find them together in a recent issue of *o·blēk.* They seem natural compatriots of an unimaginable country, the superficially antagonistic partners in a high-concept poetic "buddy movie."

Yet the way of understanding these poets, their worlds, and their relationship to one another is not by way of a genealogy of influence, anxious or otherwise. These two poets who, perhaps above most others writing today, would instruct us in the art of listening, who would teach us to see the world for all its strange familiarity, and who know well not only the weight of time but also the complex burden of history may together guide us to reenvision the character and terms of poetic history. They can remind us that poetry remains the hope of a noisy society and that the task John Hollander, for one, envisions for poetry—to "reinvent wisdom"[9]—is a shared enterprise, as much dependent on the narratives of poetic history we construct as on the poems we take as "events" in that history.

My purpose here is not to deny influence as a significant dynamic of poetic consciousness, nor even to suggest that we should ignore the striking similarities between, in this case, Ashbery and Bronk, who clearly can be placed in the same community of poets. Rather, my purpose is to reemphasize the critic's inevitable role as (literary) historian and to juxtapose that role to the poet's own inevitable role as (cultural) historian, one whose work reflects necessarily what Melville called the "correspondent coloring" between the artist and his or her culture and times.[10] Narratives of influence are not simply versions of historical poetic process; they are also reconstitutions of other readings of historical experience, those of the poets themselves. Fundamentally, narratives of influence are acts of appropriation in the name of historical coherence, acts geared toward identifying the contours of a possible community of understanding. The question the historian of influence faces is not how to avoid this act of appropriation—for as Foucault has argued, commentary is unavoidably a strategy for controlling the multifarious possibilities of the original text.[11] Rather, the question the literary historian faces (which Foucault himself cannot avoid) is how to manage this act of appropriation, and to what purpose. In this regard, the "correspondent colorings" between Ashbery and Bronk can provide us with a useful reminder of our roles as readers of readers, thereby helping us identify our own responsibilities as literary correspondents.

I

Reflections on the nature and workings of influence and identifications of particular sites of influence align with what Hayden White calls the "prefigurative act" by which historians determine "as a possible object of knowledge the set of events reported in the documents."[12] Applying the "modes of [historical] emplotment" identified by White (himself drawing from the work of Northrop Frye),[13] one could categorize the various literary histories resulting from notions of influence. Depending on the critic's own field of vision and poetic allegiances, the narrative of influence could be *romantic,* envisioning the transcendence of the poet and the ultimate victory (as the young poet applies the lessons of his or her elders) of light over darkness; *satiric,* emphasizing the younger poet's heightened awareness of the captive human consciousness struggling against an inevitable futility, signaling the breakdown or fragmentation of the poetic enterprise (for example, Stephen Fredman's identification of "the crisis in American verse"); *comic,* signaling the ultimate reconciliation of the younger and the elder poet, a marriage of vision spanning the years; or *tragic,* the story of a poet weakened and finally defeated by the influence of his or her poetic elders.

Overriding all these archetypal visions (or perhaps grafted onto them) is a vision of poetic history that one might call simply evolutionary, involving, above all, the quiet celebration of the survival of poetry in a challenging environment—and one suspects that literary critics, as Henry Adams says of himself in *The Education,* are "Darwinist because it [is] easier than not."[14] Indeed, literary critics, at times the dominant group of a relative handful of readers of challenging poets, might well understand, in application to poetry as a continuing ideal, Henry Adams's assessment of the attraction of Darwinism: "Unbroken Evolution under uniform conditions pleased everyone—except curates and bishops; it was the very best substitute for religion; a safe, conservative, practical, thoroughly Common-Law deity."[15] By way of narratives of influence, one can have one's practicality and one's poetry too—the best of both worlds, sacred in the defiantly eclectic regularity of the process.

Here, though, Harold Bloom would join Adams in recognizing the limitations of a Darwinian explanatory framework. As Adams puts it in *The Educa-*

tion, "Evolution was becoming change of form broken by freaks of force, and warped at times by attractions affecting intelligence . . . and the wisest of men could but imitate the Church, and invoke a 'larger synthesis' to unify the anarchy again."[16] Bloom, arguing that "the profundities of poetic influence cannot be reduced to source-study, to the history of ideas, to the patterning of images," joins Nietzsche in reacting against Darwinian evolution ("The influence of 'external circumstances' is overestimated by Darwin to a ridiculous extent," Nietzsche asserts in *The Will to Power*)[17] and finds his own "larger synthesis" in a "theory of poetry that presents itself as a severe poem, reliant upon aphorism, apothegm, and a quite personal (though thoroughly traditional) mythic pattern."[18] We have, finally, a vision not only of poetic history— "though thoroughly traditional"—but of pure history, the story of strong poets.

My point is that narratives of influence colonize individual poets and poems, assuming critical authority over them in the name of conceptual manifest destiny. At their worst, narratives of influence merely imitate uncritically the chauvinistic implications of a privileged province which is the unavoidable product of the historian's delimitation of his or her field. At their best, they refine an explanatory grammar that speaks less of either poetry or its subjects than of taxonomy. Consider, for example, this description by one of the most capable of historians of influence, Helen Vendler: "And yet it is no service to Ashbery, on the whole, to group him with Stevens and Eliot; when he echoes them most compliantly, he is least himself. In any case, though he descends from them, he is not very much like them: he is garrulous, like Whitman, not angular, like Eliot; he is not rhetorical, like Stevens, but tends rather to be conversational, for all the world like Keats in his mercurial letters."[19]

What is interesting here is not merely the unreliability of influence as a critical framework, leading Vendler to say this and Bloom to conclude that "Ashbery (who is not likely to be pleased by this observation) is at his best when . . . he dares to write most directly in the idiom of Stevens";[20] what is yet more interesting is the private grammar that confronts one here, sweeping and resweeping the fields of history, calling upon one to essentialize one's own Whitman, Eliot, Stevens, and Keats in an effort to correct the disservice of grouping Ashbery with Stevens and Eliot not by looking for him elsewhere but rather by enlarging the group. If Ashbery cannot escape Eliot and Stevens, he can at least avoid talking to them directly by corresponding with Keats.

Perhaps we could hear him more clearly, though, if we would listen for him in other contexts, in other histories. In *The Education,* Henry Adams asserts that "every man with self-respect enough to become effective, if only as a machine, has had to account to himself for himself somehow, and to invent a formula of his own for his universe, if the standard formulas failed."[21] Adams's own formula likened "man to a spider in its web, watching for chance prey," that of "forces of nature," broadly defined, "[dancing] like flies before the net."[22] This reminds one of Ashbery's description of his work as "an individual consciousness confronting or being confronted by a world of external phenomena";[23] it reminds one as well of Bronk's assertion, in the poem "Particulate. Inhumane." that

> Our stuff, all stuffs the same: energy,
> in little charges, swarms in clouds of flies
> around itself, unanalyzable
> and not becomes but is whatever it is.[24]

The problem with narratives of influence is that they are all webs and spiders, and very few flies. My point is that the paradigm of influence tells one not only what to find in one's criticism but also, unavoidably, where and how to look.

Commonplace though it may seem these days, it is useful to repeat Karl R. Popper's own reminder that "before we can collect data, our interest in *data of a certain kind* must be aroused: the *problem* always comes first."[25] Beginning with the "problem" of influence presents one with a prefigured program for reading, a program not well suited to help the poet in his or her efforts to be "effective." I share John Hollander's sense of the problem: the need, in a complex and diverse American culture, for "a poetry of restitution," a poetry capable of changing one's life. I think most of those who write about poetry would agree that poetry has that power, but too often—in our emphasis on continuity, in our search for lines of influence, in our determination to identify major poets and minor poems, in our implicit allegiance to the comforts of mastery promised by a vision of a continuous or total history—we fail to give responding voices to that which we need the most, thereby undermining the very poetry we would support.

II

To some extent, the tension between the essentially constructive mode of criticism, fashioning order from a plurality of poetic voices, and the deconstructive mode of Ashbery's and Bronk's poetry, self-reflexive performances of self-consciously fictive imaginations, is appropriate, for that tension is central to the two poets' separate visions. As James McCorkle has said of Ashbery's work, "By misremembering the known, we navigate toward the unknown";[26] similarly, Henry Weinfield has argued that the "aim" of Bronk's poetry "is not negation but, through negation, to evoke what in rational terms is ineffable."[27] But while narratives of influence may be seen as attempts to chart the successive stops on this journey toward the unknown, studies in the art of navigation, the emphasis is projective, not redemptive. While informally we may tes-

tify to the inspiring challenge of the journey, formally we stand on solid scholarly ground, viewing the journey from a distance, as the culturally authorized
terms for delineating this misremembering of the known themselves become
the known. Only the artist wanders; the critic follows along on the map of
commentary. Nothing more is at stake than the possibility of relocating the
subject on the map, adjusting boundaries, or renaming the unknown region.

Consider as another paradigm for understanding this journey one of Bronk's
poems of qualified arrivals, "Exploration," from *Living Instead*:

> The way Columbus or someone earlier
> came to a place to be called a New World
> though not more new than the old world was
> —there all along and people living there—
> is like the way a poem is come upon:
> you think there's something there, you go see what.[28]

This is a poem of exploration, but not of discovery. The "what" that one finds
is the poem itself, speaking only of the sense of "something there" that led to
its discovery, arguing at once for the significance of its discovery, the perspectival character and illusion of its newness, and its ability to speak only of its
own genesis. It is a poem that proceeds not to the endpoint of the journey but
rather to its ambiguous impetus.

This poem about discovering the poem reminds us that the first readers of
Ashbery's and Bronk's works are, respectively, Ashbery and Bronk themselves,
who read the poems into existence. As Bonnie Costello has argued, "Reading
is as much Ashbery's subject as writing is," a subject not designed to lead us to
"the tower of truth" but rather one that "exists for the pleasure of riding along
with the reader, for the sense of communion that can be had on the way to
nowhere in particular."[29] Similarly, Bronk has said, "The work and the artist
say each other as I think lovers do and, in later contact, it is the work and the
reader that say each other."[30] Reading becomes an act of community, and the
poet becomes an important member of that community not merely by provid-
ing it with something to read but rather by representing the art of reading—or,
to use Bronk's term, of "listening," for "our hearing is not absolutely accurate."[31]

It seems to me that, though they hear in different ways, Ashbery and Bronk
listen for something similar. Both look for their poetry beyond themselves. In
Flow Chart, Ashbery presents himself as one "taking dictation / from on high,
in a purgatory of words"; Bronk, when told that he seems to be suggesting that
"the poem exists outside of you and you're transcribing it," answered, "Of
course, where else? Do you think it's something in your goddamned head?"[32]
For Bronk, poetry is "like the universe: it was not created; it's simply there."[33]

However, Bronk knows as well as Ashbery the terms of the challenge to hear something outside your goddamned head. Both poets strive to remind themselves continually that, as Ashbery puts it in "The New Spirit," "in staring too long out over this elaborate view one begins to forget that one is looking inside, taking in the familiar interior which has always been there, reciting the only alphabet one knows" (TP 11). It is in their separate responses to this recognition that the two poets offer us different poetics of listening, different modes for reading our way toward the ineffable.

Entering into these poetics of listening requires an examination not only of selfhood (distinguishing between public and private, social and individual, cultural and primal identities) but also of the dynamic vagaries of individual belief. I agree with S. P. Mohanty and Jonathan Monroe that Ashbery presents us with a vision of "self as an ineluctably social construction," and I would apply to Bronk as well their description of the dynamics of that vision: "Recognizing the social not as something outside, but rather as an internal force that manifests itself above all through the multiple presence of conflicting discourses, Ashbery allows his very notion of the self to be fundamentally changed by what he hears."[34] If the application of this to Bronk's work is not immediately evident, it is because the poet's representation of the social as an internal force that shapes the self is itself shaped not only by *what* the poet hears, but also by *how* he or she hears. As Marjorie Perloff has said, "Not *what* one dreams but *how*—this is Ashbery's subject."[35] Between the *what* and the *how* lies belief: the conceptual framework that guides the poetic ear, the sense that there is a voice speaking within the conflicting discourses, a presence within the multiple presences.

This is not to say that we should consider literally the deities that both Ashbery and Bronk frequently invoke, but rather that we should take seriously the act of invocation. Doing so helps us to recognize the presence of another reader in our readings of these poets' works. In an essay on Edward Taylor, a poet with whom both Ashbery and Bronk have much in common, Jeffrey A. Hammond argues that Taylor's primary reader is Christ and that Taylor's poetic "puzzlings" demonstrate not only his determination to push "his reason to its limits" but also "a wonder inseparable from true belief, the emotional response of a self in harmony with the Word."[36] Taylor writes with an eye toward how he will be "read" by Christ; his poems dramatize "a verbal intimacy with the Christic reader appropriate to the saved soul."[37] Ashbery and Bronk have no well-configured Christ by whom to be read, and for them the Word is and can only be human; but they still address themselves both to and from a presence beyond—or, rather, absent from—human configurations, something lost whenever it is identified. There is wonder in their poems, and selves in harmony with the very Word they struggle against. As the epigraph of Bronk's recent book *Living Instead* has it, "I am servant to the god; he does his own work"; or, as in the poem "Holy Ghost,"

> In the feel of desire
> he becomes so real
> we have written him books
> and built him houses.
> Times that he comes
> we can hear him read.[38]

Ashbery's and Bronk's poems speak of something that can be known only by the human gesture of invocation itself, something that can be represented only by the activity of the poem, the process of reading and being read.

III

As Bronk put it once, "The world is our work which we address, which addresses us."[39] For him, the only relationship that matters to the "poet as poet . . . isn't with the audience or the public or society or the environment or the future or, indeed, the self. It is with the work."[40] To sustain this relationship, to be open to the work's addresses, one must struggle against the known (and knowable)—a struggle that is, for Bronk, not only the good fight, but the only fight. His conception of the real is more than a little similar to his description of Thoreau's conception of silence in one of his early essays: "Silence is the world of potentialities and meanings beyond the actual and expressed, which the meanness of our actions and the interpretations put upon them threaten to conceal. Yet all actuality is to be referred to it and valued accordingly as it includes or suggests it."[41] Believing, as he says Thoreau believed, that "there is ignorant silence in the center of things,"[42] Bronk senses evidence of the real both within and around him, and his 1946 presentation of Thoreau's life as an effort to give expression to that silence has proven to be a prophecy of his own career. Bronk could as well have been speaking of himself when he wrote, "His [Thoreau's] foreknowledge of failure prevented failure from turning him aside to some other problem. There was no other problem."[43]

Indeed, when chided by Cid Corman for never attempting to go beyond what I have called elsewhere the "metaphysical stalemate" of his central theme—a belief in the fictionality and groundlessness of belief[44]—Bronk defended himself in a letter which is of a piece with the dogmatic singleminded-ness of his work:

> We have a concept of "real" and a concept of "true" though we may find it impossible to put anything very big in either category and expect it to stay there. But this is what it is about—this is what confronts us—this is the face

of the seam. "Others" is a concept of the same sort and so is "I" or "self." My poetry is about all those things of which we have concepts but which we find non-existent or unapproachable, and about our experience of finding them so. It would appear you would like me to forget about that experience—to mature out of it—as boys are exhorted to do—and go on to other things. But to me there are no other things to go on to and to pretend that there are would be the most desperate kind of evasion, the dreariest escapism and eccentricity.[45]

As silence for Thoreau, so this for Bronk "illuminates his obscurities and integrates all of his writing."[46]

Collectively, Bronk's poems seem an ongoing (without the sense of a progression) study of an inarticulate desire, of a "wish" that is not his wish for a "something" that he cannot know.[47] In his ongoing confrontation of the only alphabet he knows, failure becomes a necessary prolegomenon to hope. Bronk's inner drama, his ongoing monologue to himself, is an attempt to, as it were, deconstruct autobiography, for autobiography is finally the most intimate and direct form of self-delusion. As he puts it in "The Plainest Narrative":

I am William Bronk, have been raised to believe
the personal pronoun plus the verb to be
and a proper name said honestly is fact
from which the plainest narrative begins.
But it isn't fact; it comes to this. Is it wrong?
Not wrong. Just that it isn't true.[48]

In this approach to autobiography, the examination of the cultural and even the most intimate features of one's sense of identity reveals that life, in fact, isn't there, at least not in any recognizable or portrayable form. But this conception of autobiography seems to confound the relationship between poet and reader, placing them, by virtue of the fictions of identity, at cross-purposes. Small wonder that Bronk, the most plainspoken of poets, should hear so often that readers don't understand his work, leaving him to reflect, as if to claim it as a fundamental condition of human life, "We think we speak with unmistakable clarity and are often received with misunderstanding or incomprehension."[49] The aggressively intimate privacy of Bronk's perspective seems to argue against a relationship with readers who cannot help but approach his work by way of an uneasy alliance of their own plain narratives of selfhood and the conceptual portal of "William Bronk's poetry."

What gives Bronk's poetry its power—and, I would say, its value—is not its ability to present us with yet another reminder of what is all too familiarly known as the postmodern condition; rather, its power lies in the mode of reading it embodies. Bronk provides us with a conceptual framework for that mode of reading in his essays on pre-Columbian civilizations, in which he himself plays the role of reader. It is not difficult to understand Bronk's fascination with the ruins of these civilizations, for they are, after all, highly imaginative and magnificently articulated representations of a created world, artifices of a "reality" that has failed: "Mayan buildings were inventions of space, a notice that place existed where they had decided that there should be a place as part of a world they were constructing in accordance with an idea of what the world was."[50] The ruins offer Bronk a chance to see such inventions of a world without the distraction of continued utility and life. They serve as grand examples of the human impulse to form a world, to create an understandable, concrete representation of reality which eventually proves inadequate, even false. "Our passionately occupied Palenques," Bronk observes, "are always abandoned."[51]

In fact, the special virtue of these worlds is that, abandoned, they become for us now the most intimate and revealing of mirrors, of the sort which will unflinchingly reveal the emperor's new clothes and force one, if one is honest with oneself, to examine the habits of creative perception which allow one to embroider with ever more elaborate threads:

> Don't we look to find ourselves there, though history is the guise we give ourselves as if we meant not to speak directly of our subject, and history served as that Mayan mask, complexly devised of plumes and false faces, to cover our nakedness. For it is we who are naked here, exposed in layers by the river's cutting away of those successive domestic and ceremonial disguises in which we sought to hide ourselves. It is our absence, indeed, which is our presence: the disguises are there still and we are not there, we are nowhere.[52]

Bronk's responses to the ruins extend from this revealed nakedness; as others have noted, the essays in *The New World* are clearly more about Bronk than about the ruins. Or, rather, it is the nakedness itself he is addressing; he is able to look directly at a world without having either to believe or to disbelieve in it, and finds in it a stone metaphor for the wonders and limitations of the human mind and spirit.

To wonder at the science and cosmology revealed by the ruins is to wonder at the potentialities of human understanding; and yet, Bronk suggests, the greater part of our interest extends from the recognition, ineluctably inscribed upon our perception, that these intricate cultures failed: "Our interest in knowing how to interpret this inscription as cosmology is an interest in knowing how someone else failed as we do too."[53] We are able to understand, to place ourselves in relation to, the failed cosmology precisely because we recognize that the people at Copan were faced with the same raw material as ourselves; they measured the stars, counted the days, and enclosed a space almost wholly symbolic in the wilderness, a space which was valuable for the enclosure itself, for the space marked off in a representation of a conception of the real. We share with such failed civilizations the impulse to order, the desire to know; to look at their remains is to recognize that there is no knowing, that even that which we have not yet achieved must fail.

Our nakedness, then, is that of a frustrated impulse and an insatiable desire. We are, in other words, confronted with that part of ourselves we would control: the at once socialized and chaotic human nature that we receive passively and try actively to direct. This confrontation marks the difference between awareness and thought; the mirror of Copan, in particular, reveals the distinction and leads Bronk to a revitalized recognition of "something felt," the inner evidence of the real:

> There are things which we feel, certain angers, rejoicings, fears. These feelings astonish us. Set beside our expectation of a real world, they seem not to have the habit of reality. They seem unrelated, and there is a lapse of time before we take them as real in the absence of a more expected reality. We learn at last, and accept the learning at last, that these feelings come to us without our willing or acceding or inventing. They come from beyond our skin like approaches to us, like messages; and we respond, trembling and shaking, or vibrating in tune as though we were instruments a music were played on and we arch and turn to have the contact closer. Our responses are presences that tower around us, seemingly solid as stone.[54]

Bronk here means his metaphors literally. The structures at Copan are, in his view, a particular substantiation of a universal response. And if we recognize, Bronk suggests, that something greater than ourselves operates through us "without our willing or acceding or inventing," then we must be attentive, if not directly to such responses, then at least to the foolishness of our collective pretenses of order. Nor must we retreat to the more intimate pretense of the self, for "the attempt to put personal desires in place of the general want which we feel," Bronk asserts, "is a simplification, and makes the problem of desire appear to be something we could hope to solve."[55]

In his recent poem "Boiled Down," Bronk puts his central credo in its most basic terms:

> It's not
> about us.
> It's what
> we're about.[56]

Or, as he puts it in "Unpersonal," "The image is unimagined; that image is ours."[57] Bronk's poetics of reading, as presented in his New World essays, identifies a mode of communication engendered by the recognition of distance, the reading of a literally dehumanized text that enables one to identify the terms and habits of understanding, the discursive foundations and willful enclosures of a suspended culture. As he is led to read Copan as if it were about himself, he is led to unread himself to an awareness of "what we're about." Similarly, his poems present us with the features of an individual order. We can say he writes the same poem again and again only by privileging meaning and style over activity. In fact, each poem proceeds from a particular manifestation of human understanding, order, and existence in time. His work presents us with a sense of "poetry as something living"; the poems speak their own history, in which the poet is but a representative figure, an agency of other voices.

IV

If the aggressively individual and private persona of Bronk's poetry makes the act of reading seem something like eavesdropping, Ashbery often seems to present the reader with something more like eaves*drippings*—scattered fragments of the slogans and discursive modes of a culture whose stratifications are no longer either distinct or secure.[58] Ashbery seems to hear more than does Bronk, so much so that it is sometimes a wonder that he manages to make himself heard. But this, of course, is the point. I agree with John Koethe that "the sense of the presence of a unified subject that conceives these poems [of Ashbery] is very strong, almost palpable," and that this presence speaks of "a unitary consciousness from which his voice originates, positioned outside the temporal flux of thought and experience his poetry manages to monitor and record."[59] This "presence" is the palpable sign of Ashbery's success in suggesting, in the activity of his poems, a poetics of listening, the blessed result of his meditative mode of reading.

I would like to suggest the conceptual framework for this mode of reading by way of a selective engagement with one of his most strikingly meditative works, *Three Poems*. In her own Bakhtinian engagement with *Three Poems,* Margueritte S. Murphy argues that Ashbery "seeks to incorporate 'polyphony' into his poetic discourse" in support of "an existential desire to reach beyond the 'I,' the speaking or writing self."[60] Indeed, Ashbery's incorporation of heteroglossia into the fabric of these prose poems serves to draw the reader's attention to Ashbery's version of Bakhtin's recognition that "discourse lives, as it were, beyond itself, in a living impulse toward the object," and that "if we detach ourselves completely from this impulse all we have left is the naked corpse of the word, from which we can learn nothing at all about the social situation or the fate of a given word in life."[61]

Ashbery's meditative project is, in effect, to reverse Bakhtin's reasoning here, presenting the reader (even the first reader, himself) with "the naked corpse of the word" in an effort to reestablish the cognitive authority of the unspeakable "living impulse." As S. H. Miller has argued, "*Three Poems* is nothing less than the elaboration of the mind's activities," one that involves not only a search for the terms of selfhood and self-awareness but also "the epistemological implications of such a search."[62] In one of the most careful and sensitive readings of *Three Poems,* Stephen Fredman similarly views the work as "radically performative," and he accounts for the quasi-mystical character of this mental performance by presenting Ashbery "as a necessarily inaccurate transcriber of pure language."[63] In *Three Poems,* Fredman argues, we encounter the representation of "not-understanding," a state that "is available any time we trust in a meaning beyond our present understanding," and that "manifests as an aura around language."[64]

In this performative "attitude of creative not-understanding," as Fredman observes, "both the writer and the reader are implicated in the creation of an ongoing fiction of reality from 'lingering traces.'"[65] The "aura" is, in other words, not only a delicate but also a shared creation, one that exists, and that therefore can be flattened or destroyed, only through the act of reading. *Three Poems* works not merely to engage the reader self-consciously in the act of reading but also to inscribe upon the reader's consciousness the conceptual framework for an ongoing mode of reading. This is, after all, a book that ends with a recital, a performance that inspires a response that lingers in the air after the performance itself has ended. More pointedly, what lingers is "the idea of the spectacle as something to be acted out and absorbed" (TP 118). Accordingly, what Fredman calls a communal "fiction of reality" might more properly be viewed as a fiction of apprehension—"imperfect, like all apprehended things" (TP 8)—a mode of receptivity effected by an engaged response, itself both informed and incited (as applause is incited by the dynamics and shared conventions of recitals) by Ashbery's particularized perspective.

In *Three Poems,* the closest conceptual approximation of the aura Fredman notices is the book's attention to silence. Indeed, silence seems to linger in the air of every page of this noisy book. It is silence that makes the thought of "leav[ing] it all out" seem, in the opening sentences, not only another but a "truer" way (3). One thinks of Bronk when one encounters the lines, early in "The New Spirit,"

> Because life is short
> We must remember to keep asking it the same question
> Until the repeated question and the same silence become answer
> In words broken open and pressed to the mouth
> (6)

In the dynamic relationship of repeated questioning and persistent silence lies the only answer available to us. It is an answer not of conclusion but of experience, for asking the same unanswerable question against a persistent and familiar silence opens the question to a mantra of unknowing.

But the "we" of these lines, like all of the pronouns in *Three Poems,* de-

finable only contextually in a book of shifting contexts, is deceptive and unstable. Suggestive of a human condition and a communal need, this "we" is
unable to speak for all, leading quickly to a reminder that the community of
vision is inhabited by separate perspectives:

> But it is your landscape, the proof that you are there,
> To deal with or be lost in
> In which the silent changes might occur.
>   (7)

There is not a singular silence, but many silences—individual changes that together might suggest a common condition, a shared possibility, a conglomerate
glimpse of something like a "true" way of knowing and of being. But there
is no path, true or otherwise, from the individual perspectives to a communal mode of envisioning, for "we cannot see through each other, the way is
closed" (39). What we have instead are communal visions, "attitudes" which
"have hardened into the official likeness" of our actions (16), leaving one with
little more than a character that has "come to mean what it had been called
on for" (22).

As it begins to take shape from his own incremental conception of the problem, Ashbery's task is to distinguish between the "official likeness" and the
unofficial discursive features of our lives, to turn his attention from our identities as so many characters in a novel to the world of the novel itself, the "bundle of incidents related to but separate and distinct from you" (22). In fact,
with life now invested not in our acts but in the hardened attitudes, he suggests
that we have freed ourselves (unconsciously, or else it could not have been) to
discover a new conceptual relationship introducing itself into the "bundle of
incidents" of our experience: a "new casualness" (45), suggestive of a "new
spirit." Immersion in the discursive "credentials" of this new casualness, then,
becomes the prerequisite for communication in a world in which the messages
are too clearly defined. One must embrace heteroglossia and heterophony, lose
oneself in the discursive landscapes of attitudinal formations, landscapes as
stubborn in their deceptive familiarity and intimacy as they are powerful in
their perspectival containments, their ability to define the terms of one's self-
location in time and space.

But immersion within the casual waters of the day is not enough; in fact,
it can encourage one to return to the security of established conceptual moor-
ings. In "The System," Ashbery looks for the guidance implicit in his own act
of faith, his own willingness to surround himself in the cacophonous flux of
his world. The breakdown of the old systems can lead one to an awareness of
a "primal vein" and of "doing a lot of listening," "a lightning existence that
has come into our own" (53); but it calls for a response, "the business of mastering the many pauses and the abrupt, sharp accretions of regular being in the

clotted sphere of today's activities" (54). The response needs a method, a new system capable of suggesting awareness of the new spirit: "All the facts are here and it remains only to use them in the right combinations, but that building will be the size of today, the rooms habitable and leading into one another in a lasting sequence, eternal and of the greatest timeliness" (54). We must build our own building with the recognition that we will have to live in it, that it will define for us, whether we mean it to or not, who we are and what we are about. And we must remember that "there is no cutting corners where the life of the soul is concerned" (58). In effect, we must build a habitable Copan, capable of shaping our awareness of the "unwilled" pressing against the contours of our invented order.

Essentially, Ashbery calls for—or hears a call for—not a world to read but a world of reading, not a static, explanatory system but a dynamic, responsive one. It needs to be a system capable of avoiding the determinate forces of, on the one hand, the goal-oriented, history-as-progress " 'career' notion" of life, and, on the other hand, the historical escapism of the " 'life as ritual' concept" (70). Ashbery knows well, though, the impossibility of such avoidance, for some combination of these two notions, as of others, will inevitably be present in even our most willfully spiritual perspectives:

> But the world avenges itself on those who would lose it by skipping over the
> due process of elimination, from whatever altruistic motive, by incrusting
> itself so thoroughly in these efforts at self-renewal that no amount of wrig-
> gling can dislodge its positive or negative image from all that is contemplated
> of present potentialities or the great sane simplifications to come. (64)

We cannot escape history, nor can we escape what we have made of history, the images we have inscribed upon it, the cultural and ideological structures we have built on the grounds we and others have perceived. The conception of a new system, then, requires both diachronic and synchronic cultural perspectives; it requires the acceptance of culture as a multifarious, dynamic system capable of complicating (historically, discursively) our journey toward the illusion of understanding.

Ashbery explores the possibility of such a system by looking through official history to unofficial history, "a kind of fiction that developed parallel to the classic truths of daily life" (55). He looks to the "unrelated happenings that form a kind of sequence of fantastic reflections as they succeed each other at a pace and according to an inner necessity of their own" (56). One hardly needs to point out that *Three Poems* attempts to represent what Murphy has called "a flux of idiom," but we need to remember that this is a representation not only of different cultural discourses but of historical process as well. In Murphy's example of this analogue of historical consciousness, Ashbery's use of "the familiar strain from Ecclesiastes" calls to mind that which has made the strain so familiar to many of his readers, the Byrds' version of Pete Seeger's own adaptation of these biblical verses, "Turn, Turn, Turn." Read in its wider context (both that provided by Ashbery and that culled from the files of the reader's mind), "Biblical wisdom, rock 'n' roll lyric, contemporary slang join in a single phrase in this weather report on the psychology of love affairs," a report that might even include, by way perhaps of Bob Dylan, the sixties Weathermen.[66] Throughout *Three Poems,* we hear similar conversations, are reminded of similar appropriations, and follow similarly jagged paths to apprehension. The book stands as a model of reading, and reading becomes an analogue of historical experience itself.

This model, though, is distinctively private, reminding us that all reading is provisional, conditional, and dependent upon one's own haphazard structures of cultural identity. Certainly, part of the experience of reading this book is not only following Ashbery through his own study of overlapping layers of cultural formations but also wondering whether one is reading along with Ashbery or reading one's own cultural text. "Who has seen the wind?" Yoko Ono sings in her wavery, self-consciously wispy voice,[67] and Ashbery seems to sing along (61), though one doubts that this can be the case. Can we know, in a first encounter with this book, whether Ashbery thought of the Byrds when he played upon Ecclesiastes? If we know that he did not, should those of us who listened to the Byrds keep them from soaring in our heads as we read? Can we? Do we need a Weatherman to know which way the wind of this text blows? Well might one ask, as does John Gery, "Is there a *wrong* way to interpret a poem by John Ashbery?"[68] The uncertainty and the variables of individual understanding are part of the experience of the text, as of life: "And as the discourse continues and you think you are not getting anything out of it, . . . this knowledge is getting through to you, and taking just the forms it needs to impress itself upon you, the forms of your inattention and incapacity or unwillingness to understand" (TP 80). What one is left with is not a disappointing miscomprehension, not a failure, for miscomprehension is a constant human condition, not an occasional result. Rather, what one is left with is an awareness of the unique configuration of one's own experience of miscomprehension, something occurring and discovered in one's relation to others.

Therein is the hope of the new casualness as the vehicle of the new spirit, drawing our attention to "signs of life in which part of the whole truth lies buried" (80). The encounter with private configurations of the world leads one to participate in a newly social mode of reading, one which seizes upon the unavoidable failures of human understanding and celebrates the revelatory experience of frustration and disappointment.

It is worth the distraction of a lengthy quotation to hear Ashbery's own sense of this revelation, when one rises from the "hard wooden bench" of an encounter with a discourse one did not fully attend to or understand:

> For it is certain that you will rise from the bench a new person, and even before you have emerged into the full daylight of the street you will feel that a change has begun to operate in you, within your very fibers and sinews, and when the light of the street floods over you it will have become real at last, all traces of doubt will have been pulverized by the influx of light slowly mounting to bury those crass seamarks of egocentricity and warped self-esteem you were able to navigate by but which you no longer need now that the rudder has been swept out of your hands, and this whole surface of daylight has become one with that other remembered picture of light, when you were setting out, and which you feared would disappear because of its uniqueness, only now realizing that this singleness was the other side of the coin of its many-faceted diversity and interest, and that it may be simultaneously cherished for the former and lived in thanks to the versatility of the latter. It may be eaten, and breathed, and it would indeed have no reason to exist if this were not the case. So I think that the question of how we are going to use the reality of our revelation, as well as to what end, has now been resolved. (80)

This, I believe, is the revelation Ashbery works not merely to embody in *Three Poems* and in his other work, as he embodies these lines, but also and yet more deliberately to engender in the reader. He tries to lead the reader to "rule and be ruled by these strings or emanations that connect everything together" (96); he leaves the text to the vague mercies of his different readers, to make of it what they will. He guides the reader in the reading of immersion to wonder with him why the "silence continues to focus" on oneself, and to wonder what one has done "to have merited so much attention on the part of the universe" (94). Each reader is left with the possibilities of his or her own haphazardly configured universe, caught in the act of communication with distant others. As he puts it in "On Autumn Lake," "In each the potential is realized, the two wires / Are crossing" (SPCM 48)—then reminding us on the next page, in "Fear of Death," "But the breeze has dropped, and silence is the last word."

V

In their joint meditation on Ashbery's work, S. P. Mohanty and Jonathan Monroe remind us that, as Ashbery's work becomes the field for the critical plows of increasing numbers of scholars, "the business of explaining Ashbery becomes a significant kind of cultural self-definition. For such explanations are readings of the present moment just as much as they are interpretations of individual texts; they provide, moreover, implicit and overt programs for writing and rewriting literary and cultural history."[69] I have tried to suggest that we need to think carefully about what we will make of Ashbery, and that doing so requires us to think about our paradigms of historical process. Whatever may be the theoretical virtues of narratives of influence, once written, they have practical power and will inevitably shape conceptions of the role of poetry in our culture and will thereby shape conceptions of our roles (and attendant responsibilities) as readers. At issue is not only what visions of history we will inscribe but also what visions we will enable and even encourage.

Taking us from the postmodern condition to what might be called the postmodern *conditional*, Ashbery and Bronk offer us the challenging hope of a new spirit, sustained relationally, capable of drawing us to new communities of understanding. Unable to speak *to*, they can only speak *from*; by emphasizing the privacy of their separate enterprises, they reemphasize the social nature of the poetic experience. As Bronk once put it, addressing the concept of literary biography,

> Insofar as there can be anything about me worth writing about it would have to be the work and the importance of the work can only be to the reader who has entered into a relation with it. This is at variance with the generally—not only academically—held idea that works of art can be examined, described and assessed as though they were precious stones. Or houses. But the importance of houses is lost in their selling price. We live in them. Or we don't.[70]

Both Ashbery's and Bronk's houses of poetry seem haunted, though one notices this only when one tries to live there for a while. Haunted, we encounter poetics of listening, of scrupulous, precise incomprehension, always beginning again the same task. For all their similarities, we hear these poets best when we listen to them separately, and we learn from them how to listen for other, less familiar voices.

Notes

1. William Bronk to John Ernest, July 23, 1985.

2. Jean Hanff Korelitz, "Poetry Society of America Survey," *Poetry Society of America Newsletter* 35 (1991): 32.

3. Harold Bloom, "John Ashbery: The Charity of the Hard Moments," in *American Poetry since 1960: Some Critical Perspectives*, ed. Robert B. Shaw (Cheshire: Carcanet, 1973), 86.

4. John Ashbery, introduction to *The Collected Poems of Frank O'Hara*, ed. Donald Allen (New York: Knopf, 1979), ix.

5. I am not, of course, accounting for the full range of poets with whom Ashbery and Bronk are associated, but only for a dominant line of influence, used for the sake of

easy reference, usually noted in discussions of their work. I assume that most readers will be familiar with these tracings in relation to Ashbery—of which Harold Bloom and Helen Vendler provide the best examples. For Bronk, see the "conversations" in the following special issues: *Credences* 1, no. 3 (1976); *Talisman* 2 (1989); and *Sagetrieb* 7 (1988). For a study of his relationship with Stevens, see Burt Kimmelman, "Centrality in a Discrete Universe: William Bronk and Wallace Stevens," *Sagetrieb* 7 (1988): 119–30.

6. On Ashbery, see John Hollander, "A Poetry of Restitution," *Yale Review* 70, no. 2 (1981): 161–86; see also Charles Altieri, "Ashbery as Love-Poet," *Verse* 8, no. 1 (Spring 1991): 8–15. Concerning Bronk, one might begin by considering the following lines from the poem "Yes: I Mean So OK—Love" (in *Life Supports: New and Collected Poems* [San Francisco: North Point, 1982], 113–14):

> Some people say, "Well good,
> now you write about love."
> "Yes," I say, "what else,
> I always have; what else?"

7. Douglas Crase, "The Prophetic Ashbery," in *Beyond Amazement: New Essays on John Ashbery*, ed. David Lehman (Ithaca: Cornell University Press, 1980), 30.

8. Richard Jackson, ed., "The Imminence of a Revelation," in *Acts of Mind: Conversations with Contemporary Poets* (University: University of Alabama Press, 1983), 70. Donald Revell has suggested recently that "Ashbery's profoundest influence makes itself felt in the ways in which he discovers motives and momentums of desire in language itself" ("Purists Will Object: Some Meditations on Influence," *Verse* 8, no. 1 [Spring 1991]: 16–22). See also Crase, "Prophetic Ashbery," 30–65; Marilyn L. Brownstein, "Postmodern Language and the Perpetuation of Desire," *Twentieth Century Literature* 31, no. 1 (1985): 73–88; Norman M. Finkelstein, "William Bronk: The World as Desire," *Contemporary Literature* 23 (1982): 480–92; and John Ernest, "William Bronk's Religious Desire," *Sagetrieb* 7 (1988): 145–52. For somewhat contending views on Ashbery and the sublime, see chapter 3 of Finkelstein's *Utopian Moment in Contemporary American Poetry* (Lewisburg, Pa.: Bucknell University Press, 1988) and also Rob Wilson's "John Ashbery's Postindustrial Sublime," *Verse* 8, no. 1 (Spring 1991): 48–52.

9. Hollander, "Poetry of Restitution," 185.

10. Herman Melville, "Hawthorne and His Mosses," in *The Piazza Tales and Other Prose Pieces, 1839–1860* (Evanston, Ill.: Northwestern University Press; Chicago: Newberry Library, 1987), 246.

11. "Commentary's only role," Foucault argues, "is to say *finally*, what has silently been articulated *deep down*" (*The Archeology of Knowledge and the Discourse on Language*, trans. A. M. Sheridan [New York: Pantheon, 1972], 221). Foucault here provides a useful framework in which to view Harold Bloom's assertion that "criticism is the art of knowing the hidden roads that go from poem to poem" (*The Anxiety of Influence: A Theory of Poetry* [New York: Oxford University Press, 1973], 96). Criticism never functions in a realm of its own; it is a product itself of complex cultural influences, often working to reassign its debts to such influences. In practical applica-

tion, "hidden roads" are located in prefigured neighborhoods. Every road has its origin, and the maps are all too clearly marked.

12. Hayden White, *Metahistory: The Historical Imagination in Nineteenth-Century Europe* (Baltimore: Johns Hopkins University Press, 1973), 30–31.

13. Ibid., 29.

14. Henry Adams, *The Education of Henry Adams,* Riverside ed. (Boston: Houghton Mifflin, 1973), 225.

15. Ibid.

16. Ibid., 401.

17. Friedrich Nietzsche, *The Will to Power,* ed. Walter Kaufmann, trans. Walter Kaufmann and R. J. Hollingdale (New York: Vintage, 1968), 344.

18. Bloom, *Anxiety of Influence,* 7, 13.

19. Helen Vendler, *The Music of What Happens: Poems, Poets, Critics* (Cambridge: Harvard University Press, 1988), 231.

20. Bloom, "John Ashbery," 85.

21. Adams, *Education,* 472.

22. Ibid., 474.

23. Quoted in Thomas Gardner, "American Poetry of the 1970s: A Preface," *Contemporary Literature* 23 (1982): 407.

24. William Bronk, "Particulate. Inhumane," in *Living Instead* (San Francisco: North Point, 1991), 34.

25. Karl R. Popper, *The Poverty of Historicism* (New York: Harper & Row, 1964), 121.

26. James McCorkle, *The Still Performance: Writing, Self, and Interconnection in Five Postmodern Poets* (Charlottesville: University of Virginia Press, 1989), 61.

27. Henry Weinfield, " 'The Cloud of Unknowing': William Bronk and the Condition of Poetry," *Sagetrieb* 7 (1988): 143.

28. William Bronk, "Exploration," in *Living Instead,* 49.

29. Bonnie Costello, "John Ashbery and the Idea of the Reader," *Contemporary Literature* 23 (1982): 493, 513.

30. Bronk to Ernest, April 13, 1987.

31. Henry Weinfield, "A Conversation with William Bronk," *Sagetrieb* 7 (1988): 42.

32. Ibid., 39.

33. Ibid.

34. S. P. Mohanty and Jonathan Monroe, "John Ashbery and the Articulation of the Social," *diacritics* 17, no. 2 (1987): 44, 45.

35. Marjorie Perloff, *The Poetics of Indeterminacy: Rimbaud to Cage* (Princeton: Princeton University Press, 1981), 252.

36. Jeffrey A. Hammond, "Who Is Edward Taylor? Voice and Reader in the *Preparatory Meditations,*" *American Poetry* 7, no. 3 (1990): 10.

37. Ibid., 9.

38. William Bronk, "Holy Ghost," in *Death Is the Place* (San Francisco: North Point, 1989), 30.

39. Bronk to Ernest, September 6, 1984.

40. Ibid., October 24, 1984. As Bronk puts it in his "Of Poetry" (in *Death Is the Place*, 17), which I quote here in its entirety:

there is only the work.

The work is what speaks
and what is spoken
and what attends to hear
what is spoken.

41. William Bronk, "Silence and Henry Thoreau," in *Vectors and Smoothable Curves: Collected Essays* (San Francisco: North Point, 1983), 81.

42. See William Bronk, "There Is Ignorant Silence in the Center of Things," in *Life Supports*, 51–52.

43. Bronk, "Silence and Henry Thoreau," 83.

44. See Ernest, "William Bronk's Religious Desire."

45. Cid Corman, *William Bronk: An Essay* (Carrboro: Truck, 1976), 38.

46. Bronk, "Silence and Henry Thoreau," 79.

47. While one can find Bronk "wishing" for "something" in many of his poems, I am thinking here specifically of "The Poems: All Concessions Made" (in *Life Supports*, 179), which ends with the lines: "We concede so much. What don't we concede? / I wish I had something; and the poems are there."

48. William Bronk, "The Plainest Narrative," in *Life Supports*, 113–14.

49. Bronk to Ernest, February 2, 1985.

50. William Bronk, "The Occupation of Space—Palenque," in *Vectors and Smoothable Curves*, 23.

51. Ibid., 29.

52. William Bronk, "Copan: Historicity Gone," in *Vectors and Smoothable Curves*, 31.

53. Ibid., 32.

54. William Bronk, "Copan: Unwillingness, the Unwilled," in *Vectors and Smoothable Curves*, 43–44.

55. Ibid., 41.

56. William Bronk, "Boiled Down," in *Living Instead*, 96.

57. William Bronk, "Unpersonal," in *Living Instead*, 40.

58. Of course, reading these drippings brings us back to the sense of overhearing (in fragments) a conversation, as Marjorie Perloff, addressing "These Lacustrine Cities," argues: "Reading Ashbery's text is thus rather like overhearing a conversation in which one catches an occasional word or phrase but cannot make out what the speakers are talking about" (*Poetics of Indeterminacy*, 10).

59. John Koethe, "The Metaphysical Subject of John Ashbery's Poetry," in *Beyond Amazement: New Essays on John Ashbery*, ed. David Lehman (Ithaca: Cornell University Press, 1980), 89.

60. Margueritte S. Murphy, "John Ashbery's *Three Poems*: Heteroglossia in the American Prose Poem," *American Poetry* 7, no. 2 (1990): 55, 51.

61. M. M. Bakhtin, *The Dialogic Imagination: Four Essays by M. M. Bakhtin*, ed.

Michael Holquist, trans. Caryl Emerson and Michael Holquist (Austin: University of Texas Press, 1981), 292.

62. S. H. Miller, "Psychic Geometry: John Ashbery's Prose Poems," *American Poetry* 3, no. 1 (1985): 25, 28. Charles Altieri presents, in my view, the most careful and insightful consideration of the full complexity of Ashbery's "poetics of thinking" in his *Self and Sensibility in Contemporary American Poetry* (Cambridge: Cambridge University Press, 1984). As he argues, "The more complex and difficult the transitions, the fuller the interplay between motives: We are asked to participate in acts of mind that attribute motives for acts and invite analysis of the motives for the attribution of motives" (149).

63. Stephen Fredman, *Poet's Prose: The Crisis in American Verse* (Cambridge: Cambridge University Press, 1983), 110, 105.

64. Ibid., 106.

65. Ibid., 110.

66. Murphy, "Ashbery's *Three Poems*," 59.

67. If I remember correctly, Ono's "Who Has Seen the Wind" appeared on the flip side of John Lennon's "Power to the People," though it might have been "Instant Karma"; of course, frailties of the memory of experience are part of one's experience of this poem.

68. John Gery, "The Anxiety of Influence: Poets after Ashbery," *Verse* 8, no. 1 (Spring 1991): 28.

69. Mohanty and Monroe, "John Ashbery," 37.

70. Bronk to Ernest, April 13, 1987.

PART 3

Ashbery and Postmodern Poetries

11 | Taking the Tennis Court Oath

Andrew Ross

And I am proud
of these stars in our flag we don't want
the flag of film
waving over the sky
toward us—citizens of some future state.

(TCO 18)

LIKE SO MANY of his generation of poets, the first popular exposure of John Ashbery's work came in Donald Allen's seminal, best-selling, 1960 anthology, *The New American Poetry,* with its infamously high-handed partitioning of the national poetry scene into five geographically identifiable groups, "occasionally arbitrary and for the most part more historical than actual." More than twenty years later, George Butterick (the indefatigable editor of Charles Olson's work) collaborated with Allen to compile a new edition of this anthology, entitled *The Postmoderns: The New American Poetry Revised* (Grove Press, 1982). Some of the contributors had been dropped, others were added, and the selections from those represented in both editions were expanded to include post-1960 work that was thought to "consolidate the gains" of the original material. The geographic categories were dispensed with, while Olson, chief counsel for a "postmodern" poetics, was chosen to lead off an otherwise alphabetical list of entries. The result is an extraordinary demonstration of revisionist literary history, especially since the contradictions informing that history are plainly displayed in the difference between the respective dust jackets of the two volumes. The 1960 design sports a rippling flag motif which flows from the "flagstaff" of the book's spine to the edge of the page, while the list of contributors' names is continuous with (the plane of) the stripes; the book and its contributors are therefore straightforwardly identified with a particular representation of American values, expressive of the unfurled Renaissance spirit of the new, "open" poetics claimed for so much of the writing anthologized in the volume. The wind that blows across the cover is blowing away the "academic" poetry of the fifties and ushering in more extravagant forms of social and cultural change. It is also the older, returning wind of American naturalism, carrying with it those elemental *freedoms* of expression which are

193

the bedrock of the new poetry's appeal to the unmediated—the oral, the spontaneous, the confessional, the "natural."

Twenty-two years later, the open sore of Vietnam poisoning so many of the intervening years, that representation of the American contract with the natural is no longer possible. On the new cover design, the contributors are set apart, listed in solid colored lettering, while Jasper Johns's *Three Flags* signals its own heavily artifactual presence on a page that is demonstrably a page and not a flag. Johns's piece brings with it a highly ironic, almost parodic, and certainly revisionist, set of meanings to bear upon the task of representing the American interests of this anthology project. There is no offer of an easy continuity with a nation's history of cultural expression, "nature" is no longer present in any of its possible signifiers, and the "culture" that is invoked is one that in 1960 had only just begun to win a significant place for itself in postwar art and literature—the commodity culture of a mass society about to enter its postindustrial phase. *Three Flags* (1958) is one of the first of the iconic Pop works to celebrate the principle of reproducibility, by acknowledging the spirit of commercial mass production, and therefore to abandon the Romantic ethic of solo craftsmanship, dominant hitherto in the art world and associated with the high modernist cultural values of originality and authenticity. In fact, *Three Flags* signals the end of one of the most corrosive civil wars ever staged in American culture—the long resistance of artists and intellectuals to the pervasive presence of commercially produced culture, a period of virulent reaction characterized most recently, in the early 1960s, by the Abstract Expressionist gesture of spontaneous "action" painting and by the debate among literary intellectuals about the reformist, moral qualities still to be found and exercised in the high modernist classics. In their flight from the vanguardist realm of artistic originality into the long arms of the commodity world, Pop art and Pop culture at once collapse the distance between intellectual activity and everyday life and create a new, expanded realm of technological possibility, recognizing the *reality* of popular culture where previous commentators had seen only the clichés of kitsch commercial parasitism. The Pop work is no longer the product of good artistic intentions; it is a space upon which anonymous products, images, and languages are reproduced and displayed. In this less than pure art environment, a discourse about conventionality everywhere displaces marks of originality.

Almost in spite of these messages about artifice and reproducibility suggested by the Johns cover, the editors of the 1982 volume describe the prevailing ethic of their poetic generation in terms that belong largely to the Romantic ideology of originality and autonomous creativity. "A great flowering has occurred," in the best organicist tradition, while the overall response to the new technocratic world of the commodity culture has been generally to ignore it and to seek out instead the "preliterate, prerational, premodern" in a "heroic" gesture of nonconformity:

> They respond to the limits of industrialism and high technology often by a marked spiritual advance or deference, an embracing of the primal energies of a tribal or communal spirit, side by side with the most stubborn sort of American individualism. Their influence on English-speaking poetry at large has reversed the longstanding obeisance to academically sanctioned formalism. There are revolutionaries among them, as well as quieter (but no less deliberate) practitioners. Their most common bond is a spontaneous utilization of subject and technique, a prevailing "instantism" that nevertheless does not preclude discursive ponderings and large-canvassed reflections. They are boldly positioned and deft, freely manoeuvering among the inherited traditions, time-honored lore, and proven practices, adopting what they need for their own wholeness and journeying. They are most of them forward-looking at a time when concepts such as entropy and global village have entered daily life along with, for the first time in the history of the human species, thanks to this nuclear age, the possibility of irreversibility. If it can be said—as it commonly is—that modernism came to an end with the detonation of the Bomb in 1945, these are the poets who propose a world since then. Whether imagistic or surrealistic, mythic or populist in their approach, they all reflect America at a great turning point.[1]

It would be wrong, I think, not to set this boundless affirmation of "free" agency and energy in the context of an "America at a great turning point" in its own neo-imperialist aspirations: voraciously expansionist, since 1945, in its control of world trade markets, its near-global diffusion of cultural values, and its puppeteering of national governments throughout its hemispheric spheres of influence. While many of the poets in question were soon to count among the most visible and outspoken opponents of their country's foreign policy in the latter half of the decade, the pressure upon these same poets to "produce signs of cultural coherence that help to ratify imperium," as Robert von Hallberg has put it, issues as much from their inescapable role as ideological agents as it does from the much-vaunted "poetic license" of their "free" expressive voices. (No matter how much real diplomatic immunity such a role claims for itself, the power to address the *centrality* of American culture can come only from the center itself, a position often ceded to poets only because of their supposed ideological immunity as "free spirits.")[2] So, too, we should be able to point to the naïveté suggested by the alternative of a new "tribal" spirit, posed by the editors as a response to the creeping materialism associated with "the limits of industrialism and high technology." The new tribalism, for example, seems in no way incompatible, in spite of the editors' curiously ambiguous suggestion, with "such concepts as entropy and global village." (Marshall McLuhan's heady technological optimism was based precisely upon such patronizing First Worldist statements: "TV children" were to be the "new tribes-men," returning to the "Africa within" to reestablish a new globalism of techno-spiritual values.) And the passionate disavowal of the concrete realities of daily commodity life is entirely in keeping with the transcendental spirit of American idealism, traditionally proficient in turning its poets' thoughts to higher ground—preindustrial, premodern, precapitalist.

Indeed, it is in that archaic, Romantic haven of the *premodern* that tribal-ism holds sway, not in the *postmodern* world of the sign and the commodity. In effect, when Allen and Butterick draw attention to the "instantism" and spontaneism espoused, albeit in different ways, by the new poetics, the time which they invoke is not the "time" of mechanical reproduction—serial, egali-tarian, and characterized by instant accessibility, through the *copy*, to image, information, and discourse—nor is it the time of the consumers, unevenly re-sponsive to the siren call of the commodity in all of its forms. On the contrary, the "instantism" of the new poetics proclaims its poets' access to "original" and uncontaminated realms of reality and meaning and extends the availabil-ity of that access to every individual born to the rhetorical manner. Both popu-list and idealist, this gesture is firmly rooted in the time-honored tradition of American writing which valorizes the *unmediated* and which turns poets away from the responsibility of engaging contemporary cultural life toward other "unpolluted" realms of the imagination usually expressed in American poetry through "the natural."

In discussing Ashbery's work here, I have no real wish to prolong the mythical life of a nature/culture opposition which has already played too great a role in reducing complex debates within American cultural life to facile par-tisan positions (Philip Rahv's Redskin/Paleface distinction is exemplary). In-deed, the significance of the work of a writer like Ashbery is that it tends to redefine such terms and oppositions rather than aligning itself one way or an-other. Nonetheless, there is little in Ashbery's work, early and late, that could be characterized in terms of an "instantist" poetics. The hard currency of ex-perience and reflection is almost always revealed as counterfeit, secondhand, and therefore presented in such a way as to advertise its own consciousness of mediation. Whenever we confront what seems like the realm of raw, asser-tive fact, the shock of planned obsolescence takes over; we find that the real is packaged, or simulated, to use Baudrillard's evocative term, in order merely to guarantee the hyperreality of the medium itself. There is no reason to trust this hyperreal, but there is little else to place one's trust in. For a "society of the spectacle" raised on the schlock productions of the commodity theater, the result is an easy familiarity with the vivid power of staged illusions.[3] In such a theater, nature now becomes the best that culture can produce in the way of artifice.

Writing in 1962 of the effect of Pierre Reverdy's "poésie de l'imagination," Ashbery notes that "it is as if you were to see a natural landscape for the first time, having only seen painted landscapes before."[4] The painted landscapes are those of the allegorical spaces of Symbolist poetry, overburdened with the "external dead weight" of excess meaning. For the part of Ashbery's work that was to take up the promise of Reverdy's fresh attention to objectivity, Nature was to assume the look and feel of a household necessity, either too starved of meaning or else unable to offer more than its current market value. Landscapes (and Ashbery is nothing if not a landscape poet) are haunted by their shortage of meaning and tend to compensate, as Ashbery wrote of another anti-Symbolist, Gertrude Stein, by agreeing to "create a counterfeit of reality more real than reality" itself.[5]

Perhaps this refusal to celebrate the unmediated is indeed one of the reasons why the growth of Ashbery's reputation and current status has been so out of sync with that of others of his generation. It was not until the mid-1970s, almost ten years after he had returned to New York from a relatively isolated decade of writing and reviewing in Paris, that his poetry garnered the public acclaim that has accompanied it ever since. In the 1960s, however, the stakes of demonstrably public action were somewhat different, even for writers, and Ashbery had long since chosen to keep his distance from the political fray. In a response to the charge of his lack of commitment to the antiwar movement, Ashbery wrote in a 1966 issue of *Bookweek* to defend a fellow poet and friend's apolitical stance: "Frank O'Hara's poetry has no program, and therefore it cannot be joined. It does not advocate sex and dope as a panacea for the ills of modern society; it does not speak out against the war in Vietnam or in favor of civil rights; it does not paint Gothic vignettes of the post-Atomic age; in a word, it does not attack the Establishment. It merely ignores its right to exist and is thus a source of annoyance to partisans of every stripe."[6] Responding, in a letter, to Louis Simpson's outrage over these comments in the *Nation,* Ashbery explained that he was not at all complimenting O'Hara for "not having written poetry about the war" but rather was praising him for "giving a unique voice to his own conscience, far more effective than most of the protest 'poetry' being written today." He went on: "Poetry is poetry. Protest is protest, I believe in both forms of action. . . . Incidentally, I signed and contributed money to the petition protesting the war."[7] Expressed today, these comments may sound subtle, strategic, even judicious. In the activist fervor of the sixties, they were wasted (and to many, hollow) words. Two years later, as demonstrators fought police at the opening of the Venice Biennale—Minimalist art (ostensibly, without direct social relevance) was being featured on the American pavilion while a terrible war was being waged in Southeast Asia—it seemed the most natural thing in the world for Daniel Buren to point

out that "art is inevitably allied to power—today it is obvious that 5,000 po-
licemen are sent to defend an avant-garde biennale."[8]

This was at a time when an antiaesthetic impulse was everywhere being
directed against the institutions of the art world, while concrete poetry, Happenings, performance art, and mixed-media assemblages threatened the re-
trenched, autonomous space of the poetic event. If it really was a time for
"partisans of every stripe" to show their true colors, then this was not Ashbery's decade. Nor was he ever very comfortable with the most highly refined
and less overtly political form to emerge from the 1960s rapprochement of
intellectuals with daily life—the parodically theatrical interpretation of kitsch
and bad taste which Susan Sontag described in "Notes on Camp" as "Dandy-
ism in the age of mass culture."[9] His work incorporates many of the characteristic elements of "camp": its banal, epicene style; its passion for artifice and
mannerism; its distance from moralism; and its penchant for fantasy and posture. But Ashbery seldom takes advantage of the consummate sense of tone,
timing, and delivery that comes with the full-blown, naive (as opposed to deliberate) camp "sensibility"—a corny panache that seems to have been captured forever in at least one O'Hara line ("Oh Lana Turner we love you get
up") from a justly famous poem which responds to news that the actress had
collapsed.[10] Ashbery refuses to *humanize* the tone of camp in the same way;
there is no recognizably marked voice with which and through which all the
camp elements can be dramatically identified and articulated. Rather than
camping up a dramatic scene or set of observations, Ashbery will give things
a dressing down, precisely by teasing out the details of each level of artifice and
decor, more often than not to their utterly banal, but always debunking, limits.
Take, for example, one of the scenes offered in "Description of a Masque"
from *A Wave*:

> Walking in place on a sidewalk which was actually a treadmill moving to-
> ward the back of the stage was a couple in their early thirties. Mania (for the
> woman was none other than she) was dressed in the style of Joan Crawford
> in *Mildred Pierce,* in a severe suit with padded shoulders and a pillbox with
> a veil crowning the pincurls of her unswept hairdo, which also cascaded to
> her shoulders, ending in more pincurls. Instead of the sheaf of gladioli she
> now clutched a black handbag suspended on a strap over her shoulder, and
> in place of the hyena, one of those *little white dogs* on the end of a leash kept
> sniffing the legs of pedestrians who were in truth mere celluloid phantoms,
> part of the process shot which made up the whole downtown backdrop. The
> man at her side wore a broad-brimmed hat, loose-fitting sport coat and
> baggy gabardine slacks; he bore a certain resemblance to the actor Bruce
> Bennett but closer inspection revealed him to be the statue of Mercury, with
> the paint still peeling from his face around the empty eye sockets. At first it
> looked as though the two were enjoying the holiday atmosphere and drink-
> ing in the sights and sounds of the city. Gradually, however, Mania's expres-

sion darkened; finally she stopped in the middle of the sidewalk and pulled at her escort's sleeve. (W 26)

Here, to be sure, Ashbery is writing in his Raymond Roussel mode, after what he called the "heightened voyeurism" of the great proto-Surrealist's narrative style, marked by its obsessive attention to gratuitous notation and visual detail. In the all-revealing context of this superreal, any attempts to charge the minutiae of style and taste with particular significance are sabotaged by the general leveling out of descriptive relief. There are elements that should stand out as distinctively kitsch: the peeling statue of Mercury, which belongs as much to Caesar's Palace as it does to De Chirico's haunted neo-Classical perspectives; the *little white dog* (one of *those*) which transcends, in its scandalous displacement of a hyena, the mere bourgeois ridicule that would otherwise attach to its owner; and the painstakingly described, film-clonish fashions of the couple. Rather than crystallize our semantic interests, these elements fall into mundane place as their cumulative meaning is first gathered up with a collector's devotion and then flattened out and absorbed by the spectator/narrator's omnivorous attention. The action and detail is at once too banal and seriously watched to work into genuinely kitsch effects, while the spectator's addiction to theatricality is presented, as always in Ashbery, in terms of everyday servitude to the pablum of "free" will: "we would go on witnessing these tableaux, not that anything prevented us from leaving the theater, but there was no alternative to our interest in finding out what would happen next" (27).

Elsewhere in Ashbery's work, there is an abundance of testaments to the culture of commerce, such as in the feverish "happy-go-nutty" rush of kitsch products that inundates and clutters up the narrative space of "Daffy Duck in Hollywood":

> La Celestina has only to warble the first few bars
> Of "I Thought about You" or something mellow from
> *Amadigi di Gaula* for everything—a mint-condition can
> Of Rumford's Baking Powder, a celluloid earring, Speedy
> Gonzales, the latest from Helen Topping Miller's fertile
> Escritoire, a sheaf of suggestive pix on greige, deckle-edged
> Stock—to come clattering through the rainbow trellis
> Where Pistachio Avenue rams,the 2300 block of Highland
> Fling Terrace.
>   (HD 31)

Equally serious is the tragedy of errors that afflicts Popeye, Olive, Swee'pea, and Wimpy in "Farm Implements and Rutabagas in a Landscape" (DDS 47–48), while on a different level of formal indulgence is the extraordinary inventory of the names of the world's rivers invoked in the precious mock-Faustian voice of "Into the Dusk-Charged Air":

                    The Parana stinks.
        The Ottawa is light emerald green
        Among grays. Better that the Indus fade
        In steaming sands! Let the Brazos
        Freeze solid! And the Wabash turn to a leaden
        Cinder of ice! The Marañon is too tepid, we must
        Find a way to freeze it hard.
            (RM 19)

Perhaps the most consistently diverse of Ashbery's discourses about the
quiddities of daily life can be found in his 1975 collaboration with artist Joe
Brainard in *The Vermont Notebook*, a text which plays upon the purely *artificial* differences between "town" and "country" (unlike, for example, the
more evenhanded though still hilariously wry tone maintained throughout *A
Nest of Ninnies*, the satiric novel about suburban life cowritten with James
Schuyler). For the country dwellers of *The Vermont Notebook*, there is no rustic peace at all between language and image: "They all look like faces on
Wacky Package stickers, or a klutz in Mad Comics, tortured past reason and
exploding in a human, all too human display of facial fireworks" (VN 75).
Here, as with many of Ashbery's encounters with images and languages from
mass culture, the use of neo-Surrealist juxtaposition helps to transform the raw
material into something more rich and certainly more strange than the "cheap"
and banal face of the mass artifact; there is, at any rate, never any sense of
order, aesthetic or otherwise, an order upon which camp stylism depends for
its construction of an entirely mannered world.

    In this respect, it is not easy to place Ashbery's work in the context of the
continuing debate about the role of the intellectual in mass culture.[11] While
Pop art announced the end of a period of alienation for intellectuals generally, the wholesale adoption of the commercial vernacular of an "ad-mass" environment meant that cultural production was polemically divided between
the kind of work that uncritically embraced the forms, images, technologies,
and artifacts of the commodity world and other, more critically informed texts
which either incorporated the vernacular in a highly ironic way or else chan-
neled the hybrid mix of popular and high cultural imagery into a political cru-
sade against the institutional privileges of traditional high culture forms. On
the one hand, the new appetite of an art culture for "novelty" art, based on the
ephemeral, the expendable, and the gimmicky (as opposed to, but clearly in-
herited from, the "innovative" ethic of modernism), enthusiastically expressed
the will of consumer capitalism in its tendency to convert popular desires for
social change into a desire for mere market novelty. On the other, artists and
writers found, in various applications of the collage principle—mixed media,
found objects and languages, random assemblages of "intruder" materials and

discourses—new ways of reiterating the fifty-year-old theme of the avant-garde, committed to an antiaesthetic and to the hermetic institution of art practices; committed, in short, to operating in what Rauschenberg called the "gap between art and life." For the collagists, then, the new attention to popular imagery heralded a properly democratic discourse of *demotic* culture, genuinely accessible to a public, while harboring within itself the violence necessary to break out of the husklike forms which would inevitably and successively grow around its mutant body, reclaiming it for the hermetic art world.

Even if Ashbery, as I have suggested, did not share the radical political disposition of the neo-avant-garde or the broader spirit of the 1960s counter-cultures, at least one of his volumes directly aligns itself with the formal spirit and repertoire of techniques espoused by the historical avant-garde of Europe between the wars. In fact, *The Tennis Court Oath*, published in 1962, two years after the *The New American Poetry* had appeared, is far and away the most characteristically "avant-gardist" work to come out of the "new American poetry." That same year, in Paris, Ashbery was writing in a French journal about how American poetry of the time looked to him from across the Atlantic: "It still languished in the shade of T. S. Eliot," and while poets had "impoverished the intellectual content of [Eliot's] poetry," they had hung on to other aspects, "the dry and dignified language or the tone of Alfred Prufrock," for example, that of "a sensitive bourgeois overtaken by events."[12] Not surprisingly, Ashbery's own tone of weary disdain in these comments recalls the very same mannered contempt once expressed toward American and British "Georgian" poets by Eliot and Pound themselves. But while they and other modernists sought to generate a poetics of *nostalgia* based on the intellectual exigencies of the expatriate, Ashbery, in Paris in the sixties, was living, as he put it of the artist Joan Mitchell, as an *apatrides,* resigned to "producing a rather negative feeling of being at home," in distinct contrast to the modernist anxiety about origins.[13] So too was he remote not only from the patrilinear anxiety of influence of the American poetry "tradition" but also from the turbulent politics of the New York art world of the fifties and sixties: "a period of reversals and surprises, palace revolutions, deathbed conversions, posthumous knightings, anathemas, miraculous presages, eclipses, earthquakes and floods."[14]

The Tennis Court Oath is most often regarded by critics either as an early and therefore "immmature phase" or else by those, like Harold Bloom, who wield and exercise the appropriate institutional authority to make such judgments, as a "fearful disaster."[15] The epistemological model for both of these kinds of critical pronouncement is, of course, that of the unified, coherent field of the "author," replete with a recognizable career trajectory in terms of mature, creative development, issuing, from time to time, in masterpieces. Bloom, more than anyone, has successfully written Ashbery into that kind of heroic story which explains all of the contradictions and discontinuities of a writer's work in terms of *idiosyncrasy*. Construed by their own lights, the collagist techniques developed in *The Tennis Court Oath* would preclude any possibility of presenting such a unified author, interpreting and commenting on social reality from an aesthetically secured distance. For collage and montage, the basic formal principles of avant-gardist activity, depend upon the intrusion or intervention of found materials to break up the purified realm of the poem or artwork. They do not constitute a medium through which authors can transfigure their traditional role of alienated commentator. In the distinctive shift between the "created" and the "found," authors lose the power to elevate themselves as source and origin of all the transformative impulses that inhabit the text. In the context of the historical avant-garde, this loss of power strikes hard at the bourgeois Romantic ideology of creative autonomy. For the neo-avant-garde of the sixties, face to face with the massive neutrality of the commodity world, it makes all the difference between, on the one hand, sophisticated and urbane poets who are able, through safeguarding the integrity of their voice and its poetic medium, to *comment* upon the excesses of popular culture and, on the other, collagists who construct a poetic surface upon which the languages and imagery of popular culture can be reproduced and incorporated into the substance of the text. There are poems, then, which express an *attitude* toward mass culture, and there are poems which are *transformed* by mass culture because they have structurally absorbed if not wholly integrated a wide range of demotic elements into the medium itself.

That *The Tennis Court Oath* belongs to the latter category in no way elevates its critical worth as a set of poems over and above the work of other poets of the sixties who chose the former path, those who elected to retain the position of social commentator in verse, as if they were somehow expressing the consensus voice of the day—that heady mix of admiration and revulsion for consumer culture which informed critically acute opinion during and after the "Pop" years. On the contrary, what *The Tennis Court Oath* presents is an alternative to the politics of content which would limit that kind of poetic commentary to a mere ethics of opinion, the higher democratic option. Thirty years earlier, Walter Benjamin had outlined a similar alternative for the political avant-garde of the thirties in "The Author as Producer." Confronted with the obligation to exhibit both *tendency* (the politically correct opinion, i.e., socialist realist, populist) and *quality* (the aesthetically superior expression), writers, Benjamin argued, are unable to acknowledge their position as producers within the literary relation of production of their time. For writers to enter into these relations and thereby escape the problematic role of being intellectual leaders/servants of the proletariat, the relation between tendency and quality must be redefined. A politics of form or technique must emerge, whereby political "correctness" would necessarily involve writers' attention to the entire cultural apparatus which governs the production of meaning in their work. It is not enough, Benjamin observes, simply to support this or that dogma in print. Properly political writers must engage, change, and transform the technical conditions under which their work is produced in order to respond to the call for technological progress which was the watchword for the socialism of Benjamin's day. With this set of arguments, and with his symptomatic assumption that "literary tendency can consist either in progress or in regression in literary technique," Benjamin reaffirmed his commitment to the ideal of progress shared by the innovative spirits of the European avant-garde movements.[16]

In itself, this unquestioned belief in technical progress would serve today to distance us from Benjamin's arguments. The modernist passion for innovation, as I have suggested, has long since been rearticulated in the culture of the "novelty" or the gimmick, while the allied Utopian project of finding ever more ingenious technical *solutions* to modernist problems of form took on its most unsavory, if not inevitable, expression in the Fascist utopia of social engineering—the final solution. So too, the hortatory tone of Benjamin's rhetoric would be marked as histrionic in a postwar American culture in which intellectuals have relieved themselves of the priestly burden of emancipating mass consciousness. Nonetheless, the issues which he addresses are more than pertinent to the situation of sixties intellectuals, honestly confronting, for the first time, the commodity world. Denied autonomy in the same way as writers and artists of the thirties, the sixties intellectual was now compelled to take up a position, either on the side of tendentious social commentary or else on the side of transforming his or her medium of expression. These are clear alternatives, even if they were not articulated as mutually exclusive options for sixties artists and writers. For those who responded, however, by transforming their respective media—Pop artists and, later, Conceptualists, writers like the Ashbery of *The Tennis Court Oath*, Burroughs of the cut-up, Cage of "collaged sound," the concrete poets, the performance artists, and many others—the choice was one which radicalized their response to non-art environments.

Writing in Paris at the turn of the decade, jotting down overheard conversations, pirating fragments from newspapers, and lifting, cutting, and pasting whole passages from pulp novels, Ashbery could hardly be closer in form and technique, if not spirit, to the strategies of Hugo Ball, Kurt Schwitters, Paul Marinetti, Raoul Haussman, Tristan Tzara, and the other topographers of chance who populated the European avant-garde before and after the First World War. Throughout *The Tennis Court Oath*, named after one of the great historical covenants with revolutionary action, there are self-conscious echoes of the way in which these poems flaunt their resistance to the overlegislated, repetitive codes of poetic form:

I was almost killed now by reading on trial.
   (TCO 16)

Police formed a boundary to the works
Where we played
A torn page with a passionate oasis.
   (59)

The editor realised
Its gradual abandonment.
   (65)

The homage encoded in the jacket reproduction of David's famously un-finished painting of the Tennis Court Oath is conducted through a bleached, blurred, and markedly denuded image of the artist's sketch, further obscured by the shading of two-thirds of the reproduction and broken up by the diago-nal intrusion of a visiting card announcing the title of the volume. More than any of Ashbery's other dust covers, this one advertises its place in an age of mechanical reproduction in which the pristine genius of the image is at once "cheapened" and democratically disseminated through its loss of affect. So too, the poems in the volume both honor and merely contain the everyday. Their perpetual effort is to renovate the quotidian through the technologically produced shock. The most well-used techniques conform to what the Russian Formalists had called defamiliarization, the decontextualization, or alien sub-stitution, of one or more elements of a phrase:

                    the postman bent down
Delivered his stare into the grass.
   (TCO 24)

The factory to be screwed onto palace.
   (39)

The igloo sun, while I was away
Chastened the wolverine towels.
   (36)

Guns were fired to discourage dogs into the interior.
   (56)

The arctic honey blabbed over the report, causing darkness.
   (33)

Wine fished out of the sea.
   (62)

Because of the riot of meaning encouraged by these effects, this kind of writing strategy is less planned than unconsciously agreed upon. Any liberal reading, in effect, will make us consciously aware of what we unconsciously write in our reading. A naturalizing reading, however, will be very much like the process of secondary dream revision as it works to displace meaning further in order to conceal better from waking recognition the more unacceptable truths of unconscious desire. The result of this is not at all to draw attention to the "originality" of the poem itself, in the sense in which we might admire the striking way in which a writer chooses and presents a particular metaphor. On the contrary, the shock effect of defamiliarization is precisely to demonstrate how "original" effects are always a function of the given and the conventional, and that they are constantly being generated out of our newly estranged relation to the everyday consumption of the real.

In this respect, the deepest poetics in *The Tennis Court Oath* is to eradicate, at all levels, formal and material (through decontextualization and collage), the experience of an original work created through autonomous authorial agency. It would be a fatal mistake, however, to dehistoricize Ashbery's use of the found and the given within the classical context of shock, chance, and defamiliarization. For these classical strategies of the historical avant-garde are already employed here with some of the retro consciousness which we have come to associate with a commodity culture that has learned to absorb and assimilate all of the attempts of high modernism to escape the domestic homogeneity of mass culture. To reiterate these techniques three or four decades after they were first adopted is also to recycle them and thus to regard them as if they were already a second-order reality, in the same way as we read the advertising strategies of an advanced consumer society. For it is these same strategies that seek to rejuvenate or spice up the everyday real, transforming what we recognize as banal into a garden of earthly delights. Indeed, for the purposes of representation, Madison Avenue shares more than a few of the formal objectives of the avant-garde's treatment of everyday objects. To recognize this is to recognize some of the new tension that exists between the "banal" and the "strange" in Ashbery's use of shock: "you called midway between the jaws" (TCO 51). Even if shock doesn't always work, the aims that lie behind its commitment to accidentalism are relatively clear-cut in the historical avant-garde context. The instances of shock on the accidental surface of *The Tennis Court Oath* are more ambiguous: it is the commitment itself that seems random and, often, conspicuously absent when, for long stretches of verse, the effects do not come off at all:

> Only beauty offered sin
> Out of the round and the oval
> Something to match the edges of dawn
> The house where it took place
> Pardon on the face of the tall wall

That land burned season on it scum
The fence removed and all the tile gone.
    (TCO 60)

The lack of semantic rhythm in these passages does not allow the poetry to take on an organic feel; the result is more like a death mask, with distorted features that are still held together by their familiar internal structure, as if to record, perhaps, how "the body's products become / Fatal to it" (TCO 20). Similarly, the "characters" who populate the volume wear the rigor mortis of their decontextualized anonymity; to name only a few, "the mulatress," "the doctor" (11); "the janitor," "the conductor" (17); "the inspector" (22); "the postman" (24); "the dwarf" (26); "the judge" (32); "the epilectic," "the nude" (36); "the travellers," "the children" (38); "the workers" (39); "the merchant" (40); "the naked girl" (41); "the phantom," "the heroine" (47); "the technician" (49); "the barman," "the pilot" (55); "the suffragette," "the Ethiop" (60); "the sheriff" (61); "the ashman" (63); "the surgeon," "the waiter," "the editor" (65); "the librarian" (67); "the stranger" (69); "the professor" (75); "the visitor" (80); "the patient" (88); "the uncle" (90): These unformed, narrative agents have nothing to do with the grand concrete universals of a more neoclassical poetry. Here they are, stranded in an alien context where their roles have no direct relation to the (non)narrative action; where they belong, of course, is in the no less socially detailed world of popular fiction—the pulp mystery, children's story, spy or detective novel, where stock figures (more often than not, figures of authority like "the doctor," "the professor," "the judge," etc.) are necessary to the familiar morphology of the plot. Unchallengeable, even as barely animated figures, within that morphology, their legislative functions are presented in *The Tennis Court Oath* without any of the structural support which they depend upon.

Other, more recognizable avant-garde techniques often contain a description of their very function, as here, in a Dadaist word salad:

       broom
   recent   past symbolized
hair banana
does not evoke a concrete image

the splendid
    (TCO 79)

Or here, in a synesthetic mélange:

Between the legs of her
Cobwebs the lip reads chewing

and taste seems uncertain;
powerless creating images
     (81)

In such lines the *taste* for verbal pleasure is erotically produced: "the darkness
will have none of you, and you are folded into it like mint into the sound of
haying" (57); or "the eyes and clitoris a million miles from / The small persistent tug" (59). Such taste is elsewhere sabotaged by a self-conscious assault on
the very equilibrium of meaning: "the arboretum is bursting with jasmine and
lilac / And all I can smell here is newsprint."

The reader of these variously disjunct, cognitive effects will be able to take
as their directly conventional referent the semantic aporias of the historical
avant-garde: Apollinaire's simultaneist and "orphic" poems; Marinetti's typo-
graphical collages; the destructive speed of Ball and Malevich's sound texts;
Haussman's octophonetic poetry; Schwitters's found, "merzed" fragments;
Tzara's "*je m'en foutisme*"; and the automatic writing of Breton and Eluard.
Because of this second-order knowledge, such a reader will view *The Tennis
Court Oath* as much in the autodestructive spirit of Tinguely's mechanical assemblages as in the constructivist spirit of the original *cadavre exquis*, with its
purist faith in the dogma of juxtaposition. What I mean by this is that for the
historical avant-garde, there is no question of its strategies failing; the reader's
response is either to accept the task of producing new meanings out of these
collages or else to opt for a more traditional cultural expression for which
reading is more like consuming. But *The Tennis Court Oath* already harbors
within itself historical knowledge about the failures of the avant-garde, not
only on the level of cognitive/aesthetic strategies of shock, but also in the context of the politically utopian project of constructing a new social reality. This
assimilation of failure is the historical difference which any reading of the neo-
avant-garde of the sixties makes, and it is a difference that is conventionally
written into Ashbery's volume. It seems to come as no surprise, for example,
when a long text entitled "Europe" begins with an invitation to a scene of
ongoing destruction:

To employ her
construction ball
Morning fed on the
light blue wood
of the mouth.
     (TCO 64)

Violence and lyricism are spliced together in a way redolent of the opening
of *The Waste Land*. Here, just as in that earlier poem, the bourgeois facades

of European culture are slated for demolition. But Eliot's real motive was the reconstruction, or rather, restoration, of the still-resonant power of a high culture tradition through the use of allusion, lyrical invocation, and montage. By contrast, the contemporaneous Dada cabaret had taken great pains to shatter any last, vestigial exercise of bourgeois sympathy with those highly resonant forms. Both of these projects are, in a sense, historical referents of Ashbery's poem. In "Europe," however, there is no recognizable European culture myth left to demolish. Rather, the struggle for cultural hegemony, for the English speaker at least, is being fought out between two imperialist discourses: on the one hand, the lingering power of the "heroic" British popular fictions (the marvellously obscure spy adventure story, William Le Queux's *Beryl of the Biplanes* supplies fragments and whole passages as raw material for the poem) and, on the other, the growing attachment to American newspaper culture with its own scaled-down discursive forms. Similarly, the collaged landscape of the poem, while it in no way laments the "fragments shored against my ruins" as Eliot's had done, flattens out the celebrated shock treatment of constructivist montage by distributing its effects as evenly as possible over the taxonomically sectioned-off surface of the poem. As a result, both *history* and *shock*, the radical moves, respectively, of high modernism and the avant-garde, are immobilized alongside the aleatory speed of the poetic surface.

A similar loss of affect occurs when Ashbery attends to more semantically continuous poetry, as in "How Much Longer Will I Be Able to Inhabit the Divine Sepulcher":

> How much longer will I be able to inhabit the divine sepulcher
> Of life, my great love? Do dolphins plunge bottomward
> To find the light? Or is it rock
> That is searched? Unrelentingly? Huh. And if some day
>
> Men with orange shovels come to break open the rock
> Which encases me, what about the light that comes in then?
> What about the smell of the light?
> What about the moss?
> (TCO 25)

In this remarkably fluid opening, a vernacular rhythm is transformed into an astonishing rereading of a very traditional poetic line, but the operation is executed with the same kind of banal nonchalance that Ashbery will develop in his later rhythmic successes. The interest of this lies in the way in which these lines go so far as to mimic or "impersonate" the technical proficiency which such an operation would otherwise suggest. What they actually do for the reader, then, is to offer a statement about continuity, both semantic and technical. The checkered, discontinuous surface of the rest of the poem—business as usual for *The Tennis Court Oath*—reflects back upon this statement by demonstrating its exact inverse: the sheer banality of formalistic anxiety.

In reading such poems, we are shown how and why language has nothing at all to do with unmediated expression, except when it chooses to voice parodically the fallacy of such an idea. This paradox is best demonstrated in some of the most celebrated lines of *The Tennis Court Oath*, the opening of "They Dream Only of America":

> They dream only of America
> To be lost among the thirteen million pillars of grass:
> "This honey is delicious
> *Though it burns the throat*."
>   (TCO 13)

Four different, and successively more marked, levels of conventionality are stressed here, from the general assertion of the freestanding first line to the specific, quoted, emphasized, and dependent clause of the fourth; each line is decontextualized, automatically, as it is succeeded by the next. Because of the syntactical "rhyme" between the two couplets, moreover, the stanza is allowed to flaunt its own symmetry. But it is only under the pressure of this stanzaic logic that the aching lyricism of the first couplet prefigures and is thrown up against the deadpan irony of the second. Semantically, of course, the reader has the choice of naturalizing the various elements of meaning suggested in these lines. An "American dream" (exceptionalist—"they dream only") of pastoral innocence and plenitude (the land of milk and "honey") is stripped once again of its hopes of a Whitmanesque pluralism by the reality and sheer numericality of mass culture ("thirteen million"), while the new consumer religion either chemically simulates or doctors "natural" products in ways that are harmful to our health ("burns the throat"). To recuperate the world of meaning in this way is, however, to short-circuit those strategies of poetic artifice which offer us less in the way of interpretive freedom than does the *acte gratuite* of the more discontinuous areas of *The Tennis Court Oath*. What we are asked to accept and acknowledge in this passage are the various levels of artifice and convention which separate us from any unmediated expression of sympathy with, or complaint against, the protocols of mass culture. To recognize this is doubly important if it involves the reader in critically following through exactly the same procedures by which we constitute ourselves conventionally as citizens in a mass consumer society. Writing and reading at the beginning of the 1960s, this consumer imagination made all the difference for involved readers who were not only aware of the limited democracy of the historical avant-garde project but also responsive to the demotic passion of those artists and writers, like Ashbery, busy revising the medium forty years later.

Notes

1. Donald Allen and George Butterick, eds., *The Postmoderns: The New American Poetry Revised* (New York: Grove, 1982), 9-10.

2. Robert von Hallberg, *American Poetry and Culture, 1945-80* (Cambridge: Harvard University Press, 1985), 28. Von Hallberg's introduction and first chapter are expressly devoted to discussing the sociopolitical "centrality" of the American poet.

3. See my "Alcatraz Effect: Belief and Postmodernity," *SubStance* 13, no. 1 (1984): 71-85, and also my chapter on Ashbery in *The Failure of Modernism: Symptoms of American Poetry* (New York: Columbia University Press, 1986), in which I discuss at length the discourse of illusion which permeates Ashbery's work.

4. "Reverdy en Amérique," *Mercure de France* 344, no. 1181 (January 1962): 111.

5. Ashbery's review of Stein's *Stanzas in Meditation* is called "The Impossible," *Poetry* 90, no. 4 (July 1957): 254.

6. "Frank O'Hara's Question," *Bookweek*, September 25, 1966.

7. *Nation* 204, no. 19 (May 8, 1967): 578.

8. Daniel Buren, "Is Teaching Art Necessary?" *Galerie des arts* 7, no. 12 (September 1968).

9. Susan Sontag, "Notes on Camp," in *Against Interpretation* (New York: Farrar, Straus & Giroux, 1965).

10. *The Collected Poems of Frank O'Hara*, ed. Donald Allen (New York: Knopf, 1972), 449.

11. Ashbery's own comments about Pop art display his concerns about commercial complicity. In his "Paris Notes" column for *Art International* for June 1963, he regrets that his absence from America since the advent of Pop art has prevented him from seeing the work firsthand. Of one Paris show, however, he questions the moral position of Pop: "Are we to like Hine's root beer, or hate it, or hate ourselves for liking it?" In his view, Pop art must address with more complexity the hackneyed issue of "modern man vs. the supermarket" (76). In a later review of a Martial Raysse show in *Art News* (October 1965), he suggests that Raysse's work "does not have the banality, the aggression, nor the moralising undertones of the American product. He is concerned exclusively with pleasure, and if his work is still a little frightening (like most Pop Art), this is because of the ruthless way he suppresses everything but supposedly agreeable images, and because of our deep puritanical reservations about pleasure. . . . Raysse apparently does see himself as the apologist for the satisfactoriness of these pleasures, commercial and hollow as they may seem" (59).

12. "Reverdy en Amérique," 110.

13. "An Expressionist in Paris," *Art News* 64, no. 2 (April 1965): 44.

14. "Post-Painterly Quattrocento," *Art News* 65, no. 8 (December 1966): 40.

15. Harold Bloom, *Figures of Capable Imagination* (New York: Seabury Press, 1976), 191.

16. Walter Benjamin, "The Author as Producer," in *Reflections: Essays, Aphorisms, Autobiographical Writings*, ed. Peter Demetz, trans. Edmund Jephcott (New York: Harcourt Brace Jovanovitch, 1978), 222.

12 | The Music of Construction

Measure and Polyphony
in Ashbery and Bernstein

John Shoptaw

> To read your meter, mark on the enclosed card exactly where the arrows on your meter are pointing. Then write in the box above each dial the number the pointer has just passed.
>
> —Peter J. Lyndon, Jr., ComGas instruction manual

WHAT IS THE music of construction of a poem? What does a poem's music have to do with its production of meaning? What do we listen for when we construe a poem's sonic sense? How do we measure its coming into meaning or its resistance to meaning? Neither traditional nor linguistically renovated prosody sufficiently describes the music of metrical poetry. Identifying Hopkins's "Spelt from Sibyl's Leaves" as an octameter sonnet helps us appreciate its hypermetrical force. But the invocational power of its beginning, "Earnest, earthless, equal, attuneable, vaulty, voluminous, . . . stupendous / Evening," has less to do with syllables, sprung or not, than with words. Hopkins's ellipsis suggests his list is immeasurable.[1] So too, knowing that Dickinson's poem "Hér—'last Póems'— / Póets—énded— / Sílver—perished—wíth her Tóngue—" (#312) uses the ballad rhythm known as 8s and 7s enables us to hear the crucial emphasis on "Her" in this elegy for Elizabeth Bárrett Brówning, whose nominal trochaic rhythms Dickinson echoes.[2] But Dickinson's music depends on the counterrhythms marked by her dashes, which unexpectedly isolate words and phrases. With American postmodern poetry, in which the familiar metrical and stanzaic markers are often missing or self-consciously adapted, the need for a new system of measurement is even more apparent. In this essay I will notch a new rod for divining postmodern poetry by comparing John Ashbery's and Charles Bernstein's musics of construction.

Ashbery and Bernstein have both characterized their poetry in musical terms. In a 1965 statement, Ashbery emphasized the relational structures of music: "What I like about music is its ability of being convincing, of carrying an argument through successfully to the finish, though the terms of this argument remain unknown quantities. What remains is the structure, the architecture of the argument, scene or story. I would like to do this in poetry."[3] And

212 I *John Shoptaw*

in a 1972 interview, conducted soon after he had finished his dialectical prose *Three Poems,* Ashbery draws attention to musical progression: "The thing about music is that it's always going on and reaching a conclusion and it helps me to be surrounded by this moving climate that it produces—moving I mean in the sense of going on."[4] For Bernstein as for Ashbery, poetry consists of inherently meaningful arguments and measures. In "Thought's Measure" (1980), Bernstein speaks of poetic measure as "the *unit* of ordering—phoneme, morpheme, word, phrase, sentence, etc." (CD 75).[5] In "Semblance" (1980), which helps dispel the idea that Language poetry is nonreferential and meaningless, Bernstein offers a fuller description of a poem's thoughtful music:

> the music of meaning—emerging, fogging, contrasting, etc. Tune attunement in understanding—the meaning sounds. It's impossible to separate prosody from the structure (the form and content seen as an interlocking figure) of a given poem. You can talk about strategies of meaning generation, shape, the kinds of sounds accented, the varieties of measurement (of scale, of number, of line length, of syllable order, of word length, of phrase length, or measure as punctuation, of punctuation as metrics). But no one has primacy—the music is the orchestrating these into the poem, the angles one plays against another, the shading. (CD 38)

The amplest description of poetry demands attunement to its music. But no description is as ample as its poem. Nor would it be of much use to us if it were. In this study, I plan to modify, and to some degree codify, Bernstein's and Ashbery's descriptions of a poem's music, its measured argument, to develop some new methods of poetic measurement.

Following Bernstein, I will define a poem's measure as its smallest unit of resistance to meaning. I say "smallest" because we make sense of a text by absorbing larger and larger units of meaning; we don't usually pause to check the spelling of words in novels. Insofar as a unit of meaning calls attention to itself and either delays or disrupts the argument or movement or progressive development of a text, it establishes itself as a measure of construction. James constructed his later novels and stories largely out of unwieldy, writerly sentences, while Joyce composed at the level of the portmanteau word and even the letter. Reading *Finnegans Wake* for the plot requires overcoming a lot of resistance. Poetry, as most readers will attest, resists—delays, redefines, calls attention to—the construction of meaning more tenaciously than prose. Experimental poems, which misrepresent not only ordinary language but ordinary poetic language, offer resistance from the smallest to the largest units of significance. Even if a poem makes little or no sense in the usual sense of the word, it always makes music.

My units of poetic measurement in this essay will be the character, the word, the phrase, the line, the sentence, and the section.[6] Each measure raises its own set of expectations, so that departures from the rules are audible. If the measure is a character, for instance, we expect an entire upright letter or number to be printed (not handwritten or partially erased) in the same typeface as neighboring characters, and we expect these characters to combine into, or punctuate, words; if a word, we expect it to be spelled correctly and separated from other words; if a phrase, we expect regular word order and grammatical completeness (if not independence); if a line, we expect it to be straight and horizontal, and (less confidently) we expect a complete metrical, grammatical, semantic, or imagistic segment; if a sentence, we expect an implied or explicit subject, verb, and possibly an object to convey a complete thought or expression; and if a section (marked by a space or page break, a number, a title, and so on), we expect its varied rules to remain relatively consistent. Across sentences and verse or prose paragraphs, traces of a story or a situation—what Ashbery calls an argument—or versions of a discourse (e.g., a lab report, a sermon, or a commercial) create expectations of logical and narrative and discursive conclusions and resolutions. Such expectations, of course, are conditioned by literary and cultural history and by individual reading habits. Reading and writing can fail if expectations of measure are either disappointed or satisfied too consistently. These measured expectations are not strictly or equally audible. The fragmentary lines "red, black" and "red. Black" differ by more than the indefinite length of their caesural pause. The first "sounds like" (and a poem's constructive music has often to do with recognition) part of a list, while the second sounds like the border between two sentences. A poem's unheard music is made sweeter when its silences are diversified by particular missing sounds.

Poets measure in conjunction with, and counter to, other measures. A poem may consist of one-word or one-sentence lines. But measures often overlap. In Homeric verse, for instance, the poet knits hexameter lines together by threading sentences through them. We may describe such poetry as measured by the line or verse and countermeasured by the sentence. Poems more than a few lines long may be read as composed of several measures, from the character up to the verse paragraph perhaps. And sometimes the difference between a measure and a countermeasure is relative, since both measures lay equal claims on our attention. Yet a poet will often focus the resistance of a measure with a single, unequal and opposite countermeasure, so that we find ourselves pulled in one or more pairs of distinct, rather than no, directions at once.

The horizontal, successive dimension of measure and countermeasure is only a partial measurement of a poem's music of construction. The vertical, simultaneous dimension of overtones and resonances plays its part in playing off the reader's expectations. Ashbery's trademark "personal-pronoun lapses" (FC 150), which shift the lyric key, multiply the solo lyric voice. Ashbery has described his own negative capabilities as polyphonic: "I guess I don't have a very strong sense of my own identity and I find it very easy to move from one person in the sense of a pronoun to another and this again helps to produce a kind of polyphony in my poetry which I again feel is a means toward greater naturalism."[7] Polyphonic resonances layer the smallest compositional intervals. Ashbery has recalled his habit of resonant revision: "I just wrote a poem this morning in which I used the word 'borders' but changed it to 'boarders.' The original word literally had a marginal existence and isn't spoken, is perhaps what you might call a crypt word."[8] I will use Ashbery's nonce term to identify this largely neglected polyphonic dimension of a poem. I will call the unwritten word or words the crypt word and crypt phrase, their replacements the markers, and the revisionary procedure or process (sonic, semantic, etc.) cryptography. Though missing from the final text, and often from the original manuscript, crypt words and phrases are nevertheless audible by virtue of their markers' deviation from expected stock phrases, idioms, and grammatical or syntactic patterns. Like a counterpointed metrical foot, the crypt word reverberates in its marker. All poets, not only resolute experimenters, compose with crypt words. Reading for similar sounds, rather than simply for associated meanings, is indispensable to reconstructing poetic meaning.[9]

Ashbery's crypt words are common in his most obviously experimental book, *The Tennis Court Oath*. Some markers rhyme or slightly alter their crypt words, reverberating in letter measure: "Boots on the golden age of landscape" (TCO 22; "Books"), "screwed onto palace" (39; "into place"), "Time stepped" (66; "stopped"). Others involve metonymic substitutions and syntactic rearrangement: "the great outside" (19; "outdoors"), "Burnt by the powder of that view" (29; "powder burn"), "As we gallop into the flame" (58; "sunset"). But Ashbery has continued to compose with crypt words, even in later works which are less immediately disconcerting. Homophonic crypt words occasionally pipe up in the conversationally diffuse *Flow Chart*: "Sad grows the river god as he oars past us" (FC 3; "rows," "roars"), "idle retreats" (109; "threats"), "the evangelist profited" (47; "prophet," "prophesied"). But associative, word-measured substitutions are more frequent: "cultivates certain smells" (7; "tastes"), "walking away from a cure" (32; "fight"). Sometimes turns of phrase are noted even as they are mangled: "gilding the / pill as you might say" (129; "sugarcoating the pill," "gilding the lily"), "the path is what you call freckled with blemishes" (138; "fraught with danger"). Ashbery drew attention to this phrase itself in "Variant":

> The way
> Is fraught with danger, you say, and I
> Notice the word "fraught" as you are telling
> Me
>   (HD 4)

But in *Flow Chart,* it is we who notice the difference between "fraught with danger" and its hilarious reformulation.

In discussing his own vectors of composition, Bernstein describes a similar cryptographic process. In "Semblance" he writes of "working at angles to the strong tidal pull of an expected sequence of a sentence—or by cutting off a sentence or phrase midway and counting on the mind to complete where the poem goes off in another direction, giving two vectors at once—the anticipated projection underneath and the actual wording above" (CD 38). At the larger level of discourse, Bernstein notes that "by combining those sentences with other types of language, the clash in the sounds of the discourses creates a polyphony that interests me" (CD 456). In a 1981 interview, Bernstein expands this musical analogy:

> Polyvalences and polyrhythms occurring overall throughout the poem create a music of the text, a music that has to do with both the rhyming/comparing/vectoring of possible meanings, creating *chords* of the simultaneous vectors of the several interpretations of each polyentendre, and with the combination of these chords with other chords, durationally, in the sequence of the writing, and simultaneously, in the overall structure. The overall "sound" of the work is actually more important to listen for than the linear prosodic sequences, since the relation of the "chords" reinforces the sound resonances and echoes creating an intense overall vibration that adds a dynamic dimensional depth to the sound of any given linear movement. (CD 396–97)

As his own work demonstrates, Bernstein is not merely waxing analogical. Like Ashbery, Bernstein is fond of the polyphonic possibilities of stock phrases and proverbs, which he sometimes echoes with a parenthetical variant:

> Knocks
> on the door of deferred opportunity
> (mops on the floor of perfumed
> importunity).
>   (I/I 46)

Or consider the following, where we hear " . . . is better than none":

> half a loaf
> would be not
> so good as
>
> no loaf (half
> a boast not
> so good as
>
> no boast).
>   (RT 57)

In "Semblance" he invents illustrative phrases which "allow for this combination of projection and reflection in the movement from word to word. 'For as much as, within the because, tools their annoyance, tip to toward' " (CD 37). These polyvalent phrases are burdened with undertones, among which are "inasmuch as, within the clause, fuels their annoyance, tip forward." More than Ashbery's, Bernstein's verbal resonances cross grammatical boundaries. While "tools" may be an unexpected verb, "because" and "toward" aren't nouns at all, though forced to function as such. Bernstein sometimes employs these dissonant chords as a closural device, to stall out a phrase, a sentence, or a poem. "But Boxes Both Boats," an early hymn to domesticity, closes with this iambic spell: "Contain this charm, permit / what clutches spore" (R 3). Usually a noun, the marker "spore" philters this embrace with reproductive powers, but its resonant crypt word "spare" marks how dangerous such clutches, including Bernstein's own apprehensive grasp, may be.

The intricacy, and seriousness, of Bernstein's cryptography may be illustrated by the opening sentence of "The Harbor of Illusion" (crypt phrase: "to harbor illusions"), which makes its music not only from its trochaic tick but from its tidal undertones:

> At midnight's scrawl, the fog has
> lost its bone and puffs of
> pall are loamed at
> tidal edge.
>   (S 177)

The keys to reading this polyphonic sentence are not in one's dictionary but in one's ears. The crypt word we expect and hear under "scrawl" is the clock's "stroke," a temporal mark which the fog blurs into a "scrawl." The misted word-boundary between "midnight's scrawl" exposes "crawl." The "fog" buries "dog" as a dog its bone, and "pall" clouds "smoke" looming in the loam at the "tidal ledge." Eliot hid a "yellow dog" in the "fog" of "Prufrock" and transformed its gestures into a cat's. Sandburg's harbor-bound "fog" with "little cat feet" also seeps into Bernstein's "Harbor." But Bernstein's resonances go beyond wit or figuration or "poetic vision." The metonymic associations— "scrawl" for "stroke" and "dog" with "crawl"—are made possible by sonic deformation. The harbor fog, that is, resounded in the ear before it was imagined in the eye.

Bernstein's and Ashbery's polyphonic measures are differently paced. One of the most interesting contrasts between the musics of Ashbery and Bernstein comes from Bernstein himself. In one interview, Bernstein concedes Ashbery's influence but hastens to articulate their rhythmic distinctions:

Sure, Ashbery, too, where although the image generation is fairly fluid and the transitions elegant, a framing mechanism is still active, though most especially and usefully in *The Tennis Court Oath, Rivers and Mountains* and *Three Poems.* . . . I don't want to produce an unending flow of dream/psychic/automatic material or images . . . but the questioning, the stopping, built into the structure of the poem, seems to me crucial to seeing the constituting nature of language, which is the reading value I've been suggesting, and that indeed this stopping/framing allows the *music* of the poem to be heard, the music being hearing the sound *come into* meaning rather than a play with already existing meanings by way of meter. (CD 389–91)

Most readers would probably agree that Ashbery's poems have had more flow and Bernstein's more hover. But it is also true that Bernstein's distinction carries a string of implications. Flowing and stopping also characterize modes of being and behaving: smooth and rough, elegant (graceful) and rude (awkward), romantic and realist, diffuse and concentrated, accommodating and oppositional, even and odd, dreaming and waking, unconscious and conscious, emotional and intellectual, temporal and spatial, and so on. But neither poet wants to, or does, confine himself to his own side of the fence. Bernstein's poetry is as strongly emotional, for instance, as Ashbery's is analytical.

Bernstein's first long self-characterizing sequence, "Substance Abuse," written around the time he composed written answers for the interview quoted above, shows a poet of two minds about flowing and stopping. One section begins with self-doubting reflections. "Everything I write, in some mood, sounds / bad to me," the diarist confesses. "Rough / cuts satisfy, intrinsically, no more / than seamless webs" (I/I 79). In the seventh stanza of the poem, Bernstein suddenly shifts from double- to single-spaced and capitalized lines, claiming the best of both worlds:

> To move from moment to moment without
> Break is the ideal from which there is no
> Escape. But isn't what is wanted to
> Stop and hover, go back and forth at mea-
> Sured speed, to dwell everywhere or only as
> Chosen.
>   (I/I 80)

The period punctuating Bernstein's question marks it as rhetorical; he means to persuade us, not himself. Bernstein has recently tested Ashbery's influential currents in "The Influence of Kinship Patterns upon Perception of an Ambiguous Stimulus."[10] After a long preamble, Bernstein rocks Ashbery's Marvellian boat, "As One Put Drunk into the Packet-Boat" (SPCM 1), with parodic Bloomian anxiety:

> Ashbery. While the packet
> Boat sunk I can still imagine I am
> Crawling into it
> (DC 132)

No indebted sailor would desert a sinking ship. Finally, Bernstein confronts his distant kin:

> Let's face it—
> From the word *go* you've
> Resented me—resented my being finished
> In the face of your—what?—continuing
> On?
> (DC 134)

(Cf. Ashbery's "What Is Poetry": "It might give us—what?—some flowers soon?" [HD 47].) Bernstein may have started late, but by stopping early he finishes first.

Under different names, flowing and stopping mark dialectical poles in both Bernstein's and Ashbery's poetics. For Bernstein's fullest statement of the poetics of stopping, we turn to his magnificent verse essay "Artifice of Absorption" (1985), the best introduction to Language poetry likely to be written. Early in this loosely pentametered work, Bernstein distinguishes between the "absorptive" and the "antiabsorptive" or "impermeable"—dialectically related terms which "should not be understood as mutually exclusive, / morally coded, or even conceptually separable" (P 22). Absorption is a capacity both of texts and of readers. Bernstein asks us to "think / of a text as a spongy substance, absorbing / vocabulary, syntax, & reference" (22). As such, a "poem can absorb contradictory logics, / multiple tonalities, polyrhythms" (22), which stop the text or jump it to a larger measure. These jumps from smaller to enveloping measures and back again provide their own rhythm. As Ashbery put it in "The Skaters," the "falling snow" of the poem consists neither of "the individual flakes" nor of "the whole impression of the storm" but of "the rhythm of the series of repeated jumps, from abstract into positive and back to a slightly less diluted abstract" (RM 39). Full of "interlinear or interphrasal 'gaps' that act / like intervals in musical composition" (P 22), Bernstein's and Ashbery's poetry may be (initially) antiabsorptive to readers who cannot absorb themselves in the text. Yet since much conventional poetry may also be antiabsorptive (uninteresting) for many readers, Bernstein means to use "antiabsorptive / techniques . . . toward / absorptive ends" (P 30). The "reading value" (20) of this dialectical absorption is that the reader will become absorbed in the poem, and by analogy the world, as an artifact; the construed poetic construction becomes an absorbing collaboration or language game for reader and writer.

Bernstein's relational dyad of absorptive and antiabsorptive poetry may be fruitfully compared with Ashbery's notions of frontal and latent happiness, which he developed in his 1971 homespun prose poem "The System." "Frontal happiness" is a state of ecstatic absorption: "Its sudden balm suffuses the soul without warning, as a kind of bloom or grace" (TP 71). For the frontally happy, the world—resembling, and including, an overwhelming lover—is totally absorbing, both fascinating and engulfing. But such absorption, Ashbery argues, characteristic of the hippy mystics of the sixties, may be an ahistorical rapture which stops time. One seizes the moment of higher awareness at the expense of mundane, ongoing life. In latent happiness, the beneficent frontal moment is absorbed into one's memory or an era's expectations, as though the latent ecstasy were about to reappear: "its *nearness* is there, tingeing the air around them, in suspension, in escrow as it were, but they cannot get at it" (73). The antiabsorptive text of the world is a porous but impermeable artifact. Yet by absorbing the moment of frontal clarity (e.g., the moment of sexual choice) into "the fabric of life" (96), latent happiness, like Bernstein's dialectical absorption, becomes "a fleshed-out, realized version of that ideal first kind" (81). Ashbery's latent, endlessly absorbing text is amply illustrated by the all-consuming prose of *Three Poems,* which we might term hyperabsorbent. In this vast oceanic prose, Bernstein's "frontal" gaps and fissures are confounded and erased rather than smoothed over. Readers of *Three Poems* are absorbed by the wait for their own frontal moment of understanding, which, miragelike, seems always a little ahead or behind. The ceaseless fluidity of *Three Poems* is no less unsettling than the endless varieties of hovering and stopping in Bernstein's poems; in neither place can we find a place to stand for long.

Near the beginning of his writing life, Bernstein occasionally stopped and hovered over Ashbery's fluid measures, as is evident in an early poem which explores the phenomenon of frontal and latent awareness, "As If the Trees by Their Very Roots Had Hold of Us." This 1977 poem, which Bernstein chose to introduce *Senses of Responsibility,* begins retrospectively in sentence measure:

> Strange to remember a visit, really not so
> Long ago, which now seems, finally, past. Always, it's a
> Kind of obvious thing I guess, amazed by that
> Cycle: that first you anticipate a thing & it seems
> Far off, the distance has a weight you can feel
> Hanging on you, & then it's there—that
> Point—whatever—which, now, while
> It's happening seems to be constantly slipping away,
> "Like the sand through your fingers in an old movie," until

> You can only look back on it, & yet *you're* still there, staring
> At your thoughts in the window of the fire you find yourself before.
>   (SR 1)

Bernstein's argument recalls not only "The System" but Ashbery's timepiece in three stanzaic tenses, "Blue Sonata," a poem which takes up the didactic, objective discourse of Eliot's *Burnt Norton*:

> Long ago was the then beginning to seem like now
> As now is but the setting out on a new but still
> Undefined way. *That* now, the one once
> Seen from far away, is our destiny
> No matter what else may happen to us.
>   (HD 66)

Bernstein's dactylic lines in falling rhythm sound in fact more fluid than Ashbery's doggedly philosophical measures. Both poets overflow their lines, for instance, but for different ends. Whereas Ashbery's line endings underline his argument ("now," "still," "once," "destiny"), Bernstein's endings mime his experience of formulation ("so," "it's a," "that," "seems," "feel"). Ashbery's "we" is homiletic; Bernstein's is interpersonal. But Bernstein's poetic rhythms and emotive register are counterpointed by his prosaic diction, "Always, it's a / Kind of obvious thing I guess," which is itself indebted to Ashbery's breakthrough into demotic American speech in "The System." Bernstein breaks up his cadences with his punctuation, not only the dashes and commas but the musically chosen quotation marks and italics. Ashbery too will italicize and punctuate to slow a phrase to words in line ("*That* now"), but Bernstein seems to resort to typography as a stop-gap measure against the Ashberian tide. It would be difficult to find a Bernstein poem nearer to Ashbery's fluctuations than "As If the Trees," as Bernstein soon realized. *Controlling Interests* included an untitled poem, which begins to sound strangely familiar:

> So really not visit a remember to strange
> A it's always finally seems now which ago
> Long that by amazed guess I thing obvious of kind
> Feel can weight a has distance the off.
>   (CI 37)

In this truly halting poem, countering line with word measure, Bernstein reverses nearly verbatim his brilliant prior exercise, "As If the Trees," as though by this charm the spell of influence might be undone. Other poems in *Controlling Interests* reverse prior claims, but nowhere else has a poet so deliciously eaten his words.

Rather than limiting myself to showing how Bernstein has evaded Ashbery's fascinating rhythms, I want to juxtapose their poems, measure by measure, exploring how they have responded to similar musical possibilities. Both Ashbery and Bernstein have graduated, more or less steadily, from smaller to greater measures—from character to discursive section. Ashbery experimented with smaller measures most intensively in the later fifties, in *The Tennis Court Oath*. Since then, he has tended to employ characters and words as polyphonic counterstatements (e.g., in crypt words) within larger measures. Bernstein (over the course of twenty rather than forty years) has kept smaller measures more prominent in his later work, but he too has taken on greater and greater measures, with necessarily more complicated resonances. This common development is not surprising. Both renovating poets, with or without design or destiny, have continually expanded their horizons by absorbing some techniques and then undertaking others. Both have worked from the ground up in order to reconstrue and reconstruct poetry in revolutionary fashion.

Character

Literally an onomatopoeic name for an engraving tool's chiseled mark, "character" measure foregrounds the materiality of the character stroke. Characters raise the written, spatial, and visible, as well as the material, economic, and sexual possibilities of a poem. Pound's ideograms oscillate between marks and rebuses, both punctuating and illustrating his lines. In "An Ordinary Evening in New Haven," Stevens imagines material, unimagined reality as the first literal letter:

It is the infant A standing on infant legs,
Not twisted, stooping, polymathic Z,
He that kneels always on the edge of space[11]

Just as painters such as Matisse and Cy Twombly have explored the scriptural recesses of marks, so concrete poets from Apollinaire to Johanna Drucker have drawn out the shapes of letters and punctuation marks. Rachel Blau DuPlessis in *Tabula Rosa* and Kathy Acker in *Don Quixote* have exploited the intractably deviant, pornographic character of handwritten letters. But while measured characters are iconic and brutely material, they are also isolated. Poetry in purely character measure soon lapses into a predictably antiabsorbent stream or field; character measure requires the attraction of another measure, such as a word or sentence, into which it refuses to be absorbed.

Whether capitalized, italicized, bold, underscored, enlarged, or otherwise differentiated, individual letters, like punctuation marks, break up the poetic continuum. Nonalphabetic characters—punctuation marks, arabic and roman numerals, virgules, hash marks, dollar and (per)cent signs, and so on—also interrupt sense consumption; "2" does not equal "two," and "(" does not function like "parenthesis." Punctuation is essential to a hovering poetics. Bernstein, who has always textured his poems with dysfunctional, decorative punctuations, gives a recipe for punctual seasoning on the last page of *The Occurrence of Tune* (1981), a book coproduced with Susan Bee, whose absorbing pictograms resonate with Bernstein's ideographic text: "So we; juxtapose a, healthy sprinkle of: punctuation to. break up, the: normal—usage &; see; what! you get"; here the punctuation—what kind doesn't matter—calls attention to itself not just as a stop but as a measured mark, an interval between words and phrases. In "Artifice of Absorption" Bernstein thanks "ee cummings for his typ,,OgRAPHic(((,, / in()ventio.,.ns;" (P 56). Another modernist, Joyce, particularly in *Finnegans Wake*, seasoned his text freely, leaving marks that

> ad bîn "provoked" ay ∧ fork, of à grave Brofèsor; àth é's Brèak—fast—table; ;
> acùtely profèšsionally *piquéd,* to=introdùce a notion of time [ùpon à plane
> (?) sù' ' fàç'e'] by pùnct! ingh oles (sic) in iSpace?!¹²

Puncturing the textual surface amounts to more than a typographic oddity. Emily Dickinson revolutionized the measure of American poetry with her irregular punctuation, as Bernstein acknowledges in "Artifice of Absorption":

> The capitalization & dashes
> seem to insist on a jerky, or hesitant, reading,
> cutting sharply against the grain of the singsong
> prosody
> (P 25)

Like Dickinson, Bernstein uses punctuation as much to mark the measure as to reinforce the meaning. Within a single poem, Bernstein widely, and wildly, varies his punctuation and spacing in order to change the tempo, much as Dickinson changed meters from stanza to stanza.

Most of Bernstein's character measures and countermeasures may be found among the early poems (1975–77) of *Poetic Justice*. Written entirely in prose that is anything but prosaic, the characters themselves sometimes make the music. "LIFT OFF," for instance, aided and abetted by the IBM Selectric with its electronic upper case and repeating keys, purports to transcribe a roll of lift-off eraser tape. Here is the end of the tape recording: "olarofpgo u3in lksg==urr in-cc-eworksforme330! Oe6) Yanapply, 1000,ndam llle?WSrrrrrrrr" (PJ 36). The nearly unbroken chain dices the text into character measure, where a punctuation mark is just another key stroke. The inadvertent mistakes on the polyphonic tape now cover the hypothetical corrected text, rather than the reverse. We can momentarily pick up the revised, sentence-measured, text beneath its original—something about a job application—before the whirring machine drowns out the communication. In the lexically polyphonic "AZOOT D'PUUND" Bernstein overlays the densely substituted measures of letter upon that of a sentence: "iz wurry ray aZoOt de puund in reducey ap crrRisLe ehk nugkinj sJuxYY senshl." (PJ 25). The sentence measure, signaled by the verbal spacing and the period, is contorted to letter measure by nonexistent and sometimes unpronounceable combinations. These collocations of letters keep us listening, rearranging, and reading aloud ("I worry about the pound . . . "?), because their seemingly garbled words and sentences suggest there's more here than meets the ear. In the most extensive of Bernstein's and the IBM's collaborations, "eLecTrIc," a series of unpunctuated prose blocks is interrupted only by randomly capitalized letters. While the lack of punctuation encourages an unchecked flood of thoughts or words, Bernstein's unabsorbed capitals continually dam up his Proustian meditations:

> but the waY you SEe the eVent & after a WEek its FOrgotten youRE SEEing diFFerent EVents movING on as a DIFFErent persON almost by the waY you DEfine your dislikes if you can gET it Up to own tHEm its a KINd of inertIA not that CONtinues movement but that WAnts to STop it at any minute & SO a CONtinuaLLy PREssing to CONTinue to allOw to BE hERE rathER than in ALl the FANtasIES of WHere it MIGHT be nice to Be (PJ 22)

What do we do with these capitals? Unlike Cage's mesostics, they spell out no name or superscript message. Nor do they mark stresses or emphases. Nevertheless, their countermeasure is registered. The self, which wants both to join and to resist the defining time and tide, reflects itself in the struggle between surging miniscules and upstanding majuscules.

Ashbery's most ecstatic experiments in character measure came in the late fifties, when he was living in Paris on a Fulbright scholarship. One little-known musical offering, "Three Madrigals," written in 1958, oscillates between word and character, with punctuation marks making their own measure, as in this last page of the "Third Madrigal":

```
                         mattress
        hawk

                personality        table        pregnancy
        apron    bin
                ,,,,,,,,,,))))))))))*************
            ''''****  *  :: ::::..:,.,:::.,. . . . ,./:/.:-*
            shoo      Amy any analyse amiably accentuate
        foregone     tide          enfant
        ........../
                         cooperate     building     lynx     stuffed
                             *board*
        osprey ostensible Orkney of olfactory ore or orator advantage[13]
```

A secular polyphonic song for three to six voices, "Third Madrigal" encourages us to hear its lyric lines simultaneously. Literally "of the womb" (*matri-*

calis, matrix), the ending of "Third Madrigal" seems to have almost erased a story of an unwanted pregnancy (the open-mouthed "a" and "o" have their usual iconic, originary values). Ashbery's surreally invariant alliteration, itself a kind of character measure, keeps the horizontal lists of words from linking into syntax. The last word, "advantage," acts to close the text by returning to the earlier alliterative sequence (and the first letter). Within their separate lines, the punctuation marks mark no grammatical or musical pauses. Rather, they mimic musical notation. Commas perhaps indicate an andante and periods a dotted rhythm, asterisks words sung brightly, but above all the piece asks to be performed merrily.

After he returned to the United States, Ashbery occasionally returned to his earlier character-measured experiments. Perhaps his most entertaining interlude in character measure is his 1967 work "ONE HUNDRED MULTIPLE-CHOICE QUESTIONS."[14] Printed like an aptitude or "personality" test, the poem bristles with possibilities. It begins reasonably, and absurdly, enough in incomplete sentence and phrase measure:

1. Thinking can help to solve problems because

A) problems exist only in the mind

B) problems must be taken seriously

C) mind triumphs over matter

D) not to think would be to avoid the problem

E) no problem can be completely solved anyway

F) it is our duty to think our way out of problems

Anyone who approaches Ashbery's or Bernstein's poems as so many problems to be dutifully solved had better reread the question. Gradually, it seems, the letters attached to the choices suggested character-measured possibilities, as in this $64,000 question:

64. The phrase, "All happy families are obioud, py od pm; u yjr imj½½i pmrd ejp str akule," has been attitued to

A) high cost of living

B) *Typhoon*

As the multiple-choice sentence trails off into character-measured obscurity, Ashbery plays both upon literary allusion and upon "foreign" language. The language in question is not the Polish writer Conrad's English but the misrepresented Russian of Tolstoy, who began *Anna Karenina* with the reflection "Happy families are all alike; every unhappy family is unhappy in its own way." Like Bernstein's "LIFT OFF," Ashbery here dips into the character-measured resources of misspelling and puzzling. Though his experiments in smaller measures are much less frequent and pervasive than Bernstein's or other Language poets, it is clear that Ashbery is adept at raising their (non)signifying stakes.

Word

Like characters, isolated words have a material presence. But their referential status lends them an additional thinglike, objective solidity. The word "pumice" not only refers to a spongy volcanic glass but takes on something of that material's abrasiveness. Qualifiers, quantifiers, verbs, and so on have their own semantic and sonic texture; even nonreferential words, such as prepositions or articles, have the palpability of their sound in the oral reader's mouth. Also like characters, words in isolation—whether syntactically resistant or widely spaced—soon lapse into impermeable uniformity, requiring the pull of larger measures for definition. Accentual-syllabic meter ignores word boundaries. Poets such as Pound, and later Olson, have returned individual weights to words by employing stress meters. In the latter sections of *A*, Zukofsky constructs an objective pentameter of five-word lines. Susan Howe has drawn us to her penchant for words, "First I was a painter, so for me, words shimmer." In "Thorow," she arrays widely spaced concatenations of letters into word groups—"anthen   uplispth   enend"—in which the transgressing or erasing of word boundaries and formation has postcolonialist implications.[15] Thoreau himself, whose variantly spelled name Howe adopts as her title, articulated an evolutionary onomatopoetics (a poetics claiming the motivation of the signifier) of the word and letter in the "Spring" chapter of *Walden*, as he studies his mother globe: "*Internally*, whether in the globe or animal body, it is a moist thick *lobe*, a word especially applicable to the liver and lungs and the *leaves* of fat, (λείβω, *labor, lapsus*, to flow or slip downward, a lapsing; λόβος, *globus*, lobe, globe; also lap, flap, and many other words,) *externally* a dry thin *leaf*, even as the *f* and *v* are a pressed and dried *b*."[16] The word strings and hyphenated neologisms of Hopkins revived an English line of stress-based onomatopoetics for poets like Dylan Thomas, Seamus Heaney, and the American transplant Sylvia Plath, whose hard-edged words assert their impermeability, as at the edge of "Edge": "Her blacks crackle and drag."[17]

Ashbery's word-measured poetry comes predominantly from the period of *The Tennis Court Oath*. In one poem, marking the crypt phrase "dirty words," adjectives and nouns pile up in a parody of romantic excitement: "the clean fart genital enthusiastic toe prick album serious evening flames" (TCO 34). In the 111 brief, often interchangeable sections of his detective epic "Europe," words themselves take the form of scattered, indecipherable clues and suspects. Here are two sections (TCO 82), with Ashbery's arabic numerals:

101.

the doctor, comb
        Sinn Fein

102.
dress

If (as we suspect) the comb and dress both belong to the same missing person, and "the doctor" is really a member of "Sinn Fein," then we're on to something. But we never have enough to go on, and soon we're in the next section, with its own evidence. The comma in the line "the doctor, comb" marks more than a pause; we now detect the line as a textual fragment in which either end has been erased or destroyed.

Ashbery's later work also breaks up, if less obviously, into word measures. In "Sand Pail," for instance, published in 1974, a redeveloped beach is set in word-measured concrete:

Prócèss
of a réd strípe thròugh múch whíplàsh
of environmental sweepstakes misinterprets
slabs as they come forward.
    (SPCM 54)

The jammed monosyllables and the polysyllables of haphazardly mixed diction show the ugly resoluteness of this capitalist "Process." In Ashbery's hands, the concreteness of word measure also mocks the interpretative fixity that misses the abstract expressionist process in the final "concrete poem." Idle words are dirty words. On one page of his catalog *The Vermont Notebook* (1975) Ashbery's words thinly veil a sultry narrative: "many, before, few, undid, seam, artery, motor, before, sleep, come, mouth, asshole, behaving, foundered, sleep, reef, perfect, almost" (VN 29). Not only lovers are involved here; this freely wandering list mimes the free associations of psychoanalysis.

Bernstein's first chapbook, *Disfrutes* (Spanish *disfrute*, "enjoyment"), was composed primarily in word measure. Its alphabet's worth of twenty-six unnumbered pages, containing only a few untitled words each, adds up to either a sequence of poems or a poem in sequence. Reading these poems is a matter not of figuring out what they mean, since none of them "makes sense," but of recognizing their music of construction. One unpunctuated page (19) plays word against both line and sentence measure:

she
shells
smells
by the by

This page counterpoints the word-measured tongue twister "She sells seashells by the seashore." Its polyphonic ending, "by the by," seems ungrammatical (how can a preposition be the object of a preposition?) until we remember that it is itself an idiomatic variant of "by the way," a twisting byway where she shells smells. Bernstein's spatial arrangement encourages us to read vertically by letter measure, to see how "she" grows into "shells," which twists into "smells." The latter rhyme plays grammatical difference off phonemic resemblance; "shells" and "smells" look the same (both plural nouns or singular verbs) but cannot be the same ("smells" needs to be a noun) for the sentence to work. By the by, one can smell shells, but can one shell smells? She can.

On another page (12), the music depends upon the combined forces of letter, word, and phrase:

> of it
> on
> the it
> she
> on the
> it she

Once again, reading this page means more than asking what (if anything) these words together mean. Such an approach dead-ends in a declaration that the work is "nonsense," "nonrepresentational," and so on. An affirmative, textually specific reading asks instead about its music of construction. The opening line leads us to expect a sequence in phrase measure, an expectation the following lines pleasantly disrupt. The juxtaposed words "the it" make phrasal sense only if we think of "it" in quotes as a word pointed to rather than pointing. But the line's resistance to syntax suggests in turn that we should reread the first line in word measure. The lines "on the" and "it she" sound like fragments (e.g., "on the table," "after she read it she left"); we should pronounce them accordingly, with unmarked beginnings and endings. Then again, we might read the entire sequence in word measure, performing each word separately and equally. Such a performance spotlights the abstract patterning of these place-holding monosyllables (xa/b/ca/d/bc/ad). But the polyphonic key to this page lies with the grammar of "she," a third-person pronoun. Instead of employing the entire third-person sequence "he, she, it" (or "on" in French) in his variations, this male poet buries the crypt word "he" under the homophonic marker "the." In this generation "of" gendered meaning, Bernstein is the definite article.

Phrase

Poems in phrase measure are typically driven by what Bernstein calls "the propulsion of a comma" (CD 48). The mere presence of a medial stop (a comma, dash, ellipsis, etc.) raises phrasal expectations, as with Ashbery's line "the doctor, comb." Minimizing subjects and main verbs, phrase-measured poems are reflective interiors. If word measures reproduce things, phrase measures record the hovering flow of impressions. Stream-of-consciousness prose may be identified by phrases and phrase-measured elliptical sentences. Nineteenth-century psychological realist style was stitched together out of main clauses hemmed with qualifying phrases. The prose of James, Proust, Joyce, Faulkner, and Woolf abounds in phrasal and phrase-filled sentences. Since a line break is roughly equivalent to a comma, "free verse" and "open form" lines tend to consist of phrases. But since phrases are grammatically incomplete and unassertive, such lines are short and indefinite and can easily stray from the left margin or slip into prose. Commas, however, also partition lists, collections of things. Whitman's phrasal catologs often reproduce the exuberance of itemization. Phrases also mark the gradual process of poetic formulation. Dickinson's dashed phrases, for instance, dramatize the suspense of her own super(ior)stitious invention:

> The Body—borrows a Revolver—
> He bolts the Door—
> O'erlooking a superior spectre—
> Or More—
> (#669) .

Leslie Scalapino has adapted Dickinson's dashes to capture the act of narration, using indefinitely dependent clauses to gesture toward a vast interdependence of events, where the hovering main subject is public property: "being downtown—it's during the day—there were many people out; so my having a conflict in the sense of being nothing if I were not in that setting—regardless of others having such a view—"[18]

Bernstein's early volume of prose poems, *Poetic Justice,* is predominantly in phrase measure, culminating in the last, longest (eight-page) piece in the volume, "The Taste Is What Counts." The poem is segmented into thirty-three prose blocks (unindented prose stanzas), each bounded by an opening capital and a closing period, within which a single argument is pursued. "The Taste" reflects on, and at, the phenomenological border of the constituting and constituted individual in the temporal world of glancing events. Consequently, its sentences are overwhelmed by its phrases, in which subjects and verbs are fused into participles, the poem's salient grammatical feature. A modifier participating in the action without itself acting, the participle stands in for consciousness without a subject. Before settling into its phrasal rhythm, "The Taste" (PJ 40) begins with a word-measured dam of consciousness:

> Obviously hover hanging on as times is like an icon or Terry etc that going on
> dropping of names, aroma, can't really cut out, choppiness, drunken into sexual

> frenzy, the trick now I repeat this unless I force myself, its discipline, what I
> remember of it, a kind of sick feeling, purely to possess a movement,

This comma-propelled prose has the immediacy of a diary or an interior monologue. Its musical phrases are layered with crypt words—"overhanging," "hangover," "at times," "as time [goes by]," "name dropping." The self over-hangs the page and its impulse to recapture its former fluid state. But Bernstein's drama is not the reconstruction of the past—a dull name-dropping party from which he wanted to "cut out"—but the construction, phrase by phrase, of a hovering but fluid, "unconscious" prose. Though the poem begins with "Obviously," there are few objects in the way of the surging impressions. The prototypical thing in "The Taste" is the phenomenal seashore, confronted in section 14: "The slope of the sand, migrations of bars, flow, uprush, storm surge, swash and swell, drift of current, wane of the shore. Ridges, runnels, beach rock, silt, clay, cusp of the ranges, dune, granite, glauconite, basalt" (PJ 44). Only the list in the second pseudosentence slows the temporal flow to immovable objects in word measure. Hovering is not simply an alternative to Ashbery's fluid-state poetics, but a struggle against it.

In his later poetry, Bernstein tends to subordinate resistant phrases to their bursting sentences. But a few phrase-measured poems stand out. In "Asylum," a disturbing poem composed of broken lines unjustly arranged upon the page, Bernstein confronts the objectifying capacity of the list. In one line, a person is reduced to punishable characteristics—"inferior, weak, blameworthy and guilty"—and in others, physical barriers reproduce individual alienation:

> intercourse with the outside and to departure
> such as locked doors, high walls, barbed
>   wire, cliffs, water, forests, moors
>   (I/I 36)

Escape coincides with the end of the line, beyond the barbed commas. But Bernstein also landscapes interiors with commas. In one passage from the diversely measured sequence "Amblyopia" (an inturned, "mystical" eye), the phrases resist their sentence frame with private notations:

> Related to this—the excitement, the dancing
> around, articulating itself in terms of these,
> & getting, this might, the sanctioned
> "drive and concentration", more
>   (S 116)

And so on for another seven lines until we reach the period, "an unresolvable fend."—a fended off conclusion which resolves nothing grammatically or semantically. Bernstein again figures fluidity as Dionysian frenzy, but now his impressionist phrases and phrasal fragments gather force by working against the forward momentum of the sentence and the identity of the line. The inner phrasal life of Bernstein's poems is neither obliterated nor deconstructed in his later work; it exists not by itself or at the borders of social life, but as an indissoluble element within it.

The phrase is essential to Ashbery's fluid poetics. Whereas Bernstein in his early poems in *Poetic Justice* tended to submerge his phrases in comma-rested prose, Ashbery in *Some Trees* and *The Tennis Court Oath* usually underscored his phrases by isolating them in lines as impressionistic, incomplete units. In the first stanza of "Pantoum," for instance, an adopted French form in which the second and fourth lines of the first quatrain become the first and third lines of the next, Ashbery dissipates the sentence and its thesis into piecemeal impressions and signs:

> Eyes shining without mystery,
> Footprints eager for the past
> Through the vague snow of many clay pipes,
> And what is in store?
>   (SoTr 42)

The phrases, punctuated only by final commas and the question mark, are charged with narrative latency, a happiness forever withheld in the future or the past. These phrasal lines present pieces of a puzzle, each used twice, which don't quite fit together or stand on their own. The opening quatrain lacks a narrative subject, or even a pronominal perspective. Ashbery might have personalized his narrative with a main clause and pronoun: "My eyes shining, my footsteps eager for their destination, I bounded through the snow, wondering 'what is in store.' " But by displacing his impressions, he places them all over the repeating landscape.

The phrase-measured poems and passages of *The Tennis Court Oath* stop short of direct, public statement. In an all-American nocturne, "Night," first published in 1960 in Paul Carroll's magazine *Big Table,* short phrases follow long ones like afterthoughts. Here is a stretch from the second verse paragraph:

> Bringing night brings in also idea of death
> Thought when she was sixteen . . . he'd take her out
> But it did no good . . . Fuss was
> Over the comics like in board you seen
> Growing in patch on them laurels. And after
>   (TCO 22)

The elided article before "idea" jots it down and frames its thesis as a secret, private truth. The "idea" of death leads to the "thought" of taking her out, a venture into sixteen-candled, heterosexual Americana that "did no good." The phrasal punctuation in these conventionally capitalized verses is not the comma but the ellipsis. A printer's mark indicating the elision or erasure of an indefinite number of words, the ellipsis is in some ways an inevitable punctuation for Ashbery's elliptical, foreshortened verses. But ellipses also indicate voices trailing off into thought—a literary convention reinforced by "idea" and "Thought."[19] But this rustic dialect is as foreign to Ashbery, a thoroughly cultivated farm boy, as is its experience. "Night" thus counterpoints external and internal ellipses, citation and thought, and heterosexual and homosexual experience.

Ashbery's later measures fluctuate between sentence and phrase. His loquacious *Flow Chart*, a 216-page voyage without a chart, seems to lapse at times into almost unmediated improvisational phrases, as at the beginning of this early verse paragraph:

> But at times such as
> these late ones, a moaning in copper beeches is heard, of regret,
> not for what happened, or even for what could conceivably have happened, but
> for what never happened and which therefore exists, as dark
> and transparent as a dream. A dream from nowhere. A dream
> with no place to go, all dressed up with no place to go, that an axe
> menaces, off and on, throughout eternity.
>   (FC 12)

In this stretch, Ashbery improvises negation. The stereotypical retrospective summation "I wouldn't change a thing" makes stoic virtue of necessity. But Ashbery's pseudo-statements can't quite take no for an answer. As the midline stanza break and the long miniscule lines suggest, the dominant measure in *Flow Chart* is the sentence. The first full line, for instance, varies some statement such as "a moaning of regret is heard in the copper beeches." The denial is not so much of regret as of pain. The passive voice "is heard" fails to locate the moan inside an "I," with the result that the pain is everywhere outside. The first person first appears in this passage triply circumscribed by quotation marks, italics, and parentheses, in a quotation from Cowper's "Castaway": "(*'when such a destin'd wretch / as I, wash'd headlong from on board'*)" (FC 12). The displacement of the phrase "of regret" to the end of the line emphasizes its invention, as though the "moaning" were just understood. But as soon as it is identified, subsequent phrases seek to qualify it out of existence. Though Ashbery's phrase measures evade the conventional formula, "I regret that I never . . . ," what "never happened [to me]" nevertheless coalesces into a "dream" of a ghost, as in Henry James's late regretful suspense story "The Jolly Corner." Including "a dream" thrice in a single line, Ashbery's improvisational syntax conjures his dream lover and alter-ego-ideal. The "axe / menaces," guilt-laden and darkly latent, yet never happens only in the sense that it never stops happening. Ashbery's phrases cannot put a period on the moaning.

Line

One inadequate but persistent definition of a poem is that it is made of words divided into lines. As the definitive poetic measure, lines promise integrity, enclosure, and completeness. Meter once determined line length, determining the number of beats and/or syllables if not of letters or words. But once rhyme (another popular defining characteristic of poetry) gave way in English verse, poets began to underscore their lines as units of thought and speech. The end-words of Milton's disobediently unrhymed *Paradise Lost,* for instance, might be read as forming a vertical plot line, as in the first sixteen-line sentence (I use Milton's punctuation): "Fruit taste woe, Man Seat, top inspire Seed, Earth, Hill flow'd thence Song, soar pursues Rhyme."[20] One contemporary response to the insular boundary of the line has been to avoid it altogether. As Bernstein remarks in "Of Time and the Line":

> Nowadays, you can often spot a work
> of poetry by whether it's in lines
> or no; if it's in prose, there's a good chance
> it's a poem.
> (RT 42–43)

Bernstein's poem first appeared in *The Line in Postmodern Poetry,* a collection which "ended" with an anthology of Language poetry lines and (anti)-linear statements of poetics. Some Language poets, breaking free from linear constraints, realize that liberation isn't everything. Bruce Andrews, whose improvisational poetry rarely toes the capitalized line, exhorts us to improve on lines, "Better, constant crease & flux, a radical discontinuity as lack" (177), but realizes the "bogus immediacy of gesture" (178) such freedom suggests. When he describes the poem as incorporating "meaning's outer structure (language/society) as model and limit" (178), the line, dividing the poem from the world as such, reemerges as a locus of resistance and reformulation. Rather than fighting or walking away from the line, Lyn Hejinian embraces it as her basic poetic measure, "given my inclination to reject the sentence . . . except as it is modified by the line (which discontinues the sentence without closing it)" (191). The "chapters" of her long sonnet sequence *Oxota: A Short Russian Novel* are poems of fourteen capitalized lines of wildly varying length, while *The Cell* exploits the printer's convention of indenting run-on lines to construct composite capitalized and uncapitalized lines, each with its own margin. Susan Howe, primarily a word-measuring poet, has, in "Thorow" and elsewhere, written skewed and overlapping, palimpsestic lines. The "concrete" Language poet Johanna Drucker has put some meat on her lines by manipulating the complex, familiar conventions of newspaper prose with its headlines, subheadlines, and parallel columns. Steve McCaffery drolly constructs his prose poem *Black Debt* from a series of strict Miltonic pentameter sentences: "From honour's zenith sly suspicion creeps. / Such sail spred roars in birth's black mantle flight" (200). McCaffery's prosodic prose sentences the line to solitary confinement, where it began.

North American poetry began by redefining the line. Dickinson's syncopated lines—with open-ended dashes at the ends and halting capitals in the middles—and Whitman's fugitive catalog lines cut out the patterns from which American poets have worked. I can only mention here a few innovations important for Bernstein's and Ashbery's practice. At the end of *The Waste Land,* Eliot collaged lines together, making linear insularity a poetic value. Stein juxtaposed her own capitalized verses without knitting them syntactically, so that they stood as variations on each other, as in *Stanzas of Meditation:*

> Full well I know that she is there
> Much as she will she can be there
> but which I know which I know when
> Which is my way to be there then
>   (Part II, Stanza I)[21]

William Carlos Williams renovated Dickinson's rhythmic hesitancy and jazzed up Pound's imagism by substituting frequent linear pauses for dashes and capitals. Most brilliantly in "Words," Robert Creeley lowered long sentences rung by rung down short lines, producing vertical as well as horizontal lines of force. And Frank O'Hara lineated prosaically and parodically, as in these two lines from "Why I Am Not a Painter": "and life. Days go by. It is even in / prose, I am a real poet. My poem".[22] These lines are not so much "enjambed"—an inadequate term for describing the relations between entire lines—as cross-measured; O'Hara plays the line off the sentence by seeming to neglect their relative measurements.

Ashbery too, who likens verses to railways, "as though our train were a pencil // Guided by a ruler held against a photomural of the Alps" (HD 24), has railed against poetic linearity. Nevertheless, the line is arguably Ashbery's defining measure, a measurement which places him securely in the lyric tradition. Ashbery employs the line either as the dominant measure or as an equal and opposite measure to the sentence, which also qualifies as the major measure of the author of *Three Poems.* His later verses tend to cross-measure lines and sentences, whereas Bernstein's recent poems are measured more exclusively in densely polyphonic sentences. Otherwise put, there is more semantic

distance between Ashbery's lines than between his sentences, and more semantic distance between Bernstein's sentences than between his lines.

Ashbery's first poems were composed of surreally artificed lines, a mannered tendency furthered by his penchant for rare, Audenesque fixed forms.
But these early lines, either too empty or too full, were never complete. As we
saw above, Ashbery divided the doubled lines of "Pantoum" into dependent
phrases. In "Canzone," which strings five end-words along twelve-line stanzas,
he yields to the end-stopped form rather than trying to overcome it. He learned
the form from Auden's "Canzone" (1942), in which Auden subjected his lines
to sweeping periodic sentences:

> If in this dark now I less often know
> That spiral staircase where the haunted will
> Hunts for its stolen luggage, who should know
> Better than you, beloved, how I know

Auden continues, delightfully, for another four and a half lines, to the rhetorical question's mark.[23] But instead of hurdling his own verbal barriers, Ashbery
hovers at them, in short lines composed almost entirely of end-words:

> Until the first chill
> No door sat on the clay.
> When Billy brought on the chill
> He began to chill.
>   (SoTr 55)

In Ashbery's thin canzone, "chill," with its encrypted undertone "child,"
marks his poem's transgressive limit. There are lines, we are told, we must not
cross. In "The Instruction Manual" (1955, SoTr 26–30), he stretched the lyric
line to prosaic dimensions. It is not surprising that this poem, modeled on the
travelogue, is his first in a nonliterary discourse. Ashbery continued experi-
menting with longer than lyric lines in "The Skaters," resorting to the type-
writer to transcribe these elusive lines more quickly. The poem incorporates
sentences from an actual instruction manual, *Three Hundred Things a Bright
Boy Can Do,* as in this lesson on perspective:

> The lines that draw nearer together are said to "vanish."
> The point where they meet is their vanishing point.
>
> Spaces, as they recede, become smaller.
>   (RM 48)

So too, the lyric, expressive persona has vanished from these lines, which lengthen
and contract but never touch.

It is fascinating to hear Ashbery absorb his earlier lessons and measures into his later constructions. In "Farm II" (1975), for instance, Ashbery resumes the unpunctuated phrasal lineation of *The Tennis Court Oath*:

> A lattice-work crust
> Holes are blobs of darkness
> Has been placed across the road
> You can't walk out too far that way any more
>   (SPCM 29)

Like Ashbery's poems from the fifties, this passage uses a buried American metaphor, "crust of snow," to justify its unpunctuated, whited out landscape. It takes a couple of readings, for instance, before the syntactically unhinged second line drops into its parenthetical hole ( ). Though planed level by its monosyllabic measured words, the long fourth line seems to reach into unmarked wildernesses. But the extravagant line of laconic American farm talk is actually a pentameter—for American pathfinders, a road too often taken.

Periodically throughout his career, Ashbery has generated poems defined by their lines. In "Into the Dusk-Charged Air" (1961), for instance, each of his fluid lines names a river, which makes for surreal confluences:

> Flows too fast to swim in the Jordan's water
> Courses over the flat land. The Allegheny and its boats
> Were dark blue. The Moskowa is
>   (RM 17)

"Sortes Vergilianae" (1968), deriving from "the ancient practice of fortune-telling by choosing a passage from Vergil's poetry at random" (DDS 95), elongates each verse line into a life-line: "You have been living now for a long time and there is nothing you do not know. / Perhaps something you read in the newspaper influenced you and that was very frequently" (DDS 74). These opening lines unroll without subordination or medial punctuation, so that we race to the end to keep the meaning in our heads, a more and more difficult task. Life may have a fortunate design, but it's too long for any one liver to apprehend.

In a recent volume of lyrics, *Hotel Lautréamont* (1992), Ashbery continues his manipulations of the one-dimensional line. Coming after his longest sentence-measured poem, *Flow Chart,* the volume absorbs the lesson of American talk to bring out a new line of verses. The title poem is a pantoum, line-measured by definition. But Ashbery reverses his earlier phrasal practice by overextending his lines and by adopting a clunky academic discourse:

> Research has shown that ballads were produced by all of society
> working as a team. They didn't just happen. There was no guesswork.
> The people, then, knew what they wanted and how to get it.
> We see the results in works as diverse as "Windsor Forest" and "The Wife of
> Usher's Well."
> (HL 14)

It is typical of Ashbery's indirection to simulate the history of the ballad, another quatrain form, in a pantoum. Unlike conventional cross-measurements in which sentences extend across and join lines, these long lines can absorb more than one sentence. The vitality of "Hotel Lautréamont" may be seen by contrast with the volume's other pantoum, "Seasonal":

> What does the lengthening season mean,
> the halo round a single note?
> Blunt words projected on a screen
> are what we mean, not what we wrote.
> (93)

This well-wrought tone poem of four quatrains certainly illustrates Ashbery's largely untapped facility with metrical verse. What I miss here is Ashbery's formal self-consciousness. With "Hotel Lautréamont," by contrast, Ashbery takes "fixed forms" to lengths undreamt of by New Formalists.

Most of the line-measured forms in *Hotel Lautréamont* are Ashbery's own invention. In a one-page poem "Another Example," Ashbery places end-stopped lines further and further apart in meaning, leaving them as scattered instances of some unglimpsed precept:

> The train is turning away—
> There are no familiar quotations.
>
> Here, put some on a plate, he said. That's the way.
> (HL 49)

"The Departed Lustre" begins with Gertrude Stein's paraphrasal lines, where one sound rather than one thought leads to another ("Oh," "so," "Some-," "sum-"):

> Oh I am oh so
> oh so
> Something is slightly wrong here,
> a summer cold.
> (99)

"The Man Whose Pharynx Was Bad," as Stevens called the postlyric poet, can no longer simply sing a song, oh so "happy" or "sad," but Ashbery makes a

hoarse new music out of that shortcoming. In "Quartet" he adds a line to each
stanza until he reaches twelve (willfully admitting imperfection with two
quinzains), thereby affirming the accumulation rather than the diminishment
of the years. Only his quatrain is punctuated:

> only don't make me think it
> always
> I'm figuring out what went just before
> with that which comes too late:
> (HL 124)

With neither sentence markers nor capitalized lines, the two principles of sequence—line and sentence—compete for primacy, so that the reader doesn't
know where to start or how to stop. The lines, as though superstitious of full
stops, take on more and more of the burden of punctuation. The book's closing
instruction manual, "How to Continue," likewise contains a single punctuation mark, a period, placed at the end of the first rather than the last stanza.
After opening with a lyrical "Oh," each of the poem's stanzas continues with
"And," leveling syntax into parataxis. The absence of punctuation denies not
only finality but subordination, whether logical or biological. In this poem of
freely rhymed and metered verses, Ashbery writes a hazardous fairy tale. Here
is its final continuation:

> And when it became time to go
> they none of them would leave without the other
> for they said we are all one here
> and if one of us goes the other will not go
> and the wind whispered it to the stars
> the people all got up to go
> and looked back on love
> (157)

The so-called private poet makes his poetry public here by writing in recognizable, if irregular, narrative discourse and metered, if stubborn, lines. The
lines of poems are supposed to rhyme, and so the ghost of the canzone enters
with "go." But the counterlogical, polyphonic negation in the fourth line, in
this AIDS-era fable, is what stays. Headed for his *Paradiso*, Dante looked back
on earth. Hazarding for a moment the perspective line of those departing, Ashbery instructs the rest on how to continue.

Beginning his poetry in radically alternative forms and antilyrical measures, Bernstein has always seemed somewhat embarrassed about versifying in
lines; even "Of Time and the Line" (RT 43; cited above), generated proce-
durally from different senses of "line," is written in sentence measure. Bern-

stein has had his fun upsetting lines. In his musically eclectic "Blow-Me-Down Etude," Bernstein records the following observation (RT 103–4):

> Once
> I
> saw
> a
> man
> walk
> into
> a
> pole.

The "punchline" of this "Polish joke" (two generative crypt phrases here) upends the sentence so that we "read" (interpret and perform) it either as one vertical line or as nine one-word lines. In an early poem, Bernstein generated an untitled sequence of sentences in prose from another play on "line":

> Comraderie turns to rivalry when 12 medical students learn that only seven of them will be admitted to the hospital.
>
> A CIA agent is ordered to feign a breakdown to trap a spy at a mental hospital.
> (I/I 25)

Sooner or later we realize that Bernstein is producing "plotlines." With his versified narrative summaries, Bernstein blurs the lines between poetry, fiction, and prose.

Bernstein's self-conscious, antiabsorbent use of lines does not prevent him from putting himself upon them. In "The Years as Swatches," for instance, he follows Creeley in tapping into a phone line:

> Voice seems
> to break
> over these
> short lines
> cracking or
> setting loose.
> (S 31)

Lines in this sentence are word-measured two by two like a person-to-person long-distance phone call. As the voice breaks at each "line break" (the generative crypt phrase), the difficulty of any telecommunication, typographic or electronic, is audible. Even Bernstein's most disjunctive, impermeable poems are faintly outlined. In his recent field composition "The Puritan Ethic and the Spirit of Capitalization" (R 51; cf. "Cooperation," "Capitalism"), only line segments are visible. The poem screeches to a start:

constancy—or, rather

questions about
    notably, mark
  at which the
      locus
    which this
        put
 not all. If

The spacing in Bernstein's poem is particularly unsettling. Not until the eighteenth line does the uncapitalized phrase "by looking" establish its rightful place at the left margin of the page. Successive lines are either too distant or too overlapped to be read sequentially as caesural, dramatic breaks. Radical disjunctiveness sometimes defeats itself by reinscribing unity at a smaller level; lines may be perfectly self-sufficient in order to disjoin their neighbors. But these lines are neither quite part nor whole. Nevertheless, their music of construction is audible. As with Ashbery's "Europe," a great deal of evidence seems to have been covered up. And as in "Europe," several of the phrases bear self-referential traces, either to themselves or to the act of reading them. The reader thus has "questions about" the notable lack of marks on the page, the "locus" within "which this" inquiry arises; the poem's first capitalized word is "If." What largely distinguishes "The Puritan Ethic" from "Europe" is that each line constitutes a fragment of discourse. To read each line persuasively, the reader must hear unwritten discursive registers before and after each fragment. The music of the first line, for instance, requires a lecturing distinction—"[The Puritan ethic demanded] constancy—or, rather, [fidelity to its principles]." In the professional discourse of the second line, the historian notes that "[many] questions about [the Puritan work ethic]" are raised. After such fragments of public discourse, even the spatially and syntactically isolated words "locus" and "put" move beyond word measure. Thus as a fragment of academic discourse and a self-referential document, Bernstein's uncapitalized, uncapitalist poem works.

Sentence

If the line is the definitive measure of poetry, the sentence is the identifying unit of prose. Like words and lines, and more than phrases and characters, sentences are relatively independent and complete. If phrases seem to record thoughts and impressions, sentences may make assertions about the world, declare one's feelings to the world, and perform acts in the world. If phrases are private, sentences are public. One doesn't talk from oneself to oneself in complete sentences, at least not in poems. Interior sentences, written or unspoken, are imported from the public domain. In his statement of prose poetics, "The New Sentence," Ron Silliman argues that the "sentence is a unit of writing" distinct from the "utterance" in speech.[24] While the immutable visuals of electronic media are rendering this distinction less and less distinct (who speaks, or writes, commercials?), it is still valuable. Readers of poetic sentences hear in them traces of oral, written, and broadcast social discourse. Ashbery's "Evening in the Country," for instance, opens with the following line and sentence: "I am still completely happy." (DDS 33). This sentence doesn't fit its situation, presumably an evening of rusticated reflection on life after a trying time in the city. We would expect a phrase or an elliptical sentence ("Still happy"), simulating private language. As it stands, Ashbery's sentence sounds like an affirmation in the form of a resolution, which keeps "the smokestacks and corruption of the city" (33) very much in mind. The following poem, in prose, is composed in phrase-measured sentences from which the first person is missing: "Kind of empty in the way it sees everything, the earth gets to its feet and salutes the sky. More of a success at it this time than most others it is. The feeling that the sky might be in the back of someone's mind." (35). Omitting a personal pronoun ("I got to my feet . . . "), this reflecting prose also exists in the back of someone's mind and in the sky.

   Sentences, incomplete or not, are punctuated by full stops. As with commas and phrases, the mere injection of a period into a string of words will make readers construe it sententially. Sentences in verse tend to override lines. If we pause along the way to dwell on the sentence's subordinate phrases and intervening lines, we may have to reread it for its "overall" meaning. Sentences often make statements about what is the case and frame laws and rules about what will be the case. People who read poems for their stories or ideas are reading sentences. When joined together, sentences become stages or steps in an argument, which promises logical or narrative sequence. We expect sentences to make sense. In an essay on Ron Silliman's Chinese box, *The Age of Huts*, Bernstein speaks of releasing sentences from their obligations of arguing and telling: "If syntax is a neutral term for intrasentential relationships, narrative, in this structural sense, would be the term for intersentential relationships. That is, narrative is not intrinsically tied to causality, development, chronology, characters, setting—concepts that might be associated with narrative conventions within fiction or the novel" (CD 307). I will use Ashbery's term "argument" for this structural, musical relation between sentences because it represents not only the (il)logical but the (non)narrative relation between sentences. But I share Bernstein's sentiments. A poem's argument, too quickly dismissed as its "content," is its reel, which develops its broken and spliced line in its own time and space. A poem need not have an argument, but the expectation of one particularizes gaps and swerves between sentences; we hear what went wrong. Most model sentences exist in prose. The sentences of Proust,

James, Stein, Kafka, and Beckett are as important as those of any poet for Bernstein and Ashbery. Of innumerable versified sentences, I mention Stevens's dramatized Whitmanian sentences:

> To discover an order as of
> A season, to discover summer and know it,
>
> To discover winter and know it well, to find,
> Not to impose, not to have reasoned at all,
> Out of nothing to have come on major weather,
>
> It is possible, possible, possible.[25]

Note also Stein's abbreviated utterances:

> Call me Helen.
> Not at all.
> You may call me Helen.
> That's what we said.
>   (GS 29)

Bernstein took the measure of the sentence in his first full-length book, *Controlling Interests* (1980). The most frequent format in the book is what I will call the accordion stanza or poem, an inflatable sounding sentence box. Sentences promote accordion forms by ignoring linear and stanzaic divisions. Seven of the seventeen poems in *Controlling Interests* are accordions, stretching from one to nine pages. The three prose poems in the book also employ accordion right- and left-justified containers. Two of them string sentences together without a space, and the third is divided into unindented prose blocks (as if acknowledging the justified margins of verse).[26] Lacking the paragraph indentations of classical accordion stanzas, familiar from Greek and Latin epic poetry and from Milton and Wordsworth, Bernstein's poems play off expectations of an argument. Each new sentence in Bernstein's stanzas is itself an event.

These sentences exhibit great variety of measurement and style, but all approach the condition of nonpoetic or nonliterary prose. In the accordion prose of "The Italian Border of the Alps," for instance, Bernstein employs Steinian periodic sentences—short, sweet, and disjointed: "I've spent the years since. Primarily rowing. I'll phone. Next week after the tube roses are installed. Vivid memories. People remain. I have occasionally. Shops, sorting out how to become useful. A prolonged bout. Interest in useful plants. Aside from, a couple of trips, I do what I must. This is a pleasure. Exactly two weeks but more like." (CI 14). With the simple device of the period as the measure bar, Bernstein transforms these phrases and pseudosentences into incomplete, telegraphic statements. But little is left out that we couldn't fill in, after a fashion, in this travel discourse: "What vivid memories! Only a few people remain after the end of the season. I have occasionally descended on the little village. I've pored over its charming little shops, sorting out how to become useful around your house. But unfortunately, I've suffered a prolonged bout with the flu." These representative details, or others equally familiar, go without saying. By omitting the connecting joints, the monotony of travel writing shows through. When you've read one vacation, you've read them all.

Another accordion prose poem, "The Blue Divide," dilates its sentences to Jamesian periods but cross-measures them with the phrases and dependent clauses of psychological realism: "Several hours pass the mood indiscernibly shifting to less substantive pleasures, the hallway rotating airily to the tempo of unforeseen reverberations. A small coterie remains behind to see that the ship departs smoothly, counting their change with an alternating frenzy and tedium. You ask for the lighter but remain seated, seem to recollect what you refused to say, purse your lips and, with a forlorn look, lapse back into thought, then begin to make suggestions for lunch" (CI 55). "You," the specular, self-addressed, armchair traveler, personifies each inner perception and motivation. Each main clause, where something might happen, trails off in a string of clauses, participial phrases, and qualifying second thoughts. Like the phrase-measured prose of *Poetic Justice,* this mannered, patient novelistic relation hovers before the possibility of action, lost in its clauses.

If the accordion prose poems of *Controlling Interests* are primarily parodic, the accordion verses parodically advance an argument, against policy statement and for change, that matters. The book's opening poem, "Matters of Policy," makes light of the endlessly recycled custom of modernity. The title varies that dreaded phrase, "As a matter of policy . . . ," which signifies that the speaker disavows all responsibility for making or challenging the rules he or she perpetuates. What if the universe, the material world as we know it, consisted only of matters of policy? Wittgenstein wrote, sententiously, "The world is all that is the case." According to this thesis (subject to his later modifications), the world would be a collection of sentences. For Bernstein, "Matters of Policy" describes the way sentences take root, so that we no longer give them a second thought: "A poem like 'Matters of Policy' is exactly about this process, how conventions and language itself induce trances under which we glide as if in automatic pilot" (CD 391).

"Matters of Policy" is a hymn to particular things and events, subject to misadventures and unforeseen mishaps,

> the number
> that are wonderfully changed without any
> motive, view, design, desire, or principle of
> action.
>   (CI 2)

Its middle is occupied by a policy functionary—part newscaster, part local booster—who lays down the new policies by which matters shall be ordered. In this long stretch, independent sentences are strung loosely together as statements of fact, with the objectifying phrasal list erasing the constructive principle of the sentence. The petty official begins by announcing a new austere grammar for the depleted era of Carter malaise:

> Let me just for a minute.
recount the present standings. There is
no more white chocolate & the
banks are on holiday in Jamaica. All
the cigarettes have already been lit &
the mountains climbed & the chills
gotten over.
>   (CI 3)

Bernstein's anticlimactic, O'Hara-like enjambments ("There is / no more") underscore the postmodern condition each sentence reinforces, that there is no more news. With this depletion of novelty as a backdrop, the speaker, now a political orator, projects far-reaching but less than earth-shaking changes in policy:

> We live in a
time of great changes. Revolutions have
been made in the make-up of the most
everyday of vegetables. The sky itself is constantly
changing color. Electricity hyperventilates even the
most tired veins. Books strewn the streets.
Bicycles are stored beneath every other staircase.
>   (CI 4)

Bernstein's argument here follows Ashbery's in "The Skaters." Writing in the aftermath of President Kennedy's assassination, Ashbery assumed a similarly revolutionary tone:

> Thus a great wind cleanses, as a new ruler
Edits new laws, sweeping the very breath of the streets
Into posterior trash. The films have changed—
The great titles on the scalloped awning have turned dry and blight-colored.
No wind that does not penetrate a man's house, into the very bowels of the
>   furnace,
Scratching in dust a name on the mirror—say, and what about letters,
The dried grasses, fruits of the winter—gosh! Everything is trash!
>   (RM 37)

Nothing is untouched by the Zeitgeist. American poets in particular have as-

244 | *John Shoptaw*

sumed that change is a necessary good. But Ashbery, writing in Paris in mid-1963, lectures on the cultural amnesia of America's urban renewal in cross-measured sentences:

> These lacustrine cities grew out of loathing
> Into something forgetful, although angry with history.
> They are the product of an idea: that man is horrible, for instance,
> Though this is only one example.
>   (RM 9)

In "Matters of Policy," Bernstein diagnoses a similar amnesia in modernity. Thus he trails a prophetic main clause, "What stretches will also, & quicker / than you think, come apart," with an ablative, amnesiac absolute:

>   the new
> lights & new gaiety masking the utterly out-of-mind
> presence of the ancient city's darker history.
>   (CI 7)

New sentences forget their antecedents.

In Ashbery's "These Lacustrine Cities," the policy makers themselves, an ominously anonymous "we," threaten their poet-prophet with an assignment in the wilderness: "We had thought, for instance, of sending you to the middle of the desert" (RM 9). But Bernstein, in "Matters of Policy," keeps to the city streets, pinning his hopes on anti-institutional countermeasures. The poem sighs against the battered fortresses of officialdom:

> The surrounding buildings have a stillness
> that is brought into ironic ridicule by the pounding
> beats of the bongo drums emanating from the candy
> store a few blocks away.
>   (CI 9)

Bernstein's "ironic ridicule" marks the crypt word "(comic)relief." The verse skyscraper of "Matters of Policy" ironically contrasts with the renovated establishment it hopes to rock.

In the most autobiographical accordion poem in *Controlling Interests,* "Sentences My Father Used" (written in the summer of 1978), Bernstein shifts the familiar thirtysomething male poet's topic from his father to his father's sentences. His subject is the discursive formation of the time, most likely in the fifties, when the sentences were passed on and learned by the son, who may revise but not disown them. To bring up the sunken hoard of those sentences in himself, Bernstein contracts his own sentences into phrases so that the text becomes a memory pad, and handwriting akin to mine (or metal) sweeping:

> Ruminate around
> in there—listens for mandatory disconsolation,
> emit high pitched beeps.
> (CI 21)

The portmanteau marker "disconsolation" calls up "disconsolate," "consolation," and (following "mandatory") "sentence." The son is sentenced to the
father's sentences. But the disconsolate treasure hunter, shifting from an interior monologist ("Ruminate") to an external narrator ("listens"), homes in on
an elegiac "disconsolation."

Both father and son make statements in "Sentences," but these statements
are societal explanations. As a social history, the poem recalls Ashbery's "System," and as an oral (auto)biography it anticipates his *Flow Chart*. Here are
its elliptical opening sentences:

> Casts across otherwise unavailable fields.
> Makes plain. Ruffled. Is trying to
> alleviate his false: invalidate. Yet all is
> "to live out", by shut belief, the
> various, simply succeeds which.
> (CI 21)

The first three sentences begin in medias res by omitting, or refitting, their
pronominal subjects. The opening line, a Zukofskian five-word pentameter,
resonates variously. Hearing "Casts" as a verb brings in the elided subject
(writer or topic) with its obscuring but spellbinding shadow; reading it as a
plural noun turns the poem's own sentences into fly casts upon the still past of
the poem's "plain" surface. After the first end-stopped line, which announces
the end-stopped sentence as the poem's measure, "Sentences" constricts into
Steinian periodic utterances. The music of content here may be summed up by
the patriarchal finality "That's that."

But the paternal phrases aren't put down, composed and subdued, without
a struggle. The following sentences, firm and definitive, state their case without
admitting the shadow of a doubt, though the father, questioned, gets "Ruf-
fled." The father's approach to life, "to live out," is exhibited in quotes, with
grim undertones of "to live out" one's time, to serve one's sentence. The word-
measured close of the sentence, "simply succeeds which," defines and illustrates what Bernstein means by "the various": that "which simply succeeds"
or follows the previous sentence or event without a logical or physical cause.
Many of the incomplete sentences in "Sentences" list "Surprising details that /
hide more than announce" (CI 21), exemplifying Bernstein's idea of narrative
succession. By the seriatim spell of these simply seeing sentences, the son hopes

to avoid the sins of the father, turning his testimony into "A canvas of trumped up excuses, evading / the chain of connections." (CI 26). In this elliptical sentence, devoid of pronouns, "excuses" marks "charges," and "evading" calls up "responsibility." If sentences and events and generations simply succeed each other, perhaps responsibility may be evaded. Varying an American revolutionary slogan, J. L. Austin in "A Plea for Excuses" claims that there is "No modification without aberration."[27] Bernstein's "Sentences" is a series or "canvas" of aberrant, encrypted excuses, both the son's and the father's, in which each makes his own pact with his past, "simply succeeds which."

In elegiac poems, crypt words merge with their subjects. The word drowned out in the pounding, revisionary close of the sentence "Is trying to / alleviate his false: invalidate" is "pain," nearly audible in "Makes plain." By evading the unpredictable details of life, the father can "alleviate his pain" and rule it out. But can the son make his sentences true merely by exposing his father's painful sins of omission? Put another way, is Bernstein's blunt, jump-cut sentence truer than a more fluid one such as "He is trying to / invalidate his pain," which would mark "alleviate" and suggest "false"? Yes, since the smoother sentence would establish just that safe, known distance between father and son, between the conventional and the radically innovative, that Bernstein cannot honestly claim. Rather than narrating it, Bernstein's sentence performs his father's falsification of pain. Bernstein will later characterize poetry as nonconformist: "*Poetry is aversion of conformity* in the pursuit of new forms" (P 1). But to his credit, the practicing poet gives his father's conformity its due in "Sentences": "We just conformed because of the / respect we had for each other." (CI 24). This sentence, and sentiment, is difficult to dismiss.

The most moving parts of "Sentences" are those in which the father takes the stand. Bernstein's father, who died in 1977, was a dress manufacturer in the garment district in New York City. He specialized in making "knock-offs" (affordable copies) of fashion dresses, an innovation his son has brought into poetry manufacturing. Bernstein's patriarchal rhythms work hesitantly, as when the father reminisces over what seems to be his high-school yearbook photo:

> Patent leather shoes. In a gentle way. I
> wasn't very, I didn't have a
> very, my appearance wasn't one of, that
> one could take, well I didn't make
> the. Nothing stands out. Nice
> type of people. Rather isolated. Pleasant.
>   (CI 24)

What makes the music of these broken, unfinished sentences so powerful is that their speaker just begins, with his hesitations, to question the "gentle," "gentile" values of his class; sentences in "Sentences" only end in periods. A complex, contradictory speech act, the poem explains and excuses behavior:

> I felt badly about it but never made a
> protest for my rights. We never thought
> of that. I kept in short pants: what
> was given we ate. Nobody had
> to tell me this. Everything went into
> the business: being able to take advantage
> of an opportunity, create an opportunity.
> It was just a job I had to do.
> (CI 25)

These cross-measured sentences and lines present a compound "I," remembering and relating, inside and outside his life, unable to finish the disjointed sentences he had counted on "to live out" his life.

"Sentences" ends with an episode reminiscent of another father-son encounter, the episode in Faulkner's *The Sound and the Fury* in which the father gives his son, Quentin, his watch so that he may occasionally forget about time. Bernstein concludes his vigil with a watch:

> Misled by the scent, you
> spend the whole day trying to recover
> what was in your pocket, the watch your
> parent gave you if you would only mind
> the hour. Months sink into the water and
> the small rounded lump accumulates its
> fair share of disuse. Dreadfully private,
> pressed against the faces of circular
> necessity, the pane gives way, transparent,
> to a possibility of rectitude.
> (CI 27)

The narrative close surfaces only partially, its sentences ("false scent," "sentence") densely encrypted. The waterlogged watch, the father's "abused" heart or "ticker," must be retrieved from its pocket of memory. The self-characterization "Dreadfully private" covers "sorry," as a final apology is kept to itself. The glassed "circular / necessity" of the clock face is a window on the parent's, father's, past. The intervening "pane," marking "pain," finally gives way, and a "trans-parent" relationship becomes possible. With the surprisingly Utopian "rectitude," Bernstein answers in part his father's request for the "correct time." Insofar as rectitude is possible, the resonant pain is put into remission.

Bernstein's "Sentences" may be juxtaposed with Ashbery's "Fragment," which is also in part an elegy for his father. I will confine myself here to its opening dizain, an invariant form Ashbery adapted from the French Renaissance poet Maurice Scève's sequence *Délie:*

> The last block is closed in April. You
> See the intrusions clouding over her face
> As in the memory given you of older
> Permissiveness which dies in the
> Falling back toward recondite ends,
> The sympathy of yellow flowers.
> Never mentioned in the signs of the oblong day
> The saw-toothed flames and point of other
> Space not given, and yet not withdrawn
> And never yet imagined: a moment's commandment.
>   (DDS 78)

Like Bernstein, Ashbery announces, and refers to, his predominant measure in his first sentence. The closed form of "Fragment" fits its sentences into ten-line blocks. As Bernstein's "opening" of "shut belief" keeps closing the subject, Ashbery's first line closes the calendar and memorial block. But Ashbery outlasts its sentence with a specular "You." The interior second-person perspective is doubled, superimposing the tearful widow upon a younger permissive mother. What is silenced in Bernstein's "Sentences" is "the various," for which excuses and apologies are unnecessary; what is "Never mentioned" in "Fragment" is the son's variant sexuality, which ends the reproductive line. Ashbery describes his parental, patriarchal sentence as "a moment's commandment." It is an interesting conflation of the biblical commandment to "Honor thy father and thy mother" (Exodus 20:12) with Dante Rossetti's definition at the beginning of his sequence *The House of Life,* "A Sonnet is a moment's monument." As Bernstein refuses to order his sentences in an argument, Ashbery refrains from telling a single, sequential story in his dizains. Nevertheless, his nonsequential sequence pays its tribute to sentence framers, both literary and patriarchal.

Ashbery's first fully sentence-measured poem in verse was his seven-page accordion stanza of "lines contracting into a plane" (RM 28), "Clepsydra," which probably encouraged Bernstein's own experiments in the form. Once again, I will confine myself to Ashbery's opening sentences, which introduce the measure. Written in the spring of 1965, after both "The Skaters" and "Fragment" (published, out of sequence, in *The Double Dream of Spring*), "Clepsydra" proceeds slowly in dense, elliptical, phrasal, but often fluid sentences. Ashbery's immediate formal model was probably the accordion stanzas of *La Vue* by Raymond Roussel, but "Clepsydra" derives ultimately from Wordsworth's "spontaneous" stanzas in "Tintern Abbey" and *The Prelude.* A clepsydra was a water clock used to time legal arguments, and Ashbery's poem

marks various senses of the word "argument": legal, narrative (plot), philosophical, and romantic. The plot concerns a long-term love affair, which
started out fresh and became ossified by custom. The sentences begin in its
wake with elliptical, waking questions:

> Hasn't the sky? Returned from moving the other
> Authority recently dropped, wrested as much of
> That severe sunshine as you need now on the way
> You go.
>   (RM 27)

"Clepsydra" is a good example of Ashbery's metrical practice of composing by
both the metronome and the musical phrase. The initial choriambic rhythm
("Hásn't the ský?") is repeated in "récently drópped" and varied in "móving
the óther," which itself echoes in "wrésted as múch of." The third line introduces an obstinate rhythm of evenly stressed syllables. Their sonic resonance—
"other / Authority," "you need now on," "recently" and "reason," "sky" and
"why"—advances a musical argument with its own parallelisms. Though the
capitalized lines of "Clepsydra" consistently oscillate between pentameters
and alexandrines, their phrasal patterning keeps the reader from thinking of
them as measures. Lines end, but sentences continue.

    The constructive music of "Clepsydra" goes beyond its melody to the dia-
lectical rhythm of question and answer. Ashbery's apocalyptic question echoes
Chicken Little's exclamation, "The sky is falling!"; the following lines vary the
traveler's question, "Is it light enough to go on?" Accordion stanzas always
concern themselves with (dis)continuity. In this case, the overwhelming question of "Clepsydra" might be formulated, Hasn't my life broken up with what
it was? The unbroken accordion form itself answers in the negative. Ashbery's
first two phrase-measured, interiorized sentences are musically but not grammatically punctuated. Normative grammar would put question marks after
"dropped" and "go." Ashbery's punctuation divides the monologue into two
"parts" or roles: one asks elliptically, the other responds rhetorically. One may
wake up alone, but the musically implied other allays his or her doubts.

    The lengthy, complex argument of "Clepsydra" led Ashbery to the mean-
dering prose sentences of *Three Poems*. In his 1972 interview with the *New
York Quarterly*, Ashbery recalled that he turned to prose poetry partly to dis-
pense with verse: "The arbitrary divisions of poetry into lines would get abol-
ished. . . . [The] poetic form would be dissolved, in solution" (126). But it took
a while before the solution took effect. While much of the first poem, "The
New Spirit," prosifies the meditational style of "Fragment" and "Clepsydra,"
a new prosaic discourse and constructive music emerges in the accordion prose
blocks of "The System." The public-address system of "The System" presents
an "inside" history of the sixties "love generation." Opting for free, cosmic

love, religious or otherwise, this younger generation (Ashbery wrote *Three Po-ems* in his forties) saw itself as "the logical last step of history" (TP 62) and sought therefore to maintain its "nirvana-like state" (61) in spite of the historical cataclysm of Vietnam. In order to describe an alternative to this ahistorical bliss of permanent "frontal happiness," the historian mounts the pulpit with a sermon on the virtues of latent, historically implicated happiness. But the philosophical problem of style in "The System" is that the subject may get lost in its syntax, as in this serial sentence:

> Here it is that our sensuality can save us *in extremis:* the atmosphere of the day that event took place, the way the trees and buildings looked, what we said to the person who was both the bearer and fellow recipient of that message and what that person replied, words that were not words but sounds out of time, taken out of any eternal context in which their content would be recognizable—these facts have entered our consciousness once and for all, have spread through us even into our pores like a marvelous antidote to the cup that the next moment had already prepared and which, whether hemlock or nectar, could only have proved fatal because it *was* the next, bringing with it the unspoken message that motion could be accomplished only in time, that is in a preordained succession of moments which must carry us far from here, far from this impassive but real moment of understanding which may be the only one we shall ever know, even if it is merely the first of an implied infinite series. But what if this were all? (TP 76)

Ashbery's Proustian argument—that we may save our treasured moment by remembering its sensuous, sensual details—is reversed by its syntax. The first sentence moves from "Here," the sensuous moment, to "far from here," the inevitable next moment in an "infinite series." But as we know, the series is finite. The music of construction of the sentence has first to do with our afterlife in the wake of the frontal moment, no longer "Here." Ashbery's subsequent, appropriately shrunken question, thus carries theological import. Is there life after ecstasy? Though Ashbery's public speaker argues that "our sensuality can save us *in extremis*," no details are forthcoming. I do not mean by this to deconstruct Ashbery's sentence, but to show the complexity of his thinking. Proust recaptured time in his sensuous sentences. Ashbery's abstract periods keep the moment, perhaps of sexual and textual initiation, without any saving concrete knowledge of it.

Ashbery uses first-person sentences most extensively in his anonymous autobiography *Flow Chart*. Now a "senior public figure," as far as poets go, the poet's first person includes a historical dimension it lacked, for instance, in "The Skaters" and *Three Poems*. At the threshold of his longest poem, Ashbery asks a question:

> Still in the published city but not yet
> overtaken by a new form of despair, I ask

the diagram: is it the foretaste of pain
it might easily be?
   (FC 3)

The constructive music of this question lies in its delayed subject. The first line reads like an elliptical sentence: "[I'm] still [here] but not yet [ready to leave]." The opening phrasal measures, which promise an interior dialogue, get publicized by their trailing independent clause, "I ask / the diagram." The lowercase lines of *Flow Chart* are more cross-measured than enjambed. But the hesitant sentence holds surprises. We expect a narrative, past tense verb here; in the present tense, "I ask," with "you" the polyphonic object, takes on the character of a plea. The sentence thus reports with the urgency of a plea: Is this the end? Is this "Still" silence an omen or not? Given its pronominal subject, the question is public, as the crypt phrase "in the public eye" suggests. Unlike "Hasn't the sky?" for instance, the question opening *Flow Chart* is not only asked but reported, even performed: "I hereby ask. . . . " The one responsible for answering the question is not only "the diagram"—the ever-unfinished city and the outlined, projected poem—but the reading public. The life of Ashbery's poem, whether we feel up to it or not, is now in our metropolitan hands.

Section

Since my measurements are expanding along with Ashbery's and Bernstein's measures, I will limit myself to outlining this largest measured unit, which I call the section. Not exactly measures themselves, sections are spatially defined, sometimes numbered and even titled, relatively independent poetic units. Poems may be divided into rhymed or unrhymed identically measured stanzas, or topically measured blank or free verse or prose paragraphs or blocks. The English verse paradigm for poetic sections is the sonnet sequence, and sections of poems often stand more or less alone as independent poems. Poetry books may also be divided into sections. Though Ashbery has done so only implicitly, by placing long poems at the end (or beginning) of his books, Bernstein recently trisected *Rough Trades* with subtitles. Among nonverse sections, the chapter and the (sometimes numbered) paragraph have been the most obvious models; the heavily segmented productions of electronic and mass print media will doubtless have an increasing influence on poetry. Collage techniques are especially productive in sectioned poems. Since most poems keep all their eggs from one basket, I will confine myself to those in which measures, tempos, styles, discourses, and so on differ from section to section, like musical movements. These differently measured sections are often visible at a glance, as with *The Waste Land,* whose impact on both Bernstein and Ashbery is immeasurable. Especially in his recent work, Bernstein has assem-

bled multimeasured long poems, which stop and start over at each break. Ashbery has less overtly divided his long poems, but he has used sectioning to
diversify his music. Sectioning enables Ashbery and Bernstein, both notoriously "difficult" poets, to contrast "easy," often pop or pulp sections with
more densely constructed passages. Lucid intervals make their own measure.

In an essay on artificial intelligence, "Blood on the Cutting Room Floor,"
Bernstein (who worked from 1973 to 1989 as a medical editor) adapts a little-
known medical term to define differentiated poetic unity: "*Dysraphism* may
be a useful term. . . . Medically, it would mean a congenital misseaming of em-
bryonic parts—*raph* means seam, a rhapsodist being one who stitches parts
together, that is, a reciter of epic poetry" (CD 359). We might describe certain
Bernstein and Ashbery poems, sectioned or not, as dysraphic, catgutting several announced or unannounced measures together. But mere juxtaposition, as
Bernstein argues, would simply atomize the poem's social text, "undercut[ting]
the overall system of relationships—the total prosody—that makes a poem a
whole" (CD 358), and turning antiabsorption into absorption. Dysraphic poems have their own rhythmic unity; not all patchworks are equal.

Bernstein's first sustained experiment in dysraphic sections was "Standing
Target" in *Controlling Interests,* a composite self-portrait. While brief excerpts
from "Standing Target" will hardly convey its antiabsorptive unity,[28] a few
spot checks may give some feel for its dysraphic measures. The poem opens in
heavily polyphonic line measures countermeasured by words:

> Deserted all sudden a all
> Or gloves of notion, seriously
> Foil sightings, polite society
> Verge at just about characterized
> (CI 39)

In this opening paranoid movement, the individual, "deserted all of a sudden"
like a word, is a sitting duck for the plane that masks its radar-sighted approach with tin foil. Surviving on the verge of being characterized, however,
entails foiling the sightings of polite society. Soon, "Standing Target" itself
foils our expectations with a collaged, phrase-measured section from a summer camp manual: "1. Throwing a tennis ball into the / air and clapping
hands—up to four / times—before catching it again. 2." (CI 40–41). After
this standardizing test of boyhood comes an antiphonal response in sentences:

> (saying:)
> *I am hungry, let me eat*
> *I am thirsty, let me drink*
> (41)

This response leads to cross-measured sentences:

> How sad lines are, crisscrossing
> out the hopes of an undifferentiated
> experience, the cold sweeps
> past, eyes tear, the night begins
> again.
>   (41)

The hovering poet is always in search of an undifferentiated fluidity. This stanza gives way to a psychoanalytic characterization, objectifying its phrase-measured subject:

> Neurological impairment, speech delay, psychomotor
> difficulties with wide discrepancies and
> fluctuations
>   (42)

At the other end of this dimly lit tunnel is the well-adjusted sentence-measured man, whose description begins:

> As President and Chief Executive Officer
> of Sea World, Inc., David DeMotte is
> responsible for managing all aspects
> of the Company's operations
>   (42)

As "Standing Target" is more than the sum of its measures, the person is more than the total of society's individuating grids.

Ashbery began writing dysraphic sections for humorous effect in "Europe." After composing seven of the 111 sections of "Europe" in unfinished, ungrammatical line and word measures, Ashbery collaged in an uninflected prose passage from William LeQueux's adolescent novel *Beryl of the Biplane* (1917), before returning to differently margined line-measured verse:

> In a basket the waiter had placed some cold food with some bread and a
> bottle of wine, and this had been duly transferred to the car.
>
> All was now ready for the continuance of the journey.
>
>   9.
> The decision in his life
> soul elsewhere
> the gray hills
>
> (TCO 65)

Ashbery reformats LeQueux's sentence "All was now . . . " as prose poetry by changing a paragraph break to a stanza break. In its new position, the sententious sentence announces the "continuance" of Ashbery's arduous poetry. In the tenth section, consisting of a single capitalized but unpunctuated line, Ashbery offers a psychoanalysis of the Rauschenbergian trash artist: "He had mistaken his book for garbage" (TCO 65). This line, missing its period, is it fiction or poetry? Is "He" Ashbery or "Ronald Pryor" of the eighth "chapter," or Ashberyl of the biplaned prose poem? The music of juxtaposition here relies on multiple, analogous choices.

In "The Skaters," itself juxtaposed in *Rivers and Mountains* with the seamless "Clepsydra," Ashbery also plays verse off verse. This dysraphic poem opens with Stevensian philosophical intoning:

> These decibels
> Are a kind of flagellation, an entity of sound
> Into which being enters, and is apart.
>   (RM 34)

The eleven-line sentence-measured stanza is punctuated by an isolated line, a snatch of phenomena appropriately phrase-measured but full-stopped: "Here a scarf flies, there an excited call is heard." Another reflective stanza is followed by another phenomenal line skating on the page's surface. But this impressionist, pseudoscientific spell is broken with the fluid poet's doubts about staying: "But how much survives? How much of any one of us survives?" Ashbery soon punctures the question's suspense with the absurdist listing Bernstein employed in "Matters of Policy," an overlong line of cross-measured sentences: "One collects bullets. An Indianapolis, Indiana man collects slingshots of all epochs, and so on." While the assonance and consonance are no less dense than in the first three lines, the journalistic discourse of this long line quickens its tempo. Line length is life length. In the next stanza the dark theme of survival returns to the surface with some McGonagall doggerel: "And up the swollen sands / Staggers the darkness fiend, with the storm fiend close behind him!" (34). The phenomenal tempest, a symphonic cliché, brings on the full orchestra with Ashbery exhibiting his own Cagean collection of word-measured instrument names: "tuba notes awash on the great flood, ruptures of xylophone, violins, limpets, grace-notes, the musical instrument called serpent, viola da gambas, aeolian harps, clavicles, pinball machines, electric drills, que sais-je encore!" (35). The second run-on dissonant ("aeolian harps, clavicles, pinball machines") "line" stretches melodic verse to its limits. Though numbered into four stately seasonal sections, "The Skaters" changes measure nearly every stanza. Ashbery has continued to write multisectioned, musically self-conscious poems, such as his hilariously entitled "Variations, Calypso and

Fugue on a Theme of Ella Wheeler Wilcox" (DDS 24). But not really until *Flow Chart* would he once again ring such exuberant changes.

"You can't say it that way any more." This opening line and sentence from Ashbery's bawdy *ars* "And *Ut Pictura Poesis* Is Her Name" (HD 45) has as a correlative dictum, you can't hear it that way any more. If we simply relegate "close reading" to the annals of New Criticism, the "close writing" of poetry will also be swept from the critical scene. As contemporary poetry is still the best-informed criticism of its earlier poetry, learning how today's poets work can also teach us how earlier poetry is constructed. I don't expect all my readers to trade in their yardsticks for my new metric tape. But I do want Ashbery's and Bernstein's readers to hear more in their music than musical accompaniment. Ashbery and Bernstein might be otherwise compared; they are, for instance, among the most reflective, inventive, and funny poets now writing. Or we might beat either poet over the head with the other's "standard of comparison." My common measurement of constructive music demonstrates Bernstein's and Ashbery's extraordinary lyric range throughout their careers, well above and below the familiar scales of the syllable. From character to sentence to dysraphic stanza, Bernstein's and Ashbery's musics mount two of our most compelling apologies for poetry.

Notes

1. Gerard Manley Hopkins, *Gerard Manley Hopkins,* ed. Catherine Phillips (Oxford: Oxford University Press, 1986), 175.

2. Emily Dickinson, *The Complete Poems of Emily Dickinson,* ed. Thomas H. Johnson (Boston: Little, Brown, 1960), 146. I follow Johnson's numbering of Dickinson's poems.

3. In *A Controversy of Poets,* ed. Paris Leary and Robert Kelly (New York: Doubleday, 1965), 523.

4. William Packard, ed., *The Craft of Poetry: Interviews from "The New York Quarterly"* (New York: Doubleday, 1974), 114.

5. Throughout I use the following abbreviations for Bernstein's books:

CD	*Content's Dream* (Los Angeles: Sun & Moon, 1986).
CI	*Controlling Interests* (New York: Roof, 1980).
D	*Disfrutes* (1981; reprint, Elmwood, Conn.: Potes & Poets Press, 1985).
DC	*Dark City* (Los Angeles: Sun & Moon, 1994).
I/I	*Islets/Irritations* (1983; New York: Roof, 1992).
OT	*The Occurrence of Tune,* with Susan Bee (New York: Segue, 1977).
P	*A Poetics* (Cambridge: Harvard University Press, 1992).
PJ	*Poetic Justice* (Baltimore: Pod Books, 1979).
R	*Resistance* (Windsor, Vermont: Awede, 1983).
RT	*Rough Trades* (Los Angeles: Sun & Moon, 1991).

S   *The Sophist* (Los Angeles: Sun & Moon, 1987).

SR   *Senses of Responsibility* (1979; Providence: Paradigm Press, 1989).

6. I do not take the syllable (or morpheme) as measures, since prosodists have already spent so much time on them. Nor do I measure poems phonemically, though phonemic patterning is indispensable in describing a poem's sonic texture, since poems are written in letters and other characters, not in phonemes.

7. Packard, *Craft of Poetry*, 123–24.

8. Richard Jackson, ed., "The Imminence of a Revelation," in *Acts of Mind: Conversations with Contemporary Poets* (University: University of Alabama Press, 1983), 70.

9. For more on cryptography, see Shoptaw, *On the Outside Looking Out: John Ashbery's Poetry* (Cambridge: Harvard University Press, 1994).

10. Bernstein's poem also appears below as the Afterword to this book.

11. Wallace Stevens, *The Palm at the End of the Mind,* ed. Holly Stevens (New York: Vintage, 1972), 334.

12. James Joyce, *Finnegans Wake* (New York: Viking, 1939), 124.

13. John Ashbery, "Three Madrigals" (New York: Poet's Press, 1968). This limited edition of 162 copies was handwritten. The poem also appeared in the equally fugitive magazine *Angel Hair* 5 (Spring 1968): 47–50.

14. *Adventures in Poetry* 5 (January 1970): 102–18.

15. Susan Howe, in Robert Frank and Henry Sayre, eds., *The Line in Postmodern Poetry* (Urbana: University of Illinois Press, 1988), 209; Howe, *Singularities* (Hanover: University Press of New England, 1990), 59.

16. Henry David Thoreau, *A Week on the Concord and Merrimack Rivers; Walden, or, Life in the Woods; The Maine Woods; Cape Cod,* ed. Robert F. Sayre (New York: Library of America, 1985), 566.

17. Sylvia Plath, *The Collected Poems,* ed. Ted Hughes (New York: Harper & Row, 1981), 273. Hearing the crypt word "Egypt" in "Edge" brings into focus Shakespeare's dramatic portrait in *Antony and Cleopatra* of the Egyptian queen's suicide, with her threatened children and her asps, which distances this poem from any reductively confessional reading.

18. Leslie Scalapino, *way* (San Francisco: North Point, 1988), 16.

19. In the first edition of *Leaves of Grass,* Whitman used ellipses something in the way Dickinson used dashes, as compositional pauses, waiting for further words on the line: "I hear the bravuras of birds . . . the bustle of growing wheat . . . gossip of flames . . . clack of sticks cooking my meals" (Walt Whitman, *Walt Whitman: Poetry and Prose,* ed. Justin Kaplin [New York: Library of America, 1982], 53).

20. John Milton, *John Milton: Complete Poems and Major Prose,* ed. Merritt Y. Hughes (New York: Macmillan, 1957), 211–12.

21. Gertrude Stein, *The Yale Gertrude Stein,* ed. Richard Kostelanetz (New Haven: Yale University Press, 1980), 334. This text is cited henceforth as GS.

22. Frank O'Hara, *The Collected Poems of Frank O'Hara,* ed. Donald Allen (New York: Knopf, 1979), 262.

23. W. H. Auden, *Collected Poems,* ed. Edward Mendelson (New York: Random House, 1976), 256.

24. Ron Silliman, *The New Sentence* (New York: Roof, 1987), 69.

25. Stevens, *Palm at the End of the Mind*, 230.

26. The prose poetry in Ron Silliman's *Age of Huts* (New York: Roof, 1986) and the accordion verse of *What* are similarly unindented.

27. J. L. Austin, *Philosophical Papers*, ed. J. O. Urmson and G. J. Warnock, 3rd ed. (Oxford: Oxford University Press, 1979), 189.

28. For a fascinating conversation on this poem and related matters, see "Characterization" (CD 428–62).

Afterword

The Influence of Kinship Patterns upon Perception of an Ambiguous Stimulus

Charles Bernstein

What's money worth? Not a whole lot if
You come up a few bits short & come
Away empty handed. If that was the case
What would you have to say then? At least
The motorperson knows how to blow a whistle.
At least in the winter it's not summer
(God damn mosquitoes & horseflies). What did
The Mandela say to the Mandela? BOY
HITS IGLOO. Snowed motion, i.e., frosted or
Laminated. To be such a bitter pill
& have nothing wrong. *Don't laugh
It really hurted*. If you put on
My shirt then what shirt am I
Going to wear? The kind of people
Wear plaid Bermuda shorts. The kind of
People that judge people who wear
Plaid Bermuda shorts. The kind of
Day this has been (I think I am
Falling into a tunnel of love but
Forget to get on). For a long time I'd
Say *twirl* when I meant 'spin'. Have you
Heard the one about the fly & the
Paper? The fly bottle could not found
The fly. The Mother Bear could not
Find the rest of the story. Harry has his

Troubles too but these are not interesting enough
To bear replay. "That's a very
Suspicious-looking baby." "It's hard
Not to be a baby." "But
Are there really babies or just baby-
Behavior?" —For the purpose
Of your request I'm including this
Sentence about the influence of John
Ashbery. While the packet
Boat sunk I can still imagine I am
Crawling into it; at the same time the ice
Is too thin to
Pretend to fall through.
Meanwhile, the water is wetter in the
Rich man's pond but doesn't taste
As good. —Hey wait a minute!
That's a bit *too* close, try to stay
Back *at least 10* inches. So what
If the margins don't
Turn out right? Whadda you *mean* you're
Going to the next poem? *This is the best*
Part! Oh, I'm sorry, I guess I misunderstood
You. —But nobody seems to want to hear
About the pain we men feel
Having our prerogatives questioned.
A bunch of darn-dash pragmatists
With justice on their side (for all
The good that will do them). Don't
Frame me or I'll bust you in the
Doldrums. —*Now let's*
Switch the subject & try to find
Out what's on *your* mind. Voyage of life
Getting you down? Felt better when things
Were really rocky & now there's smooth

Sailing but it's lost its meaning? I'm a
Good listener & only mildly demanding:
There's just the one-time fee (mostly
For paper & printing & distribution
Costs) & unlimited returns. I'm bubbling over
With empathy & good advice & I'm not
Afraid to tell you where I think you've
Gone wrong. Let's face it—
From the word *go* you've
Resented me—resented my being finished
In the face of your—what?—continuing
On? But I don't mean to be complete
If that makes you feel distant; still
As I say, I
Do want some distance. She was a
Sort of Betsy Ross figure but without the
Accoutrements—no washer/dryer, just the one
TV. I said to her—What can you *expect*
From a poem?—evidently a lot less than
She did. A poem bleeds
Metaphorically, just like I do. I can
No more breathe than face
The music. But if the first
Banana smells a rat look out for
Lost leader (tossed reader). —"I
Don't think I'm ever
Going home." —I don't think
I've ever been home. *We are looking for*
Cheerful, enthusiastic self-starters
With solid backgrounds in detailed
Wails. The point
Not to change history but to change
Events. For instance, you
Can change in the car, change on the

Beach, or use a changing room
At the beach. Don't change me
& I won't change a hair on your
Chinny chin chin. Or let me
Put it this way: You can call
Me anything you want to but give me
The right change. That's right: I
Haven't changed, you have. It's
Not the time it's the beer. I'm in
A rush, don't forget to send a
Check. Not a con
Just a dodge. Not a dodge a Lincoln-
Mercury. *Take me to your leader*. Take me
To the 5 & Dime I've got to go.
Faith under leisure: as difficult as
Keeping a hat in a hurricane
Or an appointment with an erasure.
One Mandela hit the other Mandela in the nose.
What color blood came out?
R - E - D spells *red*.
Are you people? You're about the nicest people
I know & I know some pretty unpleasant
Characters.

Works Cited

Adams, Henry. *The Education of Henry Adams*. Riverside ed. Boston: Houghton Mifflin, 1973.

al-Khalil, Samir. *The Monument: Art, Vulgarity, and Responsibility in Iraq*. Berkeley: University of California Press, 1991.

Allen, Donald, and George Butterick, eds. *The Postmoderns: The New American Poetry Revised*. New York: Grove, 1982.

Althusser, Louis. *Lenin and Philosophy*. Trans. Ben Brewster. New York: Monthly Review Press, 1971.

Altieri, Charles. "Ashbery as Love-Poet." *Verse* 8, no. 1 (Spring 1991): 8–15.

——. "Contemporary Poetry as Philosophy: Subjective Agency in John Ashbery and C. K. Williams." *Contemporary Literature* 33 (1992): 214–42.

——. *Self and Sensibility in Contemporary American Poetry*. Cambridge: Cambridge University Press, 1984.

Ash, John. *The Branching Stairs*. Manchester: Carcanet, 1984.

——. *Disbelief*. Manchester: Carcanet, 1987.

Ashbery, John. *April Galleons*. New York: Viking, 1987.

——. *As We Know*. New York: Viking, 1979.

——. *The Double Dream of Spring*. New York: Dutton, 1970.

——. "An Expressionist in Paris." *Art News*, April 1965.

——. *Flow Chart*. New York: Knopf, 1991.

——. "Frank O'Hara's Question." *Bookweek*, September 25, 1966, pp. 23–25.

——. *Hotel Lautréamont*. New York: Knopf, 1992.

——. *Houseboat Days*. New York: Penguin, 1977.

——. "The Impossible: A Review of Gertrude Stein's *Stanzas in Meditation*." *Poetry* 90, no. 4 (July 1957): 250–54.

——. Introduction to *The Collected Poems of Frank O'Hara*. Ed. Donald Allen. New York: Knopf, 1971.

——. "Letter to the Editor." *Nation*, May 8, 1967, p. 578.

——. "ONE HUNDRED MULTIPLE-CHOICE QUESTIONS." *Adventures in Poetry* 5 (January 1970): 102–18.

——. "Paris Notes." *Art International*, June 1963, pp. 76–78.

——. "Post-Painterly Quattrocento." *Art News* 65, no. 8 (December 1966): 40, 61–62.

——. *Reported Sightings: Art Chronicles, 1957–1987*. Ed. David Bergman. New York: Knopf, 1989.

——. "Reverdy en Amérique." *Mercure de France* 344 (January–April 1962): 108–12.

——. Review of Martial Raysse Show. *Art News* 64, no. 6 (October 1965): 52–53, 58–59.

——. *Rivers and Mountains*. New York: Holt, Rinehart, Winston, 1966.

——. *Selected Poems*. New York: Viking, 1985.

——. *Self-Portrait in a Convex Mirror*. New York: Penguin, 1975.

——. *Shadow Train*. New York: Viking, 1981.

——. *Some Trees*. New Haven: Yale University Press, 1956.

——. *The Tennis Court Oath*. Middletown, Conn.: Wesleyan University Press, 1962.

——. *Three Madrigals*. New York: Poet's Press, 1968.

——. *Three Poems*. New York: Penguin, 1972.

——. *The Vermont Notebook*. Los Angeles: Black Sparrow, 1975.

——. *A Wave*. New York: Viking, 1984.

Auden, W. H. *Collected Poems*. Ed. Edward Mendelson. New York: Random House, 1976.

Austin, J. L. *Philosophical Papers*. Ed. J. O. Urmson and G. J. Warnock. 3rd ed. Oxford: Oxford University Press, 1979.

Bachelard, Gaston. *The Poetics of Reverie: Childhood, Language, and the Cosmos*. Trans. David Russell. Boston: Beacon Press, 1971.

Bakhtin, M. M. *The Dialogic Imagination: Four Essays by M. M. Bakhtin*. Ed. Michael Holquist. Trans. Caryl Emerson and Michael Holquist. Austin: University of Texas Press, 1981.

Barrell, John. *The Idea of Landscape and the Sense of Place, 1730-1840: An Approach to John Clare*. Cambridge: Cambridge University Press, 1972.

Barthes, Roland. *The Pleasure of the Text*. Trans. Richard Miller. New York: Hill & Wang, 1975.

Bartlett, Lee. *Talking Poetry: Conversations in the Workshop with Contemporary Poets*. Albuquerque: University of New Mexico Press, 1987.

Bellamy, Joe David, ed. *American Poetry Observed: Poets on Their Work*. Urbana: University of Illinois Press, 1984.

Bendall, Molly. "Ann Lauterbach: An Interview." *American Poetry Review* 21, no. 3 (May/June 1992): 19–25.

Benjamin, Walter. *Reflections: Essays, Aphorisms, Autobiographical Writings*. Ed. Peter Demetz. Trans. Edmund Jephcott. New York: Harcourt Brace Jovanovitch, 1978.

Bernstein, Charles. *Content's Dream: Essays, 1975-1984*. Los Angeles: Sun & Moon, 1986.

——. *Controlling Interests*. New York: Roof, 1980.

——. *Disfrutes*. 1981. Reprint. Elmwood, Conn.: Potes & Poets Press, 1985.

——. *Islets/Irritations*. 1982. Reprint. New York: Roof, 1992.

——. *The Nude Formalism*. Los Angeles: Sun & Moon, 1989.

——. *The Occurrence of Tune*. With Susan Bee. New York: Segue, 1977.

——. *Poetic Justice*. Baltimore: Pod Books, 1979.

——. *A Poetics*. Cambridge: Harvard University Press, 1992.

——. *Resistance*. Windsor, Vt.: Awede, 1983.

——. *Rough Trades*. Los Angeles: Sun & Moon, 1991.

——. *Senses of Responsibility*. 1979. Reprint. Providence: Paradigm, 1989.

——. *The Sophist*. Los Angeles: Sun & Moon, 1987.

Bertholf, Robert. "A Conversation with William Bronk." *Credences* 1, no. 3 (1976): 9–33.

Bloom, Harold. *The Anxiety of Influence: A Theory of Poetry*. New York: Oxford University Press, 1973.

———. *Figures of Capable Imagination*. New York: Seabury Press, 1976.

———. "John Ashbery: The Charity of the Hard Moments." In *American Poetry since 1960: Some Critical Perspectives*, ed. Robert B. Shaw., 83–108. Cheshire: Carcanet, 1973.

———. "Measuring the Canon: 'Wet Casements' and 'Tapestry.' " In *Modern Critical Views: John Ashbery*. New York: Chelsea House, 1985.

———. *Modern Critical Views: John Ashbery*. New York: Chelsea House, 1985.

Bronk, William. "Boiled Down." In *Living Instead*, 96. San Francisco: North Point, 1991.

———. "Copan: Historicity Gone." In *Vectors and Smoothable Curves: Collected Essays*, 30–35. San Francisco: North Point, 1983.

———. "Copan: Unwillingness, the Unwilled." In *Vectors and Smoothable Curves*, 40–44.

———. "Exploration." In *Living Instead*, 49.

———. "Holy Ghost." In *Death Is the Place*, 30. San Francisco: North Point, 1989.

———. "The Occupation of Space—Palenque." In *Vectors and Smoothable Curves*, 21–29.

———. "Of Poetry." In *Death Is the Place*, 17.

———. "Particulate. Inhumane." In *Living Instead*, 34.

———. "The Plainest Narrative." In *Life Supports: New and Collected Poems*, 113–114. San Francisco: North Point, 1982.

———. "The Poems: All Concessions Made." In *Life Supports*, 179.

———. "Silence and Henry Thoreau." In *Vectors and Smoothable Curves*, 57–107.

———. "Unpersonal." In *Living Instead*, 40.

———. "Yes: I Mean So OK—Love." In *Life Supports*, 121.

Brownstein, Marilyn L. "Postmodern Language and the Perpetuation of Desire." *Twentieth Century Literature* 31, no. 1 (1985): 73–88.

Buren, Daniel. "Is Teaching Art Necessary?" *Galerie des arts* 7, no.12 (September 1968): 42–46.

Burnshaw, Stanley. *A Stanley Burnshaw Reader*. Athens: University of Georgia Press, 1990.

Cohen, Keith. "Ashbery's Dismantling of Bourgeois Discourse." In *Beyond Amazement: New Essays on John Ashbery*, ed. David Lehman, 128–49. Ithaca: Cornell University Press, 1980.

Conte, Joseph M. *Unending Design: The Forms of Postmodern Poetry*. Ithaca: Cornell University Press, 1991.

Coolidge, Clark. *Space*. New York: Harper & Row, 1970.

Corman, Cid. *William Bronk: An Essay*. Carrboro: Truck, 1976.

Costello, Bonnie. "John Ashbery and the Idea of the Reader." *Contemporary Literature* 23 (1982): 493–514.

Crase, Douglas. "The Prophetic Ashbery." In *Beyond Amazement: New Essays on John Ashbery*, ed. David Lehman, 30–65. Ithaca: Cornell University Press, 1980.

———. *The Revisionist*. Boston: Little, Brown, 1981.

de Jonge, Alex. *Nightmare Culture*. New York: St. Martin's Press, 1973.

Deleuze, Gilles, and Felix Guattari. *Capitalism and Schizophrenia*. Trans. Robert Hurley et al. New York: Viking, 1977.

DeLillo, Don. *White Noise*. New York: Viking, 1985.

Derrida, Jacques. *Signeponge/Signsponge*. Trans. Richard Rand. New York: Columbia University Press, 1984.

Dickinson, Emily. *The Complete Poems of Emily Dickinson*. Ed. Thomas H. Johnson. Boston: Little, Brown, 1960.

———. *Final Harvest: Emily Dickinson's Poems*. Ed. Thomas H. Johnson. Boston: Little, Brown, 1961.

Easthope, Anthony, and John O. Thompson. *Contemporary Poetry Meets Modern Theory*. London: Harvester Wheatsheaf, 1991.

Ehrenpreis, Irvin. *Poetries of America: Essays on the Relation of Character to Style*. Ed. Daniel Albright. Charlottesville: University Press of Virginia, 1989.

Ernest, John. "William Bronk's Religious Desire." *Sagetrieb* 7 (1988): 145–52.

Fink, Thomas. *Surprise Visit*. New York: Domestic Press, 1993.

Finkelstein, Norman M. *The Utopian Moment in Contemporary American Poetry*. Lewisburg, Pa.: Bucknell University Press, 1988.

———. "William Bronk: The World as Desire." *Contemporary Literature* 23 (1982): 480–92.

Foster, Edward. "Conversations with William Bronk." *Talisman* 2 (1989): 18–44.

Foucault, Michel. *The Archeology of Knowledge and the Discourse on Language*. Trans. A. M. Sheridan Smith. New York: Pantheon, 1972.

Frank, Robert, and Henry Sayre, eds. *The Line in Postmodern Poetry*. Urbana: University of Illinois Press, 1988.

Fredman, Stephen. *Poet's Prose: The Crisis in American Verse*. Cambridge: Cambridge University Press, 1983.

Gardner, Thomas. "American Poetry of the 1970s: A Preface." *Contemporary Literature* 23 (1982): 407–10.

Gery, John. "The Anxiety of Affluence: Poets after Ashbery." *Verse* 8, no. 1 (1991): 28–32.

Gioia, Dana. "Poetry Chronicle." *Hudson Review* 34, no. 4 (Winter 1981–82).

Graham, Jorie. *The End of Beauty*. New York: Ecco, 1987.

Grossman, Allen. *Against Our Vanishing*. Boston: Rowan Tree Press, 1981.

Haavikko, Paavo. *Selected Poems*. Trans. Anselm Hollo. New York: Grossman, 1966.

Hammond, Jeffrey A. "Who Is Edward Taylor? Voice and Reader in the *Preparatory Meditations*." *American Poetry* 7, no. 3 (1990): 2–19.

Herr, Michael. *Walter Winchell*. New York: Knopf, 1990.

Hollander, John. "A Poetry of Restitution." *Yale Review* 70, no. 2 (1981): 161–86.

Hopkins, Gerard Manley. *Gerard Manley Hopkins*. Ed. Catherine Phillips. Oxford: Oxford University Press, 1986.

Jackson, Richard, ed. "The Imminence of a Revelation." In *Acts of Mind: Conversations with Contemporary Poets*, 69–76. University: University of Alabama Press, 1983.

Jameson, Fredric. *The Ideologies of Theory*. Vol. 2: *Syntax of History*. Minneapolis: University of Minnesota Press, 1988.

———. *The Political Unconscious: Narrative as a Socially Symbolic Act*. Ithaca: Cornell University Press, 1981.

———. *Postmodernism; or, The Cultural Logic of Late Capitalism*. Durham, N.C.: Duke University Press, 1991.

Jarman, Mark. "The Curse of Discursiveness." *Hudson Review* 45, no. 1 (Spring 1992): 158–66.

Johnson, W. R. *The Idea of the Lyric: Lyric Modes in Ancient and Modern Poetry*. Berkeley: University of California Press, 1982.

Joyce, James. *Finnegans Wake*. New York: Viking, 1939.

Kimmelman, Burt. "Centrality in a Discrete Universe: William Bronk and Wallace Stevens." *Sagetrieb* 7 (1988): 119–30.

Kinzie, Mary. *The Cure of Poetry in an Age of Prose: Moral Essays on the Poet's Calling*. Chicago: University of Chicago Press, 1993.

Koethe, John. "The Absence of a Noble Presence." *Verse* 8, no. 1 (Spring 1991).

———. "Contrary Impulses: The Tension between Poetry and Theory." *Critical Theory* 18 (Autumn 1991): 64–75.

———. *The Late Wisconsin Spring*. Princeton: Princeton University Press, 1984.

———. "The Metaphysical Subject of John Ashbery's Poetry." In *Beyond Amazement: New Essays on John Ashbery*, ed. David Lehman, 87–100. Ithaca: Cornell University Press, 1980.

Korelitz, Jean Hanff. "Poetry Society of America Survey." *Poetry Society of America Newsletter* 35 (1991): 32.

Lakoff, George, and Mark Johnson. *Metaphors We Live By*. Chicago: University of Chicago Press, 1980.

Lauterbach, Ann. "Ann Lauterbach." In *Ecstatic Occasions, Expedient Forms*, ed. David Lehman, 119–21. New York: Collier Macmillan, 1987.

———. *Before Recollection*. Princeton: Princeton University Press, 1987.

———. *Clamor*. New York: Viking, 1991.

———. "On Memory." In *Conversant Essays: Contemporary Poets on Poetry*, ed. James McCorkle, 519–20. Detroit: Wayne State University Press, 1990.

Lautréamont, Comte de. *Les Chants de Maldoror*. New York: New Directions, 1965.

Lear, Jonathan. *Love and Its Place in Nature*. New York: Farrar, Straus & Giroux, 1990.

Leary, Paris, and Robert Kelly. *A Controversy of Poets*. New York: Doubleday, 1965.

Lehman, David. Introduction to *Beyond Amazement: New Essays on John Ashbery*. Ed. David Lehman, 15–29. Ithaca: Cornell University Press, 1980.

———. *Operation Memory*. Princeton: Princeton University Press, 1990.

———. "The Shield of a Greeting: The Function of Irony in John Ashbery's Poetry." In *Beyond Amazement: New Essays on John Ashbery*, ed. David Lehman, 101–27. Ithaca: Cornell University Press, 1980.

———, ed. *Ecstatic Occasions, Expedient Forms: Sixty-Five Leading Contemporary Poets Select and Comment on Their Poems*. New York: Collier Macmillan, 1987.

Levenson, Michael. *Modernism and the Fate of Individuality*. New York: Cambridge University Press, 1991.

Lyotard, Jean-François. *The Postmodern Condition: A Report on Knowledge*. Trans. Geoff Bennington and Brian Massumi. Minneapolis: University of Minnesota Press, 1984.

McCorkle, James. *The Still Performance: Writing, Self, and Interconnection in Five Postmodern Poets*. Charlottesville: University of Virginia Press, 1989.

McGann, Jerome. *Social Values and Poetic Acts: The Historical Judgment of Literary Work*. Cambridge: Harvard University Press, 1988.

Marx, Karl, and Friedrich Engels. *The Communist Manifesto*. Ed. Samuel H. Beer. New York: Appleton-Century-Crofts, 1955.

Melville, Herman. "Hawthorne and His Mosses." In *The Piazza Tales and Other Prose Pieces, 1839–1860,* 239–53. Evanston, Ill.: Northwestern University Press; Chicago: Newberry Library, 1987.

Miller, S. H. "Psychic Geometry: John Ashbery's Prose Poems." *American Poetry* 3, no. 1 (1985): 24–42.

Miller, Stephen Paul. " 'Self-Portrait in a Convex Mirror,' the Watergate Affair, and John's Crosshatch Paintings: Surveillance and Reality-Testing in the Mid-Seventies." *boundary* 2 20, no. 2 (Summer 1993): 84–115.

Milton, John. *John Milton: Complete Poems and Major Prose.* Ed. Merritt Y. Hughes. New York: Macmillan, 1957.

Mohanty, S. P., and Jonathan Monroe. "John Ashbery and the Articulation of the Social." *diacritics* 17, no. 2 (1987): 37–63.

Molesworth, Charles. *The Fierce Embrace: A Study of Contemporary American Poetry.* Columbia: University of Missouri Press, 1979.

Moore, Marianne. *The Complete Poems.* New York: Macmillan, 1980.

Moraga, Cherríe. *Loving in the War Years, lo que nunca pasó por sus labios.* Boston: South End Press, 1983.

Murphy, Margueritte S. "John Ashbery's *Three Poems:* Heteroglossia in the American Prose Poem." *American Poetry* 7, no. 2 (1990): 50–63.

Nietzsche, Friedrich. *The Will to Power.* Ed. Walter Kaufmann. Trans. Walter Kaufmann and R. J. Hollingdale. New York: Vintage, 1968.

O'Hara, Frank. *The Collected Poems of Frank O'Hara.* Ed. Donald Allen. New York: Knopf, 1979.

Ovid. *Tristia, Ex Ponto.* Trans. Arthur Leslie Wheeler. Cambridge: Harvard University Press, 1988.

Packard, William, ed. *The Craft of Poetry: Interviews from the "New York Quarterly."* New York: Doubleday, 1974.

Palmer, Michael, ed. *Code of Signals: Writings on Poetics.* Berkeley, Calif.: North Atlantic Books, 1983.

"Paying Attention." *Economist* 320, no. 7724 (September 1991): 182.

Perloff, Marjorie. *The Dance of the Intellect: Studies in the Poetry of the Pound Tradition.* Cambridge: Cambridge University Press, 1985.

———. "Making Poetic Sense in Media Society." *Verse* 8, no. 1 (Spring 1991): 53–60.

———. *Poetic License: Essays on Modernist and Postmodernist Lyric.* Evanston, Ill.: Northwestern University Press, 1990.

———. *The Poetics of Indeterminacy: Rimbaud to Cage.* Princeton: Princeton University Press, 1981.

———. *Radical Artifice: Writing Poetry in the Age of Media.* Chicago: University of Chicago Press, 1991.

Plath, Sylvia. *The Collected Poems.* Ed. Ted Hughes. New York: Harper & Row, 1981.

Popper, Karl R. *The Poverty of Historicism.* New York: Harper & Row, 1964.

Poulin, A., Jr. *Contemporary American Poetry.* 4th ed. Boston: Houghton Mifflin, 1985.

———. "The Experience of Experience: A Conversation with John Ashbery." *Michigan Quarterly Review* 20, no. 3 (Summer 1981): 242–55.

Reinfeld, Linda. *Language Poetry: Writing as Rescue.* Baton Rouge: Louisiana State University Press, 1992.

Revell, Donald. "Purists Will Object: Some Meditations on Influence." *Verse* 8, no. 1 (Spring 1991): 16–22.

Richman, Robert. "Our 'Most Important' Living Poet." *Commentary* 74, no. 1 (July 1982): 62–68.

Ross, Andrew. "The Alcatraz Effect: Belief and Postmodernity." *SubStance* 13, no. 1 (1984): 71–85.

———. *The Failure of Modernism: Symptoms of American Poetry*. New York: Columbia University Press, 1986.

Salmond, Anne. "Theoretical Landscapes: On Cross-Cultural Conception of Knowledge." In *Semantic Anthropology,* ed. David Parkin, 82–85. London: Academic Press, 1982.

Scalapino, Leslie. *way*. San Francisco: North Point, 1988.

Schultz, Susan M., ed. "John Ashbery's Influence on Contemporary Poetry." *Verse* 8, no. 1 (Spring 1991): 1–79.

Shapiro, David. *House (Blown Apart)*. Woodstock, N.Y.: Overlook Press, 1988.

Shoptaw, John. "Investigating *The Tennis Court Oath*." *Verse* 8, no. 1 (Spring 1991): 61–72.

———. *On the Outside Looking Out: John Ashbery's Poetry*. Cambridge: Harvard University Press, 1994.

Silliman, Ron. *The Age of Huts*. New York: Roof, 1986.

———. *The New Sentence*. New York: Roof, 1987.

Sokolsky, Anita. " 'A Commission That Never Materialized': Narcissism and Lucidity in Ashbery's 'Self-Portrait in a Convex Mirror.' " In *Modern Critical Views: John Ashbery,* ed. Harold Bloom, 233–50. New York: Chelsea House, 1985.

Sontag, Susan. *Against Interpretation*. New York: Farrar, Straus & Giroux, 1965.

Stein, Gertrude. *The Yale Gertrude Stein*. Ed. Richard Kostelanetz. New Haven: Yale University Press, 1980.

Stevens, Wallace. *The Necessary Angel: Essays on Reality and the Imagination*. New York: Vintage, 1951.

———. *The Palm at the End of the Mind*. Ed. Holly Stevens. New York: Vintage, 1972.

"Symposium Responses: Poets and Writers Remark on the State of the Art." *Mississippi Review* 19, no. 3 (1991): 7–128.

Thoreau, Henry David. *A Week on the Concord and Merrimack Rivers; Walden, or, Life in the Woods; The Maine Woods; Cape Cod*. Ed. Robert F. Sayre. New York: Library of America, 1985.

Vendler, Helen. *The Music of What Happens: Poems, Poets, Critics*. Cambridge: Harvard University Press, 1988.

———. "A Steely Glitter Chasing Shadows." *New Yorker*, August 3, 1992, pp. 73–76.

———. "Understanding Ashbery." *New Yorker*, March 16, 1981, pp. 114–36.

von Hallberg, Robert. *American Poetry and Culture, 1945–80*. Cambridge: Harvard University Press, 1985.

Waugh, Evelyn. *Vile Bodies*. 1930. Reprint. New York: Delta-Dell, 1966.

Weinfeld, Henry. " 'The Cloud of Unknowing': William Bronk and the Condition of Poetry." *Sagetrieb* 7 (1988): 137–44.

———, ed. "A Conversation with William Bronk." *Sagetrieb* 7 (1988): 17–43.

Welish, Marjorie. *Handwritten*. New York: SUN, 1979.

———. *The Windows Flew Open*. Providence: Burning Deck, 1991.

White, Hayden. *Metahistory: The Historical Imagination in Nineteenth-Century Europe*. Baltimore: Johns Hopkins University Press, 1973.

Whitman, Walt. *Walt Whitman: Poetry and Prose*. Ed. Justin Kaplan. New York: Library of America, 1982.

Williams, C. K. *Flesh and Blood*. New York: Farrar, Straus & Giroux, 1987.

Wilson, Rob. *American Sublime: The Genealogy of a Poetic Genre*. Madison: University of Wisconsin Press, 1991.

————. "John Ashbery's Postindustrial Sublime." *Verse* 8, no. 1 (Spring 1991): 48–52.

Yau, John. *Radiant Silhouette: New and Selected Work, 1974–1988*. Santa Rosa, Calif.: Black Sparrow, 1989.

————. *Sometimes*. New York: Sheep Meadow, 1979.

Contributors

Charles Altieri teaches in the English department at the University of California, Berkeley. Author of two books on contemporary American poetry and *Painterly Abstraction in Modernist American Poetry* (soon to be in paperback from Penn State University Press), he has just finished *First Persons: Expressive Agency and Expressivist Ethics*, published by Blackwell.

Charles Bernstein is the author of *Dark City* (Sun & Moon Press, 1994), *Rough Trades* (Sun & Moon Press, 1991), *Islets/Irritations* (reissued by Roof Books in 1992), and *A Poetics* (Harvard University Press, 1992). He is the David Gray Professor of Poetry and Letters at SUNY-Buffalo, where he teaches in the Poetics Program.

George Bradley's first book of poems, *Terms to Be Met*, was published by Yale University Press in May of 1986. His second volume was *Of the Knowledge of Good and Evil*.

Bonnie Costello is a professor in the Department of English at Boston University. She has published two books, *Marianne Moore: Imaginary Possessions* (Harvard University Press, 1981; winner of the 1982 Explicator Award) and *Elizabeth Bishop: Questions of Mastery* (Harvard University Press, 1991), and numerous essays on modern and contemporary poetry. She is currently writing a book about landscape in contemporary poetry and working as general editor of *The Selected Letters of Marianne Moore*.

John Ernest is an assistant professor of English at the University of New Hampshire. He has published essays in *American Literary History, American Literature, Sagetrieb, PMLA,* and other journals.

John Gery teaches at the University of New Orleans and at the Ezra Pound Center for Literature at Brunnenburg Castle in Italy. He is the author of *Charlemagne: A Song of Gestures* and *The Burning of New Orleans*. He is the recipient of an NEA.

John Koethe was born in San Diego in 1945 and attended Princeton and Harvard. His books of poetry include *Domes* and *The Late Wisconsin Spring,* and he has received the Frank O'Hara Award for Poetry, the Bernard F. Connors Award from *The Paris Review,* and a Guggenheim Fellowship. He is Professor of Philosophy at the University of Wisconsin-Milwaukee.

James McCorkle is the author of *The Still Performance: Writing, Self, and Interconnection* (University Press of Virginia, 1989), a study of John Ashbery, Elizabeth Bishop, W. S. Merwin, Adrienne Rich, and Charles Wright, and he is the editor of *Conversant Essays: Contemporary Poets on Poetry* (Wayne State University Press, 1990). His poems have appeared in numerous journals, as well as being included in the 1989 and 1992 editions of *Best American Poetry.* He currently lives in upstate New York.

Stephen Paul Miller is an assistant professor of English at St. John's University in New York. He is currently working on a cultural study of the 1970s. The Domestic Press has published a book of his poetry entitled *Art Is Boring for the Same Reason We Stayed in Vietnam.* His poem "I Was on a Golf Course the Day John Cage Died of a Stroke" appeared in *The Best American Poetry, 1994,* ed. A. R. Ammons (1994).

Fred Moramarco is a poet and critic who lives in San Diego and teaches American Literature at San Diego State University. He is the coeditor, with Al Zolynas, of *Men of Our Time: An Anthology of Male Poetry in Contemporary America* (University of Georgia Press, 1992) and coauthor of *Modern American Poetry, 1965–1950* (Massachusetts, 1991); he is currently working on a sequel called *Containing Multitudes: Poetry in the United States since 1950.*

Jonathan Morse is a professor of English at the University of Hawaii-Manoa. His book *Word by Word: The Language of Memory* was published by Cornell University Press in 1990. He has recent work in *American Literary History* and *Raritan.*

Donald Revell is a professor of English at the University of Utah. He is the author of *From the Abandoned Cities, The Gaza of Winter, New Dark Ages,* and *Erasures.* He was a recent winner of a Guggenheim.

Andrew Ross teaches in the American Studies department at New York University. He is the author of *The Failure of Modernism* (1986) and *No Respect: Intellectuals and Popular Culture* (1989) and is the editor of *Universal Abandon? The Politics of Postmodernism* (1988) and coeditor of *Technoculture* (1991).

Susan M. Schultz is an assistant professor of English at the University of Hawaii-Manoa. She has published three chapbooks of poetry, including *Another Childhood* (Leave Books, 1993). Her essays on modern and contemporary American poetry have appeared in *Raritan, Arizona Quarterly, Sagetrieb,* and elsewhere. In 1992 she was president of the Hawaii Literary Arts Council.

John Shoptaw lives in New York City. His book *On the Outside Looking Out: John Ashbery's Poetry* was published by Harvard University Press in 1994.

Index

Ashbery, John (*Continued*)
114, 217, 254; "Rivers and Mountains,"
71–72; "Sand Pail," 226; "Seasonal," 48,
236; *Self-Portrait in a Convex Mirror*, 41,
133; "Self-Portrait in a Convex Mirror,"
39–41, 45, 53–54, 83, 103, 115, 133–34,
146–48, 158–59, 161–66; *Shadow Train*,
39, 41–42, 141; "The Skaters," 40, 41, 64–
65, 113, 218, 234, 243, 248, 250, 254; *Some
Trees*, 41, 61, 72, 104, 130, 136, 156, 230,
234; "Song: 'Mostly Places . . . ,'" 68;
"Soonest Mended," 1–2, 37n3, 97, 150–52,
156; "Sortes Vergilianae," 235; "Statuary,"
67; "Syringa," 97–98; "The System," 5, 95,
132, 144n15, 181–82, 219, 220, 245, 249–
50; "Tapestry," 134; *The Tennis Court Oath*,
6, 38, 41, 43, 47, 84, 86, 93, 130, 131, 193,
201–9, 214, 217, 221, 225, 230, 235;
"These Lacustrine Cities," 244; "They
Dream Only of America," 93, 209; "Third
Madrigal," 223–24; "Three Madrigals,"
223; *Three Poems*, 5, 6, 9, 39, 41, 52–53,
62, 86, 96, 107, 108, 179–84, 212, 217,
219, 233, 249–50; "The Tomb of Stuart
Merrill," 18–20; "Too Happy, Happy Tree,"
73; "Variant," 214; "Variations, Calypso
and Fugue, on a Theme by Ella Wheeler Wilcox," 72–73, 254–55; *The Vermont Notebook* (with Joe Brainard), 41, 200, 226; *A
Wave*, 6, 37n3, 39, 40, 43, 56, 62, 138, 198–
99; "A Wave," 61, 68–70; "What Is Poetry,"
127–28, 218; "The Wrong Kind of Insurance," 15–18, 130. *See also* Influence; Pronouns
Auden, W. H., 69, 169, 234
Austin, J. L., 246
Avant-garde, 91, 201–8

Baba, Meher, 152
Bachelard, Gaston, 105, 115–16
Bakhtin, M. M., 107, 179
Ball, Hugo, 203, 207
Barrell, John, 80n10
Barthes, Roland, 107, 108, 137
Bartlett, Lee, 144n11
Baudelaire, Charles, 63
Baudrillard, Jean, 16, 196
Beat poets, 84
Beckett, Samuel, 91, 92, 126, 241
Bee, Susan, 222
Bendall, Molly, 11n28
Benjamin, Walter, 202–3
Berg, Stephen, 96

Berger, Charles, 5
Berlioz, Hector, 21
Bernstein, Charles, 6, 7, 9, 125n25, 211–55.
WORKS: "Amblyopia," 229; "Artifice of Ab-
sorption," 218, 222; "As If the Trees by
Their Very Roots Had Hold of Us," 219–20;
"Asylum," 229; "Blood on the Cutting
Room Floor," 252; "Blow-Me-Down
Etude," 238; "THE BLUE DIVIDE," 242;
"But Boxes Both Boats," 216; *Content's
Dream*, 212, 215–17, 240, 257n28; *Con-
trolling Interests*, 220, 241, 242, 244, 252;
Disfrutes, 226–27; "The Harbor of Illu-
sion," 216; "The Influence of Kinship Pat-
terns Upon Perception of an Ambiguous
Stimulus," 217–18; *Islets/Irritations*, 215;
"The Italian Border of the Alps," 241–42;
"LIFT OFF," 222–23; "Matters of Policy,"
242–44, 254; *The Occurrence of Tune*, 222;
"Of Time and the Line," 232, 237; *Poetic
Justice*, 222, 228, 230, 242; *A Poetics*, 9,
246; "The Puritan Ethic and the Spirit of
Capitalization," 238–39; *Rough Trades*,
215, 251; "Semblance," 212, 215–16;
Senses of Responsibility, 219; "Sentences My
Father Used," 244–48; "Standing Target,"
252–53; "Substance Abuse," 217; "The
Taste Is What Counts," 228–29; "Thought's
Measure," 212; "The Years as Swatches,"
238
Bierstadt, Albert, 66, 75
Bishop, Elizabeth, 102
Black Mountain poets, 84
Blaine, Nell, 73
Bloom, Harold, 2–3, 83, 86, 88, 129, 130,
149–51, 186n5, 217; and American Roman-
ticism, 88, 151; on influence, 7, 8, 114, 127,
168, 170; on JA and Wallace Stevens, 5, 171;
on poetic voice, 128; on *The Tennis Court
Oath*, 6, 201–2. WORKS: *The Anxiety of In-
fluence*, 2, 143, 186n5; *John Ashbery* (Chel-
sea House), 5. *See also* Influence
Bly, Robert, 75
Bonnard, Pierre, 74
Bradley, George, 9
Brainard, Joe, 200
Bréton, Andre, 95, 126, 207
Bronk, William, 8, 168, 170, 172–79, 180,
185. WORKS: "Boiled Down," 178; "Exploration," 173; "Holy Ghost," 175; *Living Instead*, 175; *The New World*, 177–79; "Particulate. Inhumane," 172; "The Plainest
Narrative," 176; "The Poems: All Conces-